# THE TYRANNY OF NATIONS

HOW THE LAST 500 YEARS SHAPED TODAY'S
GLOBAL ECONOMY

## PALAK N. PATEL

**BIFOCAL PRESS**

*To Amrita, Mom, Dad, and Ba.*

*And to Lowell, Massachusetts — forever my home.*

*The naked passion of self-love of Nations, in its drunken delirium of greed, is dancing to the clash of steel and the howling verses of vengeance.*

*The hungry self of the Nation shall burst in a violence of fury from its own shameless feeding.*

*For it has made the world its food,*

*And licking it, crunching it, and swallowing it in big morsels, it swells and swells*

*Till in the midst of its unholy feast descends the sudden heaven piercing its heart of grossness.*

— RABINDRANATH TAGORE

# CONTENTS

# PREFACE: THE EDUCATION OF A BOND VIGILANTE

This book is a product of my experience investing in the debt of so-called emerging markets. A familiar, albeit self-aggrandizing, term for my occupation is "bond vigilante." As a bond vigilante, I policed the budgetary discipline of governments. Any fiscal improbity would threaten the repayment of principal and interest on loans that I, and other investors, had made to them. The threat of higher interest rates or a buyers' strike on their currencies would often suffice to keep these governments in check.

Over the past decade, a new phenomenon in government debt markets appeared: negative interest rates. I could not understand how investors could be willing to pay certain governments to borrow more. Furthermore, I struggled to reconcile falling interest rates in the developed countries—the United States, Western Europe, and Japan—with the exorbitant borrowing rates that prevail in their less-developed counterparts. This problem vexed me as I witnessed the market summarily throttle economies in the latter group.

The first such case was Venezuela, whose government imposed draconian controls to service large payments to debt holders (and corrupt government officials). But I could hardly believe that its flippantly anti-capitalist authorities did not bear full responsibility for its failure. Argentina's circumstances were harder to explain. There, the election of a market-friendly government in 2016 offered generational hope in redeeming a country that had long been a poster child for institutional failure. Under its new "neoliberal" president, however, the market's noose only tightened and forced it once more into debt default in 2020. After Venezuela and Argentina, many more dominoes have either already fallen or stand in line to succumb: Lebanon, Ecuador, Zambia, Sri Lanka, Tunisia, Iraq, Egypt, Pakistan, and a litany of others.

I could not help but suspect that some common force was behind such widespread economic collapse. Nor could I separate problems in the more "advanced" nations from those in the less-developed countries that depended on investment from the former. High rates of interest in the emerging world were thus inextricable from falling rates of interest—which some viewed as a sign of sickness—in the developed countries.

All the while, the shadow of the 2008 financial crisis loomed. Many had analogized this event to the Great Depression. Yet no new New Deal appeared. Instead, the party of Roosevelt supported fiscal austerity, fearing that the United States, like the less-developed nations, faced an imminent debt crisis. After the shocking political events of 2016, I, like so many others, became obsessed with searching for an appropriate historical analogy for our strange times.

Karl Polanyi's *The Great Transformation* pointed me to Britain in the second half of the nineteenth century. Polanyi chronicled how, after the 1840s, Britain and other nations adopted market institutions by deregulating both land and labor while also imposing rigid price stability via the gold standard. I felt his description of the rise of Victorian globalization, as others have noted, could fit global market expansion in the modern era. And the maladies that afflicted Britain's economic periphery then did not seem wholly different from those encountered by emerging markets today.

Further investigation into Victorian-era financial data revealed a long-term decline in interest rates and a concurrent increase in share prices after the end of the Napoleonic Wars— a phenomenon similar to what has occurred in American financial markets since the end of the Cold War. What some have described as Keynesian "secular stagnation" (*secular* here meaning *long-term*) was also present in nineteenth-century Britain. The newly resurfacing ideas of post-Keynesians like Michal Kalecki and Hyman Minsky suggested that this phenomenon resulted from policy lock-in—when policy decisions can make it difficult or impossible for policy makers to change course—and therefore had political causes.

Familiarizing myself with British politics in the 1800s, I also discovered unsettling similarities with recent American history. The politicians of the time who can be categorized under the wide umbrella of the Liberal Party were not unlike those of the American center-right and center-left. In its belligerent Palmerstonian wing, I saw Reagan, Bush, and McCain. Among the free-trading Cobdenites, I found the modern Democrats. And Trump—and Perot before him—both seemed an incarnation of the Tory traditionalist Benjamin Disraeli, who led the rump Conservative opposition to power after the Panic of 1866.

Still, I wondered whether some general phenomenon— perhaps the effects economic change has on political coalitions —could explain the shared features of the British-led world economy of the Victorian era and the American-led one after 1980. Conventional explanations relying on the classic "isms" felt unsatisfying. I had never questioned the received wisdom that the Enlightenment and Industrial Revolution represented some discontinuous break in history that marked the end of feudalism and the beginning of capitalism.

Charles Kindleberger's *World Economic Primacy* reminded me that Venice, the Flemish cities, and the Dutch Republic had all been leading economies before England and then America surpassed them. Furthermore, a distinguishing feature of these early states was that they, like the latter two, experienced falling interest rates and possessed the dominant currency. After reading Kindleberger's essay on the economic crisis of 1619 and Violet Barbour's *Capitalism in Amsterdam in the Seventeenth Century*, I learned that emerging market crises were not unique to postindustrial society.

Jan de Vries' *The First Modern Economy* and Jonathan Israel's *The Dutch Republic* showed that politics in the seventeenth-century Netherlands, too, offered a guide for the present. Specifically, a coalition called the States Party, espousing freedom of trade and freedom from executive control, rose to prominence. Once in power, it both reduced government expenditures and weakened guilds. One could be forgiven for seeing how the States Party's doctrine of "True Freedom" approximated nineteenth-century *laissez-faire* and modern-day free-market ideology.

A political-economic pattern in historical periods of expanding world trade became apparent. But what happened *between* each era of globalization? Here, Polanyi and others filled the gaps. As free trade cooperation failed in each epoch, new coalitions arose that favored militarism as a means for economic development. Marjolein 't Hart's *The Dutch Wars of Independence* demonstrated how the Dutch fiscal-military complex spurred technological innovation in the late sixteenth century. Similarly, Priya Satia's *Empire of Guns* unveiled how gun manufacturing contributed to industrial development in England. These political regimes were predecessors to the military Keynesianism that, as many have noted, was critical to the US economy in the twentieth century.

Finally, through the works of Charles Lindblom, Thomas Ferguson, Robert Brenner, and A. G. Hopkins, I learned that what I perceived as the monolithic state—the idea that governments acted as an indivisible unit—was, to a great extent, an illusion. Underlying each state are economic interests that compete for policy priority. As Minsky described in *Stabilizing an Unstable Economy*, private actors rely on the state to mitigate investment risks. "Free market" institutions are no less dependent on central authority than is the fiscal-military state. And the priorities that prevail in each country are contingent on its relative position in the global economy.

This book also owes an immense debt to the work of many others whom I have not mentioned: Joan Robinson, Thomas Palley, Karel Davids, Sven Beckert, Nicholas Lardy, Jonathan Anderson, Immanuel Wallerstein, Joseph Stiglitz, and more. Building on the foundations they have laid, I hope to illustrate how present society fits a discernible pattern of global development. This pattern challenges conventional understandings of political economy handed to society by both the academic orthodoxy and market actors. I also hope that the reader will see that what amounts to a dangerous cycle of cooperation and conflict exists because humanity, in the words of Indian writer Rabindranath Tagore, chooses to be "broken up into fragments by narrow domestic walls."

# INTRODUCTION

Economists are fond of a saying: "There are four types of countries—developed economies, underdeveloped economies, Japan, and Argentina."[1] Japan and Argentina have become totems of baffling macroeconomic phenomena that defy intuition. Japan possesses the world's highest debt-to-GDP ratio—300 percent—yet it has negative interest rates. And despite having only a third of Japan's indebtedness, Argentina has struggled to borrow at interest rates as high as 40 percent. That the quip has lingered for decades is telling. Explanations for why economic development can vary so much across countries remain inadequate.

The failure to understand these differences has had detrimental policy consequences. The International Monetary Fund (IMF) and the World Bank continue to employ a procrustean one-size-fits-all framework in their macroeconomic assessments. In the United States, opponents of welfare are never slow to point to high inflation in less-developed countries with profligate government finances. Fearmongering about runaway government finances thus keeps a tight straitjacket on even the slightest social spending. Worse, fealty to this idea remains a reliable source of patronage in Washington.

Macroeconomic discourse too often rests on the false assumption of what some have called "triple coincidence."[2] Triple coincidence is the idea that a state's geographic, decision-making, and economic areas are all the same. This assumption has allowed economic policymakers to treat America as "merely another atom in the universe of trade."[3]

Any discussion of the global economy must, of course, recognize the unique position of the United States. In particular, the dominant international role of the dollar—what economists refer to as *exorbitant privilege*—needs little introduction. Despite a current account deficit that has persisted for almost thirty years and an ever-increasing stock of liabilities owed to foreigners, the dollar has remained the de facto global currency.[4] America has consistently defied predictions of a currency collapse—predictions that would have already come to fruition for any other country with similar external imbalances. The opposite has occurred in the recent crises of 2008 and 2020. Rather than abandoning the dollar, foreigners have viewed it as a safe haven.

All the while, government interest rates have pursued an inexorable march downwards, despite forty years of hand-wringing about the unwieldy size of America's debt. In the first quarter of 2020, 30-year treasury yields fell below 1 percent even as the debt-to-GDP ratio climbed to levels unseen since the Second World War. Rather than give economic observers a cause for celebration, however, the long decline in interest rates has left them unsettled. More than a few see it as representative of an enduring stagnation of the US economy.

The special relationship of the United States to the global economy is not without precedent. As has been chronicled well, Britain once found itself in a comparable position during the Victorian era when the world was on a pound standard and at the mercy of London finance.[5] Like the modern United States, it too experienced a long decline in interest rates, with the yield on British consols—bonds with no maturity date—gradually sinking from 5 percent in 1815 to 2 percent by 1900.

Going even further back—two centuries earlier—one finds an illuminating anecdote. During the Dutch Golden Age of the sixteenth and seventeenth centuries (1581–1672), *stadtholder* (head of state) William II of Orange (r. 1647–50) struggled to find merchants willing to lend gold to his exiled brother-in-law Charles II (r. 1660–85), the king of England. The source of this problem was not Charles's notoriously poor credit but the tendency of financially sophisticated Dutch merchants to deal in paper bills rather than bullion (gold or silver).[6]

In this era of Dutch economic *hegemony*, Amsterdam's merchants wielded inordinate influence in exchange with other nations, including England. Early in the seventeenth century, English economic commentators decried Dutch speculation for draining England's money supply. Yet they also marveled at the Dutch Republic's low rates of interest and "superabundance" of precious metals.[7] Dutch financial markets defied the mercantilist doctrine that interest rates needed to be high to keep money within a country's borders.[8]

The economic reach of Dutch merchants extended far beyond just England and included extensive trade with Asia, including Japan. Evidence suggests that Dutch speculative activity also affected bullion flows in Japan's economy.[9] After 1650, rapid specie outflows prompted Japanese administrators, in an early instance of capital controls, to restrict Dutch trading. Japan's past relationship with the Dutch suggests that its economy once faced maladies not dissimilar to those that afflict Argentina today.

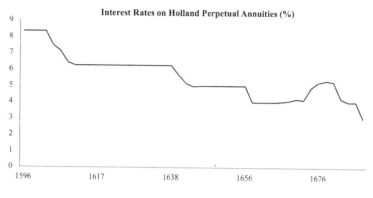

*Figure 1.1*

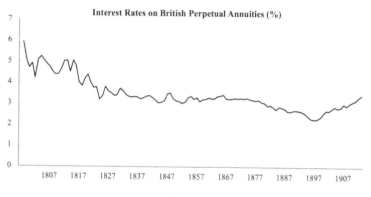

*Figure 1.2*

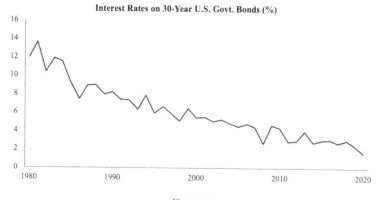

*Figure 1.3*

**Figures 1.1, 1.2, and 1.3** show the secular decline in long-term interest rates during Dutch, British, and American primacy. **Sources**: FRED, Federal Reserve Bank of St. Louis; Oscar Gelderblom and Joost Jonker, "Public Finance and Economic Growth: The Case of Holland in the Seventeenth Century," *The Journal of Economic History* 71, no. 1 (2011): 1-39; Ryland Thomas and Nicholas Dimsdale, "A Millennium of Macroeconomic Data," Bank of England, 2017, https://www.bankofengland.co.uk/statistics/research-datasets.

## Economic Hegemony

In the nine chapters that follow, I examine global development over the past five hundred years using the notion of hegemony. Hegemony, here, will mean a period of economic dominance of one state over all others. Many historians have already explored the idea of a lineage of dominant states and how it extends from the United Provinces of the Netherlands in the seventeenth century to the British in the eighteenth and nineteenth to the United States of America in the twentieth.[10] It remains popular today as insecurity about America's place in the world grows.

What I hope to show that is unique, however, is that the historical notion of hegemony is useful for resolving apparent differences in macroeconomic phenomena across countries. I also make the argument that a given country's relative position in the global economy is the principal influence on political coalitions and institutional change in that country. Further, I offer an economic explanation for how hegemony transitions—one in which institutional change is endogenous to relative technological standing. Finally, I also illustrate how the current political environment fits the pattern of the past half-millennium of global development and map the likely future course for coalitional dynamics both within states and between states.

To draw such conclusions, I detail the macroeconomic history of each hegemony and the intervening transitions. The first part of this book establishes economic phenomena common across all three cases. The historical narrative in the second part demonstrates the starkly similar political paths followed by each state.

The constituent elements of hegemony are apparent in the very beginning of *The Wealth of Nations*, where Adam Smith discusses the determinants of per-capita output:

> This proportion must in every nation be regulated by two different circumstances; first, by the skill, dexterity, and judgment with which its labour is generally applied; and, secondly, by the proportion between the number of those who are employed in useful labour, and that of those who are not so employed. Whatever be the soil, climate, or extent of territory of any particular nation, the abundance or scantiness of its annual supply must, in that particular situation, depend upon those two circumstances. The abundance or scantiness of this supply, too, seems to depend more upon the former of those two circumstances than upon the latter.[11]

A familiar term governs "the skill, dexterity, and judgment with which. . . labour is generally applied": technology. What hegemony entails is *technological* primacy. In their respective periods of economic dominance, the Dutch Republic, Britain, and the United States have each been at the cutting edge of technological innovation. Since a country's technological standing is relative, hegemony is itself a relative property and subject to continuous change alongside technology. Indeed, a central assumption of this book is that technological progress is continuous and is a property intrinsic to human society.

Nevertheless, it is difficult to avoid framing the world as "the hegemon and the rest." But tracking global development via hegemony offers a useful starting point for deeper investigation. After all, technological primacy has allowed certain states to shape the rules of global commerce. Advanced shipbuilding and nautical technique allowed Dutch privateers to employ force in establishing *mare liberum* or freedom of the seas. Likewise, the supremacy of the Royal Navy backed the informal system of international law governing trade in the nineteenth century. And few can doubt that America's technological position has allowed it to shape the character of global trade in modern times.

Furthermore, contemporary understanding of global development closely links it to the international movement of capital. But the nebulous term capital can obscure the legal foundations that underpin trade.[12] Someone gets to set the rules of the game. As this book will show, questions regarding who wins this power, why it never lasts, and what happens when it disappears are central to development.

Examining shared traits in Dutch, British, and American primacy can help uncover more general economic patterns that are obfuscated by developmental differences among countries. As suggested, the Dutch Republic and Britain both once possessed exorbitant privilege, and both Dutch guilder and British pound were monetary safe havens. Like the United States after the 1970s, both states in their primacy exhibited remarkable price stability relative to their contemporaries. Such shared properties make them better historical analogues than any other nation at any other point in history.

The Dutch Republic and the British Empire were also credit-based monetary economies. As I will later show, because of their monetary underpinnings, economic phenomena during both hegemonies conformed to Keynes's theory of demand-determined output (Chapter 2). Amid continuous technological progress, investment cycles appeared, varying with investor "animal spirits" driven by expectations for the profitable application of some new technology (Chapter 3).

I have introduced an important term here: *investor*. Throughout this book, *investor* is interchangeable with and often substitutes for terms such as *capitalist*, *firm*, and *entrepreneur* that frequently color economic discourse. I prefer to use *investor* because it is more general and because investment is the predominant driver of economic output.[13]

The centrality of investors to economic activity will also help draw attention to the significant role that distribution has historically played in the determination of output. That some individuals have greater influence over the economy than others makes distribution an important consideration. And the tendency of economic gains to accrue to privileged groups underpins political and economic change over the long term.

Intense investor activity in the international sphere is a notable feature of economic hegemony. Given their technological leadership, investors in the dominant economies have played an essential role in carrying innovation across borders (Chapters 4 and 5). Five hundred years of economic history have shown that trade between nations does not arise from comparative advantage—differences in endowments of particular natural resources for example—but rather from differences in technology.[14] The term *international trade* thus presents a misleading description of global exchange. What occurs instead is that investors from a technologically advanced economy establish interlinked production networks spanning geographic regions. Alternatively stated, they establish a global division of production. Worth emphasizing, however, is that such a division, in each incarnation, has provided disproportionate benefit to the investors of the dominant state. With foreign investors wielding monopsony power in less-developed regions—representing the sole puchasers in those markets—exchange happens on unequal terms.[15]

All three periods of hegemony experienced the phenomenon of *globalization*, in which investors from the dominant economy helped spread market activity across the world. Like the modern United States, the Dutch Republic and early modern Britain outsourced production to locations with more advantageous labor costs. After attaining technological primacy, each country followed the same pattern of development. The provision of services to the rest of the world supplanted exports, and then foreign financial activity overtook services. Thus, during their mature phase of development, the trade balance shrank while so-called "invisible earnings" grew. Hegemony culminated in the Republic, Britain, and the United States becoming bankers to the rest of the world. Indeed, drawing on the history of its predecessors, I will show that trade (and the current account) has diminished relevance for the United States today, especially in comparison to its capital account, which reflects the country's ownership of foreign assets (Chapter 10).

## Polyarchy

For much of the past fifty years, politics has played a diminished role in economics—a field that began as "political economy." Since the 2008 panic, however, politics and economics have become more difficult to separate. Stagnation amid unprecedented inequality has played no small part in that connection. History shows that the shadow of politics, especially the politics of distribution, looms over economics. In addition to economic parallels, the United States today shares uncanny political similarities with the Dutch Republic and Britain during comparable periods of hegemony. Stagnation, characterized by heightened precarity among the working masses, followed the end of a Dutch property bubble in the 1560s and a London financial crisis in 1866. Likewise, increasing asset prices coincided with rising inequality in America's hegemonic predecessors.[16] Bitter trade disputes also emerged after the end of both Dutch and British globalization. And a rise of nationalist and anti-trade sentiment like that in the United States today was evident in both countries (Chapter 8).

| Year | Schoolmaster (florins/yr) | Barber-surgeon | Clerk | Pensionary | Carpenter (daily wage) |
|------|---------------------------|----------------|-------|------------|------------------------|
| 1580 | 125 | 25 | 215 | 400 | 0.75 |
| 1595 | 275 | N/A | 330 | 650-1200 | 1.1 |
| 1620 | 405 | 75 | 380 | 1600 | 1.2 |
| 1664 | 540-600 | 150-264 | 1000 | 2000-4000 | 1.5 |
| 1712 | 700 | 150-164 | 1030 | 3000-4000 | 1.5 |

Table 1.1: Divergence of Incomes of Carpenters and High-Salaried
Occupations in Amsterdam

| Year | Income Share |
|------|--------------|
| 1800 | 15% |
| 1867 | 30% |

Table 1.2: Income Share of the Top 1% of Incomes in Britain

| Year | Income Share |
|------|--------------|
| 1975 | 10% |
| 2020 | 20% |

Table 1.3: Income Share of the Top 1% of Incomes in the United States

Tables 1.1 to 1.3 depict rising inequality in incomes in the Dutch Republic, British
Empire, and present-day United States. Sources: Peter H. Lindert, "Unequal English
Wealth since 1670," *Journal of Political Economy* 94, no. 6 (1986): 1127–62;
Emmanuel Saez and Gabriel Zucman, "Trends in US Income and Wealth Inequality:
Revising After the Revisionists," working paper no. 27921, National Bureau of
Economic Research, October 2020, https://www.nber.org/papers/w27921; Jan Luiten
Van Zanden, "Tracing the Beginning of the Kuznets Curve: Western Europe during
the Early Modern Period." *Economic History Review* (1995): 643–64.

An aspect of the Dutch and British states that is convenient for
tracking political change is that both—like the United States—
were relatively decentralized polyarchies. This term's Greek
roots *poly* and *archy* combine to mean "many rulers."[17] All
states are polyarchies to varying degrees, but the Dutch
Republic and early modern Britain were, during their primacy,

especially polyarchal when compared to contemporary states (though, critically, not all nations). In the Republic, authority rested in a very loose confederation of provinces. These, in turn, were ruled by self-selecting legislative councils that convened in a broader body known as the States General. Parliament, of course, ruled Britain, though it did not have defined powers. The high degree of polyarchy in each society made coalitional dynamics sensitive to economic change. Polyarchy, as a measure of the degree to which authority is centralized, will be useful for disproving the disconcertingly vogue idea that centralized power is more suitable to economic development (Chapter 5).

What links economic and political change is fundamental, or unquantifiable, uncertainty. Given that the future harbors immeasurable unknowns, investors rely on the state to attenuate the risk that accompanies investment. In his book *Stabilizing an Unstable Economy*, Hyman Minsky built on the foundations of Keynes's *General Theory* and observed:

> The price system of a capitalist economy must carry the carrots that induce the production of the physical resources needed for future production. To do this it is necessary that the present validate the past, for unless the past is being validated and the future is expected to validate present investment and financing decisions, none but pathological optimists will invest.[18]

For Minsky, even deliberate government neglect could be a means to validate investment decisions (Chapter 3). Whether through direct state action, indirect action, or neglect, investment requires inducements.[19] Coordination becomes necessary when investment, as Keynes argued, is subject to collective-action failure. From the Dutch admiralty boards to the English Navigation Acts to the Reagan defense program, governments have gone to extensive lengths to support commerce. And even in eras of ostensible free commerce, policy sought to instrumentalize the state in service of the market.

In the Dutch Republic and early modern Britain, commercial interests often had direct representation in government due to property restrictions on the franchise. Dutch regents—the oligarchic rulers of cities and towns—came from business and were frequently selected for their specialized expertise.[20] Members of the British Parliament were primarily landowners, but by the early 1600s they were diversifying their wealth by investing in privateering and the New World trades. By the early nineteenth century, manufacturers had gained entry into the Commons. In the modern United States, the costs of electoral campaigns and the more general costs of disseminating information to citizens give business disproportionate influence over government affairs.

Direct relationships with commerce, however, are not the only reason authorities have historically assigned a privileged role to enterprise. Even before the rise of the Dutch Republic, governments associated naval strength with the profits of their merchant marine.[21] They were also aware that commercial health determined revenues and money supply. To the chagrin of locals, the English Crown gave special privileges to Hanseatic merchants for three hundred years.[22] As the events leading to the English Civil War showed, poor economic growth could threaten higher taxes on legislators.

Concern for social stability, too, has been a significant reason behind government support for business. British Prime Minister Robert Peel attributed the high unemployment of the early 1840s to anti-Corn Law boycotts by manufacturers. In the 1990s, the US Treasury, observing the myriad currency crises in less-developed countries, was similarly gripped by a fear of "bond vigilantes." Treasury officials were afraid that fiscal spending would undermine market confidence in U.S. government debt.

On policy matters, both citizens and government officials have tended to defer to the judgment of experts, particularly those from the commercial realm. This is an inherited tradition. Before the advent of electoral politics, uncertainty made feudal and early modern populations willing to cede authority to those who could assure material security, such as an adequate supply of food.[23] Consent to rule was often reinforced from above. A Dutch political tract from 1618 railed against greater public involvement in government, asking whether "the security of the land is promoted by telling the common folk that the final word and sovereignty lies with them."[24] Tracts such as this one conditioned the population to accept narrow political participation.

## Politics as Investment

Examining the nature of polyarchal processes in Dutch and English history leads to several conclusions. First, government and the private sector have always been proximate. Their close relationship today in the United States is not a new development. Adam Smith observed in the 1770s that privileged members of the commercial elite exercised zealous influence over authorities:

> This monopoly has so much increased the number of some particular tribes of them that, like an overgrown standing army, they have become formidable to the government, and upon many occasions intimidate the legislature. The Member of Parliament who supports every proposal for strengthening this monopoly is sure to acquire not only the reputation of understanding trade, but great popularity and influence with an order of men whose numbers and wealth render them of great importance. If he opposes them, on the contrary, and still more if he has authority enough to be able to thwart them, neither the most acknowledged probity, nor the highest rank, nor the greatest public services can protect him from the most infamous abuse and detraction, from personal insults, nor sometimes from real danger, arising

from the insolent outrage of furious and disappointed monopolists.[25]

A second conclusion one can draw from Dutch and English polyarchal processes is that the principal source of political contestation is competition between investors. Specifically, investors compete for priority on the government agenda. Often lost in discourse about "the haves" and "have nots" is the reality that business interests are neither monolithic nor cohesive.

A third conclusion: continuous technological progress leads to constant competition among investors. New commercial interests arise to vie for government influence over legacy interests. I will show that this process, in turn, drives institutional change.

The ways inter-firm competition has shaped political coalitions in the modern era has been the subject of extensive research.[26] In money-driven politics, investor funds are crucial to winning elections. As a result, parties come to represent competing blocs of investors. Furthermore, parties will avoid views that conflict with their investors' direct objectives (that is, they hurt profits). If a candidate adopts a platform that conflicts with the broad spectrum of investors, he or she will lack sufficient resources to compete.

Even though they lacked formal party systems, competition among investor blocs also drove the formation of coalitions in the Dutch Republic and early modern Britain. That the link between investor factions and political coalitions generalizes to early modern times should not be so surprising. The reason is simple: political organization is costly. More generally, information is costly. Thus, the ability to disseminate information, which influences what preferences abound, becomes proportionate to material resources.

In the Dutch Republic, pamphleteering was the vehicle for information wars, and its costs helped to determine which news reached audiences. The Dutch happened to be the most prolific publishers because their print trade was also the most profitable. When William III invaded England in 1688, for example, he used this advantage to mount a successful propaganda campaign.

What happened to the radical press in nineteenth-century Britain is also revealing. It thrived in the early 1800s when middle-class manufacturers and industrialists joined radical social movements in the push for parliamentary reform. Once limited reforms allowed the former to enter the House of Commons, their shared interests disappeared. Furthermore, after 1850, the two began to clash when industry began to overtake agriculture in economic significance. Through press consolidation, industrial interests came to drown out the voice of their former allies. The volume of radical publications subsequently declined as it could not keep up with mass media.[27]

Political preferences, to repeat, are subject to market forces in which investors wield disproportionate power to affect how ideas compete. Opinions anathema to investors, as a rule, will find a small audience. Nevertheless, investor groups still have to form alliances with sections of broader population.

During the era of Dutch hegemony, the Golden Age, two separate, albeit fluid, political coalitions emerged: the Orangists and the republicans, with each representing investor blocs differing on both military and trade policy. To garner popular support, the two also allied with opposing conservative and progressive religious factions. Although elections did not exist, mob violence certainly did. Regime change occurred on multiple occasions when the Orangists successfully riled xenophobic rioters. Even contemporary observers, however, were aware that Dutch cultural conflicts served as a pretext for political ends. One English observer noted that in the Republic "no man will allege conscience, nor religion, who hath any knowledge of this state."[28]

Though investors have an outsized influence on politics, this does not preclude social progress. New investor groups, looking to compete with incumbent ones, find natural allies in those who sought change. The growth of new forms of enterprise can thus bring previously marginal beliefs into prominence.

The historical cases I investigate in this book offer several examples. As investor blocs favoring free trade rose to power in the Dutch Republic, religious toleration expanded. This development occurred as free-trade interests grew to economically rival investors aligned with Orangists. The latter included arms dealers, privateers, and various guilds.

As a colonial trade emerged, the opposite alignment occurred in England before the Civil War. Investors in the Americas allied with Protestant dissenters while the merchant companies trading on the European continent supported the Crown and Church. The demise of the merchant companies and further growth of colonial trading eventually paved the way for the English Bill of Rights in 1688.

The "old colonial system" crumbled, however, as Britain widened its technological lead over other nations in the late eighteenth century. British reform movements gained strength as free-trading industrialists and financiers saw an opportunity to almost entirely dominate the global economy. As I have hinted, they found allies among radical agitators and created a coalition that helped enact the abolition of slavery, Catholic Emancipation, and electoral reform in the four years from 1829 to 1833.

Links between investor blocs and reform movements are especially apparent in the history of the United States. In contrast to their British counterparts, those who backed the antislavery movement were railroad investors and beneficiaries of Western expansion who eschewed free trade in favor of more autarkic development. They were, in turn, displaced by new multinational proponents of free trade, who appeared as America achieved technological convergence with Britain. These interests became prominent supporters of a new political regime: President Franklin D. Roosevelt's New Deal.[29]

## Stages of Development

As the preceding examples may have already suggested, dominant investor coalitions—or party reigns—can be identified with particular stages of economic development. The three historical cases I examine here have pursued a specific sequence of stages (as I discuss in Chapter 5). In the first stage, a society, specifically one encapsulated within an autonomous political unit, begins with a considerable technological lag in relation to another society. Like England before the mid-seventeenth century or the United States before the mid-nineteenth century, it tends to export primary products, such as agricultural commodities.

Having achieved a sufficient degree of technological progress, it then pursues autarkic growth. This type of development involves exploiting the economies of scale offered by the domestic economy and proximate geographies. Such a course also resorts to protections against more developed competitors. In England's case, the exploitation of colonial markets in North America, where the Dutch had a limited presence, allowed its manufacturing and shipbuilding to catch up to the latter's. In the US case, the Western territories, followed by the South, and then the Caribbean, subsidized industrial expansion. And, though this is less clear, the Dutch seemed to have exploited their proximity to Baltic markets.[30]

The final stage, of course, is economic primacy. A country achieves sufficient relative technological progress when investors appear who have more to gain from access to global markets and less to fear from foreign competition. This stage has its own sub-pattern, characterized by the growth of multinational exporters of goods and services, followed by the expansion of international finance.

Coalitions or parties linked to each stage are not hard to discern. When the Dutch reached the last phase, the republican States Party rose to power with its support for greater pacifism and open trade. In England's history, protectionism corresponds to the rise of the Whigs. They displaced supporters of the Stuart kings—London merchants with links to Amsterdam. And technological primacy led to the ascendance of the Tory liberals, who joined with the opposition to form the Liberal Party. Finally, in the US case, the Jacksonian Democrats favoring free trade were succeeded by the nationalist Republican Party. The latter was followed by a resurgent Democratic Party, which remained dominant until the Republicans themselves embraced free trade.

## The Global Cycle

The preceding pattern characterizes special historical cases of development—economic empires—and fails to conform to most other instances. Nevertheless, given their inordinate influence, the developmental trajectory followed by the Dutch Republic, the British Empire, and the United States is useful for tracking a more general pattern in the evolution of the global economy. This global cycle is one of *cooperation and conflict* between states. And it has shaped the development of all nations since at least the seventeenth century.

The cooperative phase is more familiar as globalization. Clear technological leadership allowed Dutch, British, and American investors to coax foreign states to open their borders for investment. In the last case, the concurrent adoption of market institutions by other countries after the end of the Cold War has been well chronicled. Even countries that had been hostile to market institutions, such as China and India, welcomed foreign investment.

Similarly, cooperative institutions were adopted by other nations at the onset of Dutch and British primacy. Stuart England, Bourbon France, and a litany of other states developed a dependence on Dutch commercial and financial expertise during the early 1600s. The end of the Napoleonic Wars heralded the beginning of the Pax Britannica, coinciding with a boom in British foreign investment and the embrace of free trade agreements across Europe. When such treaties became more prevalent in the 1840s, the United States, too, participated, under President Polk, whose Democratic Party enjoyed the support of the New York agents of British banking houses.

For certain nations, the cooperative phase accelerated technological convergence. Bourbon France, Prussia, and, most recently, China all narrowed the developmental gap against their more technologically advanced peers over a relatively short period. Each of these combined comparatively centralized governance with a large labor force to attract outsourced production.

For most other states, however, the cooperative phase has historically brought false hopes. As Keynes explained, market organization ultimately gives way to the failure of collective action as investors eschew real investment for hoarding in financial assets (or claims to monopoly rents). In each epoch of cooperation, this phenomenon occurred at a global scale, with investors in the dominant economic centers—creditors to the world at large—succumbing to such behavior. The result, including the most recent case, has always been a worsening of global demand deficiency—underemployment and the underutilization of productive assets—and conditions inhospitable to the economic progress of peripheral states.

In the past, the failure of external sources to provide growth has caused centralizing forces within a state to substitute for economic coordination by foreign investors. Or, to put it more familiarly, nationalist tendencies take hold. At the same time, few investors, if any, in the dominant economy have an incentive to promote the readjustment of financial claims or, more generally, to make monetary assets less appealing. Karl Polanyi, dismissing traditional explanations of the collapse of nineteenth-century civilization in the cataclysm of the First and Second World Wars, offers a pointed summary of this process in *The Great Transformation*:

It disintegrated as the result of an entirely different set of
causes: the measures which society adopted in order not to
be, in its turn, annihilated by the action of the self-regulating
market.[31]

This explanation could apply equally to the second half of
the seventeenth century. The decline of Dutch-intermediated
trade coincided with the rise of state-building across the world.
It was in this period—an intense interval of what historians
refer to as the "General Crisis"—that Louis XIV issued his
famous declaration "L'État, c'est moi"—"I am the state." Even
Asia experienced upheaval as the fledgling Maratha Empire
captured the Mughal-Dutch trading outpost of Surat, the new
Qing Dynasty expanded from Beijing to Formosa (modern-day
Taiwan), and the Tokugawa Shogunate in Japan expelled the
Dutch to take a more active role in the domestic economy.[32]

During such periods, those who are able to take advantage
of internal scale economies can improve their relative position
on the frontier of technological innovation. England in the
second half of the seventeenth century and the United States
after its Civil War are, as mentioned, salient instances. Though
a hindrance earlier in their development, the unwieldy combination of their (forcibly acquired) population size and decentralized governance turned into a relative advantage as global
cooperation failed. Moreover, while political ossification
shackled their more advanced peers to legacy modes of production, technological change in England and the United States
led to political change. Empowered investors in each instance
then pushed the state to prioritize investments that other
nations were either unwilling or unable to embrace. England,
for example, exploited the colonial trades and its domestic
supply of coal while the United States turned to steel and oil
(among other investments).

The shifting foreign policy attitudes in these eras were
indicative of the times. George Downing, the architect of the
Navigation Acts, fomented the envy and hatred of the Dutch

Republic among members of Parliament in the mid-1600s.[33] And the US Republicans, who lampooned the Democrats as "pawns" of Britain in the 1880s and 1890s, channeled Anglophobia to advocate naval expansion.[34] Such sentiment abounded in other countries, too, in each respective period.

Perhaps it's not so surprising, then, that state intervention in response to economic failure has invariably coincided with increased arms spending. In combination with autarky—which offers few routes to growth other than expanding the definition of the state—increased militarism has been a toxic recipe for conflict. And over the past five hundred years, war is what has reversed demand deficiency and extirpated inflexible systems of global finance.

The demand shock unleashed by war has also accelerated changes in primacy. A shift in the last two instances, however, did not occur because of direct conflict between the transitioning states. Instead, the Dutch Republic and England allied against Louis XIV's French Empire and, as is better known today, Britain and the United States allied against Germany.[35] For England, the Nine Years' War (1688–97) and the War of the Spanish Succession (1701–14) created conditions conducive to the accelerated growth of its manufacturing, shipping, and export sectors. By the turn of the eighteenth century, Britain was overtaking the Republic in maritime prowess.[36] Likewise, the First and Second World Wars fueled two of the fastest periods of US export expansion.

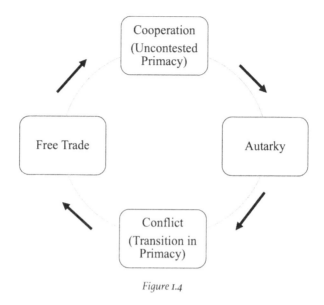

*Figure 1.4*

**Figure 1.4** diagrams the cycle of cooperation and conflict. Note that countries embrace more open trade before the beginning of the cooperative phase. Once cooperation fails, states turn to autarky before the start of the conflict phase.

Financial data from the sixteenth century on shows turning points in the global cycle. Around 1580, strong military spending coincides with a 40-percent decline in the value of the Dutch guilder.[37] Soon afterward, Dutch interest rates begin a long decline and fall from 8 percent at the turn of the century to 3 percent by its last quarter.[38] One hundred years later, interest rates in Britain peak in 1797 during the French Revolutionary Wars and subsequently fall from 6 percent to almost 2 percent in 1897. And, of course, a high point in US interest rates is evident in 1981 as the New Deal came to an end.

## The Tyranny of Nations

The pattern this book outlines will help demystify the developmental differences between nations that contemporary macroeconomic understanding cannot explain. Although half a millennium may seem an impractically long frame of reference, only such a long view can reveal the stark degree to which economic and political change across all nations is interlinked. Finally, a horizon of 500 years is necessary to answer a critical question: How can history serve as a compass for the future?

Following the financial panic of 2008, a succession of unsettling events has upset the notion that incumbent institutions represent the best of all possibilities or, to put it another way, the end of history. Many American intellectuals, especially those who inordinately shape discourse, have had to discard the idea of a permanent Pax Americana. But like the Dutch and Victorian cognoscenti preceding them, they failed to realize that their position in the world hindered their ability to discern "the long run."

Thus, rolling crises—financial instability, creeping authoritarianism, political reactions to inequality, and failure to address the outbreak of disease—now fuel a desperate search for an appropriate historical analogy for the present. Such events, however, very much conform to an identifiable pattern in place since the 16th century. This pattern offers cause for both concern and hope.

It warrants alarm because of where the world sits in the global cycle—a cycle perpetuated by the very existence of nations. As society casts off the remaining vestiges of an era of cooperation—however false such cooperation may have been —it now embarks on a long march toward conflict. And as will become evident, a new trio of nations now finds itself where the Republic, France, and England were in the mid-17th century, and Britain, Germany, and the United States were in the final quarter of the 19th.

Experience, however, also offers a reason for hope. Never before has history been generous enough to place so obvious a pattern before our eyes. Though humanity has never had so great a capacity to destroy itself, it has never been so greatly equipped with the lessons of the past to ensure lasting peace and prosperity for all.

# 2

# UNCERTAINTY, DISTRIBUTION, AND POLITICS

For John Maynard Keynes, the classical economic theory that dominated his time took for granted the immense role uncertainty about the future has on individual decisions. Thus, he observed in *The General Theory of Employment, Interest, and Money*:

> The whole object of the accumulation of wealth is to produce results, or potential results, at a comparatively distant, and sometimes at an indefinitely distant, date. Thus the fact that our knowledge of the future is fluctuating, vague and uncertain, renders wealth a peculiarly unsuitable subject for the methods of the classical economic theory.[1]

Individuals, according to Keynes, must make decisions in an environment of unmeasurable uncertainty. For Keynes, the vagaries of collective behavior were the principal source of such uncertainty. His term "animal spirits" encapsulated Charles MacKay's observation a century earlier in *Extraordinary Popular Delusions and the Madness of Crowds* that individuals "think in herds" and "go mad in herds."[2] Throughout history, as the famous Dutch tulip mania vividly illustrates, animal spirits have driven extreme fluctuations in the value of not only financial assets but also physical commodities. Keynes's *General Theory* argued that uncertainty arising from animal spirits, as well as more general causes creates demand for a unique good: money. Money, therefore, was the cause of unemployment— the principal concern of modern economics. Keynes's proposals for alleviating the ill effects of money indeed provide the foundation for economic management and policymaking today.

Oddly, the role of money as a store against uncertainty and, consequently, cause of unemployment is overlooked in early economics education, which often introduces the classical view of exchange as barter. One way to understand the distinctions between a monetary and barter-based economy is the story of Robinson Crusoe. In his barter economy, Robinson chooses between work and leisure. Because he can always spend more time working to collect items for barter, Robinson cannot be involuntarily unemployed.

Keynes's predecessors and some modern schools of economics applied this principle to the real world by arguing that market wages can always adjust to make labor supply equal to labor demand. In this view, wages, like the price of any other commodity, equal the marginal product of labor—the increment to output produced by an incremental input of effort. Such reasoning then blames unemployment on supply-side or structural conditions that make hiring unprofitable for employers. For example, unemployment may grow when individuals refuse the lower wages that reflect the diminished value that the market assigns to their work.

A popular supply-side explanation for why the market may devalue labor is technological change. Labor-saving innovation lowers the marginal product of occupations that become obsolescent. Narratives for labor distress rooted in technological shifts have had strong appeal throughout history. They caused Dutch sawyers to lobby for restrictions on mechanical sawmills and, more famously, caused the Luddites to destroy machinery during the Industrial Revolution in Britain.[3] Today, fear of the effects of automation and artificial intelligence abound.

As Keynes argued, however, the mere existence of money offers an alternative explanation for unemployment. When money acts as a store of purchasing power, the economy behaves quite differently from what the barter-based model suggests. In a monetary economy, output is determined not by supply but by demand.

Money gives investors insurance against uncertainty, especially by allowing them to earn some rate of interest. But in choosing to hold money, investors abstain from investment and, consequently, hiring, in the real economy. Money thus makes involuntary unemployment possible; the cure rests on the willingness of investors to eschew hoarding in favor of organizing physical resources. In the presence of uncertainty, however, such a solution is not easy to achieve.

According to Keynes, money has special properties that make it unlike any other good. First, and foremost, money serves as a durable vehicle for storing wealth. Second, money has a low elasticity of substitution.[4] That is, even when its value rises, few will think about substituting it for other goods. In contrast, when the prices of non-monetary goods go up, there is a natural temptation to transfer at least some of that gain into money. The first and second properties in combination cause money to constitute, as Keynes put it, "an infinite sink of purchasing power."[5]

A third special property of money is its zero elasticity of production. That is, an increase in its demand does not lead to increased employment. For nearly all other goods, higher demand creates an incentive to hire, in order to produce more. Finally, money has a rate of interest. Returns to real investment must compete against this rate, and pernicious economic outcomes occur when expectations for the former fall below the latter.[6]

The definition of money is not exclusive to public currency.

All assets, to varying degrees, can serve as vehicles for storing purchasing power. When Keynes deemed money to be an infinite sink, he was referring to the historical role of land as a store of wealth. Nevertheless, the expected return of an asset, weighed against its liquidity and storage costs, governs its attractiveness as a monetary store.

The most important forms of money in society—bank money—are private sector, not governmental, creations. Among these is bank money: any debt that settles transactions in place of physical money. During the Dutch Golden Age, Bank of Amsterdam liabilities became the most important form of money across Europe. As will be evident later, the Dutch Republic's dominant economic position allowed the Bank to back 100 percent of its liabilities with bullion reserves. Bank paper, therefore, became a convenient substitute for hauling gold around the continent.

In some instances—when lending to the government of Holland or the Dutch East India Company—the Bank did violate this practice. The practice of creating loans "out of thin air"—prior to obtaining reserves—is now much more prevalent among modern financial institutions.[7] A general assumption of the Keynesian paradigm is the availability of money (or, more specifically, credit) does not restrict investment. "Elastic" credit mechanisms supply ready finance to those undertaking investment.

## Investment and Savings

For economists of the classical school, who preceded Keynes, money was an afterthought. In their view, money only served transaction demand. Recipients of money, in other words, are quick to get rid of it in exchange for an actual product or service. Two classical-school fallacies, in particular, have caused considerable macroeconomic misunderstanding: Say's Law and loanable funds.

Say's Law is named after the eighteenth-century French

economist Jean-Baptiste Say. It says that production creates its own demand: an investor will dispose of money from profits to buy other goods. Demand deficiency, therefore, cannot exist: an excess of supply of one good creates demand for another.

In classical economics, the "loanable funds" doctrine holds that aggregate savings behave like savings at the individual level. Individuals fund their own investments out of fixed savings or borrow external savings. The idea that savings precede investment indeed possesses intuitive appeal. In this view, a market exists in which aggregate savings funds aggregate investment at a certain rate of interest. If savings increase, interest falls until investment absorbs them. If they decrease, the rate of interest rises to reduce investment demand. This mechanism is incompatible with the idea that savings can reduce output.

The reason is that the loanable funds doctrine assumes scarce and fixed savings. In reality, however, aggregate savings change with output. When economic output falls, savings fall, and when output rises, savings rise. Keynes pointed out that the extrapolation of individual to aggregate savings suffers from a fallacy of composition. In other words, economy-wide saving is distinct from individual savings behavior. Consider an extreme scenario in which everyone decided to save all of their income. Economic output would be zero and savings, consequently, also zero—there would be no income to save.

According to *the principle of effective demand*, investment demand determines savings and output.[8] What governs investment demand itself is expected returns to real investment, which consequently also determine employment. Firms hire when profits from real investment seem compelling relative to the interest on money. As individual investment decisions aggregate, savings rise to equal investment. The level at which demand settles is called *effective demand*. It is effective because it can fall short of what producers are fully able to supply.

In the absence of fixed savings, what determines interest rates? From the Keynesian perspective, saving does not create rewards for waiting.[9] Instead, the rate of interest on money is the "reward for parting with liquidity," or, put more simply, "not hoarding."[10] More specifically, changes in supply and demand across the menu of financial assets determine interest. Hoarding in perceived safe and liquid forms of money during times of risk aversion causes interest rates (or "the yield") on these assets to fall (or, alternatively, causes their prices to rise).[11] A sufficient decline could make real investment compelling again. But inevitably, according to Keynes, expected returns to real investment fall faster than interest rates on liquid forms of money. Economic depressions result when the economy reaches such a point.

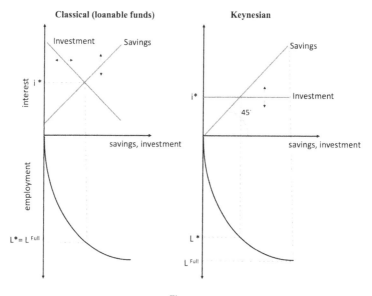

**Classical vs. Keynesian Theories of Savings, Investment, and Interest**

*Figure 2.1*

**Figure 2.1** illustrates the Classical and Keynesian theories of savings and investment. In the Classical loanable funds view, a market for savings and investment determines the *equilibrium* rate of interest (all unemployment is

voluntary). Under the Keynesian view, changes in investment demand drive changes
in savings.

**Classical vs. Keynesian Views of Output and Employment**

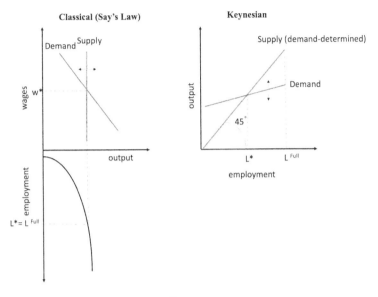

*Figure 2.2*

**Figure 2.2** juxtaposes the Classical view of output and employment with that of
Keynes. Under the former paradigm, aggregate supply adjustments settle the
economy at full employment. According to Keynes, however, changes in demand
determine changes in output. The economy can then remain in a condition of
significant voluntary unemployment. Source: Roger Farmer, "Post Keynesian
Dynamic Stochastic General Equilibrium Theory," *National Bureau of Economic
Research Working Paper Series* No. 23109 (2017).

## The Myth of Equilibrium

Depressions, in the Keynesian view, reflect a failure of collective action. When interest rates cannot fall fast enough to
compensate for declines in expected returns to real investment,

more centralized coordination becomes necessary. Keynes thus advocated fiscal intervention as a remedy for unemployment.

Until the 1970s, active fiscal policy underpinned techno-cratic management of the economy. But the economic turmoil of the 1970s challenged this approach. The occurrence of unemployment alongside accelerating inflation—a phenomenon known as *stagflation*—seemed to violate the Keynesian paradigm.

After inflation subsided and growth continued to stagnate in the 1980s—the so-called New Keynesians, the leading school whose model currently animates the policies of the US Federal Reserve—modified the traditional Keynesian view. Its propo-nents argued that money could only affect employment in the short run while, in the long run, inflation erodes the effects of money. Should unemployment and disinflation (low inflation) occur, authorities could restore the public's expectations that inflation will return and, consequently, draw individuals away from money.

The New Keynesians further argued that employment tends to reach a certain resting level of equilibrium as hoarding ceases to be relevant.[12] Structural supply-side considerations—namely, conditions of long-run production—determine this level. Through such arguments, the New Keynesians seemingly bridged the gap between the deflationary 1930s and the infla-tionary 1970s. Disequilibrium, in their view, remained a short-run phenomenon. And the right policies could ensure the proper function of markets in the long run.

Doubts about the existence of long-run equilibrium are now emerging, however. Few examples are better than Japan's economic experience over the past several decades. Despite ostensibly unconventional monetary experiments, Japanese officials have been unable to restore inflation. Furthermore, deflation has persisted even though unemployment recently fell to 2 percent and government indebtedness remained at the highest levels in the world. The coincidence of deflation with such developments casts doubt on whether a supposed natural rate of unemployment exists. In the United States, too, inflation has been absent during recent periods of gainful employment.

As will become evident later, more distant history also weighs against the idea of a natural equilibrium rate of unemployment. Unemployment in Britain fell to nearly 2 percent before the Panic of 1873 with little resultant inflation. And inflation failed to appear for almost a century during the periods of British and Dutch primacy.

All the while, the *General Theory* has been subject to myth-making around the idea that it failed the test of stagflation. Keynes himself asserted that, under significant erosion in the real value of money, "a long series of substitutes would step into [its] shoes—bank-money, debts at call, foreign money, jewelry and the precious metals generally, and so forth."[13] Indeed, money supply in the 1970s "leaked" into real assets such as gold, oil, and foreign securities.

The economics orthodoxy also sought to frame the United States in the same terms as a "less-developed" or emerging market, where stagflation, as will be evident later, is a more persistent phenomenon. In such countries, panic produces painful currency depreciation, inflation, and unemployment. But a certain fixed supply of real savings—as the loanable funds view would suggest—did not flee the US economy and force output to contract during the 1970s. Instead, inflation-protected assets appreciated most that decade when the economy expanded.[14] Such assets were also the object of risk-seeking speculation, not a panic-induced flight-to-safety, for a nascent securities trading industry (see Chapter 10).

Still, Keynes did not offer a uniform cause that could explain *why* the depression of the 1930s and the stagflation of the 1970s occurred. Equally, Keynes's fixation on employment, like the economics orthodoxy that succeeded him, ignored the broader questions about living conditions in a given society. As recent times have shown, compensation can stagnate and fail to outgrow the cost of living even when unemployment is relatively low. Such dilemmas raise questions about the long run,

which Keynes famously addressed with the unsatisfying quip,
"In the long run we are all dead." But perhaps Keynes ignored
the long run because it involved an important consideration
that he, like many technocrats today, preferred to avoid:
politics.

## Ricardo and Rent-Seeking

The roots of Keynes's *General Theory* lie in the ideas of early
English economic philosophers Nicholas Barbon and Bernard
Mandeville, who identified the problem of collective action
under uncertainty in the late 1600s and early 1700s.[15] Recognizing *the paradox of thrift,* they argued that if all individuals were
to act parsimoniously, it would produce harmful collective
effects. Barbon, in particular, noted the false analogy between
individual and collective economic behavior.[16] He saw
hoarding as an economic malady and was among the first to
articulate the idea that higher wages could increase societal
prosperity.[17]

Barbon and Mandeville, who received their education in
the Dutch Republic, lived in an era in which Dutch economic
thought had considerable influence on England and other
countries. Calvinist parsimony suited the policy aims of the
republican regents—the oligarchic town heads—who dominated Dutch politics in the second half of the seventeenth
century. Favoring low taxes (on the wealthy), free trade, and
limited executive power, they sought to curb government
spending on military adventures.

After 1660, however, Dutch hoarding in financial claims and
bullion produced economic stagnation across Europe. A resolu-
tion came in the form of war between the Protestant countries
and France. Spending needs brought an end to austerity in the
Republic and forced a reassessment of the Dutch predilection
for limited military expenditure and limited taxation. In
England, military spending would provide a means for
economic management for the entirety of the eighteenth

century. More notably, it served as a means for self-enrichment among members of Parliament. During the War of the Spanish Succession (1701–14), opponents of the Duke of Marlborough, the leader of Anglo-Dutch forces on the continent, resuscitated moral arguments against excess to condemn the military expenditures that raised his personal fortune. In response to these individuals, Mandeville wrote his poem The Fable of the Bees, which casts "private vices"—profligate spending—as "public benefits."[18]

Beginning with Adam Smith, the classical school of economics emerged in response to the corrupt political regime that grew out of the English colonial war machine. Politics, especially as it related to the distribution of economic output, figured prominently in the ideas of Smith's intellectual successor, David Ricardo. A Whig MP in the early nineteenth century, Ricardo was an influential voice not only in Parliament but also outside of Britain. When his book *Principles* reached the United States, Thomas Jefferson attempted to stop its publication, believing that its advocacy of free trade was unsuitable on American shores.[19] What likely irked Jefferson was Ricardo's attack on landowners like himself.

Ricardo's world was not one of money, like that of Keynes, but of corn. The availability of corn, necessary to feed the population of workers, determined the profits that could be gained from non-agricultural investment and hence growth. Landowners, through the mere passive ownership of quality land, took a share of aggregate profits, which Ricardo called rents.

What he feared was that a high cost of grain would limit England's development. As the population increased in response to growth (Ricardo assumed an elastic supply of labor), cultivation would spread to higher-cost peripheral land. Land rents would swell as grain prices rose to equal marginal costs on the periphery while higher costs of subsistence would then eat into manufacturing profits. A smaller piece of a fixed pie for manufacturers meant fewer savings for reinvestment

(Ricardo subscribed to Say's Law). As its most productive sector failed to grow, England would succumb to stagnation. Ricardo used such reasoning to assail the Corn Laws, which limited agricultural imports to protect the rents of landowners during the deflation that occurred after France's surrender.

Ricardo's ideas are inseparable from the historical context of the Napoleonic Wars. In 1793, rising war expenditure forced Britain to suspend currency convertibility, which, in combination with the war's effect on food prices, provided a boon to landed proprietors. During the war, landowners became a formidable investor bloc. They had a critical role in a paternalistic political arrangement that staved off the threat of Jacobinism. To combat the effect of rising grain prices on rural workers, the overseers of each parish set a minimum wage based on the price of corn and supplemented it as prices changed.[20] In reality, however, the Speenhamland system enriched large farmers and tied workers to their local parish.[21]

In acquiring a disproportionate degree of control over government, landowners had become a rent-seeking impediment to growth.[22] Although Britain's postwar depression was not the result of the Corn Laws themselves, Ricardo had introduced an important idea. He showed that distribution—how output was split between wages, rents, and profits—had an immense bearing on economic progress. Of course, what shaped distribution, in the end, was politics. Politics was the source of rents, either in the form of land ownership during Ricardo's time or financial asset ownership during that of Keynes.

## Kalecki and Distribution

Keynes is not the only economist to have formulated a demand-driven theory of economics. Michal Kalecki, his Polish contemporary, simultaneously converged on the same ideas. Like Keynes, Kalecki argued that collective investment behavior determines profits and output, but he made no assumptions about money. Instead, he argued that fundamental uncertainty leads to a society in which certain individuals have a privileged role in economic coordination. Distribution is thus central to Kalecki's version of the *General Theory*.

Monetary arrangements, in Kalecki's view, involve deliberate institutional choices. In other words, the state decides what serves as money (an observation Barbon had made in the seventeenth century).[23] But Kalecki, like Smith, believed that state decisions, such as those that concern legal tender, were subject to the influence of monopoly power.

Kalecki (1899–1970) had a range of political and economic phenomena in perspective. He experienced both the deflationary forces that accompanied the Great Depression and the price pressures of the Cold War. Kalecki doubted that any approximation of pure competition in markets existed. Imperfect competition was the norm—a view colored by the pervasiveness of cartelized industries in the 1930s. In his native Poland, for example, monopolies accounted for 40 percent of industrial goods.[24] He thus viewed anticompetitive practices as a global phenomenon and observed the presence of trusts and cartels in a host of industries including rubber, linoleum, steel, and matches. In the latter industry, one individual, Ivan Krueger, had managed to consolidate 75 percent of worldwide production of matches.[25]

The political economy of distribution played a prominent role in Kalecki's theory. First, he distinguished between those who earn profits—capitalists—and workers, who earn wages. He further assumed that workers live close to subsistence and, as a result, cannot save, and that therefore the investment activity of capitalists largely governed economic outcomes.[26] Kalecki argued that prices in an economy reflected a monopoly markup over wages. Notions of marginal product, which measure labor as a commodified incremental input to the economy, did not figure in the determination of prices and wages. And, unlike Ricardo, he made no distinction between rents and profits. Kalecki believed that markup persisted not only in the short run but also in the long run. What determined the markup over wages was an institutional condition called the "degree of monopoly."

Because he made no assumptions about money, Kalecki's theory of demand-determined output more easily accommodates the anomalies that seem to confound the *General Theory*. Imperfect competition severs the link between prices and employment, which means that low unemployment *can* be consistent with low inflation. Alternatively, high prices can coincide with high unemployment.

Kalecki attributed inflation to supply limitations in "particular groups of commodities."[27] If demand grows too quickly, it can meet capacity limits in certain goods. Prices then spill over to the level of whole industries, and more general inflation ensues. A price-wage spiral can occur if money wages cannot "catch up" to falling real wages.[28] In other words, wages attempt to catch up to prices but only manage to push prices even higher. Wartime policies provided a clear example:

> Government expenditure absorbs manpower into the armed forces and war industries on a large scale. In such a situation bottlenecks are likely to develop in various sectors of consumption-goods industries.[29]

Under such circumstances, government expenditures must accelerate to maintain target employment. What likely informed Kalecki's view of inflation was his familiarity with Poland's experience. Less-developed countries face more binding supply inelasticities and, as a result, are more susceptible to price pressures.

Kalecki, of course, did not subscribe to a notion of a long-run Say's Law, or aggregate supply constraint.[30] He, like Keynes, believed excess capacity and unemployment were persistent. But the importance of distribution, and, consequently, politics to his framework made Kalecki skeptical toward the possibilities of technocratic fiscal management. In his political-economic framework, the barriers to redistributive government programs were high. If monopoly gives firms inordinate political power, little incentive exists to cure unemployment.

Or, as he later discovered—like Smith and Ricardo earlier —fiscal policy becomes an instrument for more nefarious ends. The New Deal posed an ostensible challenge to Kalecki's views on monopoly power. Although cartels abounded during the interwar period, he admitted that the postwar decline in unemployment and concomitant rise in living standards "point to the elements of decay in monopoly capitalism."[31] Yet this left Kalecki far from satisfied, and he scathingly rebuked the postwar economic order in the West. Foreshadowing Eisenhower's warning against the "military-industrial complex," Kalecki disparaged a "military-imperialist set-up" which supported "a relatively high level of employment through expenditures on armaments" and "through the maintenance of a large body of armed forces and government employees."[32]

American Keynesianism, in his opinion, was more preoccupied with subsidizing industry than raising living standards. In comparison to the social programs being implemented in other Western societies, the New Deal was a false ideal. Kalecki did not believe that American workers exercised their bargaining power any less than counterparts elsewhere. But he did observe that mass communications campaigns—which were especially effective in the backdrop of the Cold War—facilitated more paternalistic arrangements between workers and enterprise.[33] And, although monopoly power had perhaps diminished, it still existed to some degree, with one set of firms substituting for another.

Kalecki's postwar observations can help reconcile the deflation experienced in the Great Depression and the high inflation accompanying the decay of the New Deal. More generally, they offer visibility into the forces that govern the long run. They prove especially useful when considered together with Ricardo's perspective.

The political-economic arrangements of Cold War America

can be compared to those that prevailed in Britain during the Revolutionary era. Both contained salient elements of paternalism. In the latter, the aristocracy owning coal and agricultural lands backed Speenhamland provisioning. In the former, multinational firms, principally international oil, became the most prominent backers of Keynesianism and progressive labor policies.[34]

Yet, like the owners of agricultural and coal lands in early nineteenth-century Britain, the New Deal investor bloc reaped the benefits of military spending. Twentieth-century conditions in the US, though, were complicated by another factor. Furthermore, as Kalecki identified, they were able to garner union support for their foreign policy initiatives. This symbiosis again harkened back to the Revolutionary Era when agricultural workers backed Church and Crown in sympathy with their Tory patrons.[35] By the 1970s, however, the prevailing fiscal-military regime became subject to decay. Instead of corn-growing landlords, rents went to those titled to real assets—oil interests, speculators, and US allies in the Cold War—and the unions abetting militarism.

With the onset of inflation, the problem of increasing long-term unemployment could not be solved, as Keynes's disciple Joan Robinson observed, "by operating on effective demand."[36] Robinson did not intend to question the validity of Keynes's *theory* but rather its *application*. Existing policies—the specific institutional choices made by the New Deal investor coalition —had become ineffective at raising demand. Increasing investment instead required "fundamental structural remedies" to these institutions, whose entrenchment at the hands of select rent-seeking interests was responsible for the economic distortions of the 1970s.[37]

Distribution is the common thread that ties together the ideas of Ricardo, Keynes, and Kalecki. Claimants to financial rents or real rents push institutional change to extremes in their own favor. Such extremes can manifest as the price deflation that informed Keynes's perspectives. Alternatively, they can emerge as the inflationary pressures observed in the United States in the 1970s and in Britain at the turn of the nineteenth century. These maladies are *political* in nature, and in piecing together the regular political forces that bring them about, some semblance of a long-run pattern emerges.

# 3

# POLITICS AS INVESTMENT

A simple aggregation of individual behavior alone cannot explain collective outcomes, which is why economic models premised on uniform individual actors have struggled to explain various macroeconomic phenomena. An approach biased toward analyzing static conditions is also unsuitable for a reality in which disequilibrium persists.

As dynamic processes, investment cycles offer a convenient building block for understanding change. Few explanations of investment are better than Hyman Minsky's interpretation of Keynesian animal spirits. Minsky described investment in five stages: displacement, boom, euphoria, profit-taking, and panic. Displacement, here, means some new development or "shock." It entails innovations, changes in government policy, or more general externalities.

Minsky's description, however, requires further clarification and extension. First, a given technology or domain can have a unique investment cycle, though that cycle is correlated to cycles in other technologies. At this more granular level, profit expectations invite herd investment, overcapacity, and then subsequent consolidation. As planned investment is completed, profits fall below the cost of capital, and weak players disappear. The few survivors claim industry rents.

But the cycle does not end here. The resultant monopolies can acquire a formidable position in the economy, and their position may only erode with new technology or external competition. Their ousters, too, however, maintain a monopolistic position.

The aggregate business cycle emerges from the composition of expanding, or "lead," and contracting, or "lag," investment cycles. An upswing commences when investment in a new technology passes a certain threshold. Demand from this category can then spill over to stimulate investment or delay contraction in other industries. When exuberance in a leading domain pauses or becomes exhausted, a downswing commences. An investment recession can result from either overinvestment in the leading technology itself or resumed contraction—previously delayed—in another.

Modern stock markets offer clear patterns. In the 1960s, multinational consumer companies—"Nifty 50" companies like Coca-Cola and Disney—led. Their rise delayed contraction in a domestic manufacturing sector that struggled to compete with new foreign entrants.[1] By the 1970s, after the Nifty "bubble" became exhausted, problems in the latter began to weigh on the economy. In the 1990s, telecommunications led while the foreign sector struggled. And in the 2000s, the foreign and materials sectors recovered after a downturn in telecom. Excesses in the financial sector, of course, ended this cycle. Finally, internet investment has led during the recent cycle as foreign markets and commodities have struggled.

Underlying the succession of investment cycles is continuous technological progress. Today's internet monopolies owe their origins to military research and development in the 1960s. Likewise, asset management and private equity owe their origins to the emergence of securities trading and conglomer-

ates in the "go-go years" of that decade.[2] More recently, high
energy prices in the 2000s stimulated the shale energy boom of
the 2010s, which had been substantial enough to cause a mild
downturn in 2015.

Investment cycles were present in the Dutch Republic too.
Shipbuilding and cartographic advances prompted an investment mania for new colonial routes in the 1590s. The conse-
quent slump ended in the 1620s with a series of innovations to
windmill technology. Dutch engineers applied the technology
to land reclamation, which sparked new agricultural investment. And overcapacity in agriculture was briefly staved off by
a property bubble in the 1650s.

Britain's investment cycles are somewhat more familiar. A
boom in canal construction—"canal mania"—commenced in
the 1790s, followed by investment in steam-powered machine
innovations that developed during the Napoleonic Wars.[3] Railroads emerged in the 1820s and grew enough by the 1840s to
end a painful slump. And the advent of the motor engine in the
1890s fostered a recovery from a depression that began in 1873.

Over the past several decades, many attributed business
cycle fluctuations to changes in interest rates. Economic recessions, in this view, occurred because authorities allowed wages
and inflation to grow too fast. Belated tightening then forced a
"hard brake" on the economy.

As Keynes and Kalecki explained, however, interest rates
lag changes to demand driven by varying expected returns or
expected profits on real investment. In Kalecki's conception of
business cycle dynamics, an increase in profit expectations
becomes self-fulfilling as it draws investment into the real economy, which raises profits. Ex-post extrapolation of profits
causes an upswing, which peaks with overinvestment. Aggregate savings and the money supply thus ebb and flow in
response to profit expectations.

In the process of an upswing, new financial claims prolif-
erate to meet investment demand. This idea is known as the
credit theory of money, which the early British economist

Henry Thornton first articulated in *Paper Credit* in 1802. Thornton argued that various types of financial claims can substitute for payment.[4] He sought to demonstrate that a gold standard, a subject of intense debate at the time, would not limit the creation of new money.

During a business-cycle upswing, the opportunity cost of holding relatively safe and liquid forms of money increases, which cause interest rate movements to vary pro-cyclically with aggregate investment. On the other hand, the value of existing financial claims, whose rents depend on the health of the business cycle, also increases—contributing to the unattractiveness of risk-free forms of money. Such behavior explains why the real economy seems to follow the performance of the stock market.

## The Role of the State in Investment

As mentioned in the preceding chapter, Keynes posited that money had an essential function as a haven in a world of fundamental uncertainty. In the wake of the Great Depression, he recommended that the state take active measures to stimulate investment in order to alleviate hoarding and the accompanying failure of private production. But his ideas obscure the fact that the state has always had an active role in inducing investment.

Minsky extended the ideas of Keynes and Kalecki to incorporate the essential role of government in shaping prices and output. Repudiating the orthodox view of equilibrium-determined prices, he argued that significant degrees of freedom exist in the formation of investment and prices in an economy:

> Given that such degrees of freedom in price formation exist, it is evident that simplistic policy goals such as full employment or appeals "to let the market determine" what happens grossly misspecify the economic problem. Economic policy calls the tune for what happens and economic policy always

has explicit and implicit "for whom" and "what kind" implications. Even neglect, whether benign or malignant, implies that "for whom" and "what kind" choices have been made.[5]

According to Minsky, policy choices can never escape "the normative question of for whom the game be fixed and what kind of output should be produced."[6]

Amid fundamental uncertainty, government policy is needed to sufficiently attenuate the risks investors face. Prices, therefore, are a political matter. The extent of state investment governs absolute prices, and the nature of subsidies determines relative prices.[7] Furthermore, oligopoly and monopoly become "natural market structures" since they introduce greater certainty to profits.[8]

With its powers of "purchase, tax, and subsidy" and most importantly, coercion, government serves as a facilitating arm of private investment.[9] It helps investors overcome the general problem of organizing collective action. Since the time of Dutch hegemony, states have supported private commerce in two broad ways. The first is war, and the second is the active imposition and enforcement of market institutions.

Early Dutch privateering offers a more representative example of enterprise than that of the individual barterer often presented in introductory economics courses. In fact, plunderers—"Sea Dogs"—played the most pivotal role in Dutch independence from Spain. Unsurprisingly, the newly established Republic had a not undeserved reputation as a nation of pirates. Even locals at the time observed that "no one could deny that the country had been born in war and grown rich through war."[10]

Privateering interests dominated policy during the wars of the Counter-Reformation that took place from 1566 to the 1630s. Early Dutch naval boards offered direct assistance to the Dutch West India Company, which plundered Spanish ships. Furthermore, several innovations in ship design came from naval investments made in this era.[11]

War also buttressed commerce in colonial-era England, which sought to imitate the earlier successes of the Dutch. The country that gave birth to the Industrial Revolution waged war in almost every year from 1688 to 1815.[12] Military engagement stimulated efforts to smelt iron with coal. And the demands of the War of the Spanish Succession, which immediately followed the Nine Years' War, helped produce new techniques in coke-smelting.[13] Even the steam engine owes part of its development to the Board of Ordnance—the English government's arms procurement office—at the turn of the eighteenth century.[14]

Gun manufacturing, in particular, helped create the foundations for the industrial revolution. During the 1700s, what began as an artisanal craft transformed into a mass-scale enterprise. A diffuse division of labor emerged as the government sought to strengthen supply chains.[15] In turn, innovations made in the arms trade spilled over into other industries, including textiles.[16]

And finally, governments did not embrace Keynesian policy in earnest until it suited the spending needs of the Second World War and the Cold War. Since then, military procurement has, of course, had a considerable role in American enterprise. As already mentioned, Cold War armaments expenditures provided a significant demand buffer to domestic industry. Likewise, Marshall Plan outlays supported external markets for American multinationals.[17]

The other key means of supporting enterprise has been active state intervention to widen the scope of market organization in society. Many today recognize this type of profit incentive as "market liberalization" or "structural reform." It is also the type chronicled by Karl Polanyi in *The Great Transformation*.

Polanyi detailed market expansion during Britain's primacy and noted the destabilizing effects of the "commodification" of land, labor, and money. Removal of protections on communal land in the seventeenth and eighteenth centuries allowed landlords to accumulate sizable tracts of farmland for commercial agriculture. Then, in 1834, Parliament liberalized the labor market by forcing the unemployed into workhouses. Disincentives to unemployment sought to expand the supply of labor available to manufacturers. Additional reforms, such as Peel's Bank Act, pursued stricter adherence to the gold standard. They sought to assuage creditors who required certainty in the monetary value of their loans.

Although known as *laissez-faire*, Victorian-era policies made active distributional choices and were enacted at the behest of select private interests. The myth of free markets becomes more apparent in light of Britain's interventions in the international sphere to enforce ostensibly free trade. Following the end of the Napoleonic Wars, the Royal Navy employed gunboat diplomacy to open foreign countries to British goods, ensure payment of sovereign loans, and, more generally, police the high seas.[18] Markets, both at home and abroad, relied on the protection of "the world's largest security organization."[19]

Polanyi's narrative possesses strong parallels to events in the Dutch Republic after the first quarter of the seventeenth century and the US after the late 1970s. In the former case, States Party merchants implemented a series of measures that included budgetary austerity, free trade, loosening guild restrictions, and privatization of the military. Its American incarnation—economic liberals in both parties—famously pursued the aggressive deregulation of private enterprise. Each case saw private actors use the state as an instrument for promoting market expansion.

### Political Investment

Absolute and relative profits in an economy depend on policy choices.[20] Output, prices, and incomes depend on, as Hyman Minsky put it, "*how, what,* and *for whom* questions that policy has to confront."[21] State decisions underlie the assignment of values and claims in a society. As a result, investment in desired political outcomes must enter profit calculations too.

Economic investment in any endeavor therefore entails consideration for *political* investment. Political investment consists of financial support for parties or officials who will, in kind, prioritize a given investor agenda in government. It becomes more pressing as an enterprise grows in size. Once profits appear, incentives to protect them against competitors become stronger. As will later be evident later, the tendency of new and incumbent investment interests to clash consequently makes political investment important for upstarts too.

A common pattern has characterized political investment since the Dutch Republic. Profit-motivated actors will offer support to groups—often (but not always) groups with non-economic interests—whose policy demands do not conflict with their own. In the Republic, pro-peace internationalist merchants supported the liberal wing of the Reformed Church —the main Protestant affiliation in the Republic—while their more belligerent rivals, looking to benefit from military expenditures, supported its conservative wing. In pre-Civil War England, the landed gentry composing the "war party," who had stakes in privateering outfits and colonial trade, supported Puritan settlement in the New World.[22] On the other hand, City merchants, who benefited from peace and free trade on the continent, remained close to the religious establishment and the Crown. As a result, religious nonconformists—those who were not members of the Church of England—and their pro-Church opponents proxied country and court interests, respectively. After 1688, affiliations with religious groups maintained a superficial distinction between Tories and Whigs.[23]

It is also revealing to look at which groups did *not* receive support. In the Dutch United Provinces, these were radical republicans—those who opposed hereditary executives—and rationalist opponents of ecclesiastic authority.[24] Such individuals included the Dutch philosopher Spinoza and his mentor, the ex-Jesuit Franciscus van den Enden (who was among the earliest opponents of slavery). But more liberal regents felt such groups could inflame violent religious groups, and—worse—undermine their own authority. Until the Victorian era, radical republican groups in England, too, had little backing. The Levellers found themselves marginalized by Cromwell during the English Civil War. In the following century, Joseph Priestley and Thomas Paine were forced to flee the country. And the various worker movements of the nineteenth century were anathema to both industrialists and Tories.

The intimate link between investment and politics in the Republic and Britain extends to the present. Political scientist Thomas Ferguson has demonstrated how investor blocs shape priorities in the more democratic governments of today. Given information costs, political outcomes will not reflect the preferences of the median voter. Instead, Ferguson argues, "political parties dominated by large investors try to assemble the votes they need by making very limited appeals to. . . particular segments of the potential electorate." On issues in which investors have a common interest, no party competition will occur. Furthermore, noneconomic issues will have disproportionate representation on party platforms.[25]

The preferences backed by a particular set of investors can remain in play for a long time, while the opposition is limited to, as Ferguson puts it, "variations on the same themes."[26] Such "sticky" political preferences result from imperfect competition and periods of dominance for particular investor coalitions. They're also consistent with lengthy party reigns such as those of the Whigs in the Age of Walpole, the Tories in the Napoleonic era, the Victorian Liberals, the Lincoln Republicans, and the New Deal Democrats.

Indeed, commercial groups with particular policy preferences are identifiable with the tenure of each coalition. The rise of the Whigs in the early 1700s, for example, coincided with that of protectionist manufacturers and that of West Indies planters in fierce competition with France. Likewise, the post-civil war Republicans in the US drew support from the tariff lobby and exporters supporting expansion in the Caribbean. Their reign ended with the emergence of multinationals, such as international oil, who favored free-trade internationalism and lent support to the New Deal. And like the stock-jobbing (day trading) partnerships that grew during the Napoleonic Wars and supported the Liberal program, an emergent securities industry contributed to the New Deal's demise and ushered in a new liberal era.

Resemblances between political parties across the histories of the Dutch Republic, England, and the United States are not coincidental. Underlying changes in dominant investor blocs is a process of continuous technological progress and the shifting relative position of a society on the frontier of technological innovation. Free trade eras in all three empires, for example, occurred during phases of developmental maturity when certain enterprises could exploit foreign markets without fear of competition. Indeed, as the next two chapters will show, the principal force behind institutional change is not internal but rather external: the changing relationship of a state to the rest of the world.

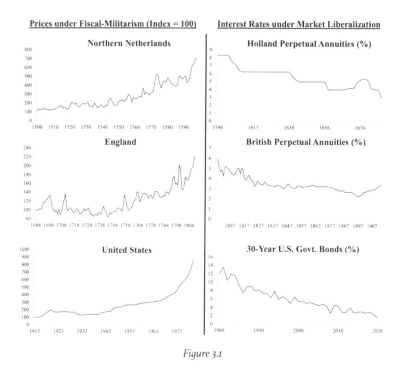

*Figure 3.1*

**Figure 3.1** illustrates the alternation of fiscal-military and market liberalization regimes through the behavior of prices and interest rates. Prices on the left-hand side show how rising military expenditures put pressure on inflation in the Dutch Republic, Britain, and the United States. Falling interest rates on the right-hand side are coincident with market expansion (and price stability). **Sources:** FRED, Federal Reserve Bank of St. Louis; Gelderblom and Jonker, "Public Finance"; "Millennium of Data," Bank of England.

## Information and Policy Lock-in

The preceding chapter suggested that inflation and depression are consistent with the decay of particular political-economic institutional arrangements. Despite being polyarchal, all three of the Republic, Britain, and the United States exhibited political inertia. In other words, dominant investor coalitions could maintain a grip on policy for long periods. A natural result was policy lock-in: fiscal-militarism begetting further fiscal-militarism and laissez-faire leading to more laissez-faire.

What enables regime persistence and policy lock-in are barriers to the free flow of information. Such restrictions tend to be associated with highly centralized societies, which use them to stifle dissent. But as Charles Lindblom asserted in *Politics and Markets*, informational bounds that allow "early, persuasive, unconscious conditioning to believe in the fundamental politico-economic institutions of one's society" are "ubiquitous in every society."[27] Though varying in degree, controls on information are an inherent part of any state. Thus, even in ostensibly free societies, where politics "is never quite a closed circle," ideological circularity, to use Lindblom's terminology, and policy lock-in can manifest.[28]

In *Manufacturing Consent*, Chomsky and Herman outline explicit mechanisms for how bounds on information can prevail in a market economy—when communication is not subject to state monopoly. Even when media is privately owned, they argue, certain news "filters" skew information. Five are notable in particular: concentration of media ownership, dependence on government sources, dependence on advertising, "flak," and "anticommunism." Flak is a catch-all term for negative responses to the media. And "anticommunism"— colored by the Cold War—refers to the practice of silencing political opponents by associating them with enemy states.

These filters approximate the principal ways in which limits to information have existed in the three dominant economies. In the early years of the Dutch Republic, anti-Catholicism and anti-Jesuitism substituted for the anticommunism in Chomsky and Herman's model. The town council of Haarlem, for example, justified censorship of a pamphlet in 1618 by asserting that it employed arguments used by Jesuits, the radical Catholic order that both Protestant and Catholic states eyed warily.

Such speech limitations in the Republic are noteworthy because it offered a high degree of personal freedom relative to other nations during the seventeenth century. The Dutch States General had little control over the largely autonomous town councils, whose interests varied with the character of local enterprise. Pamphleteers banned in one town council could publish in towns controlled by political rivals. Liberal theologians censored by conservative regents were thus able to publish their writing under the auspices of regents whose commercial interests favored peace.

But even these regents remained sensitive to criticism from hard-liners, who could provoke mob violence. After the execution of Holland's Grand Pensionary (comparable to a prime minister) in 1619, more tolerant theologians fled the country. As war with Spain flared up again, they faced increased accusations of Catholic tendencies. At the same time, the regents supporting them caught flak from nationalist rivals.

In England during the French Revolutionary Wars, anti-Jacobinism became a political weapon to stifle electoral reform. Foreshadowing later-day McCarthyism, the 1790s treason trials —Pitt's "terror"—prosecuted dissidents under exaggerated claims of sedition. Additionally, between 1789 and 1815, to slow the circulation of dissent, Parliament almost quadrupled the stamp duty on pamphlets.

Mechanisms distorting information prevailed outside of wartime too. In the Dutch Republic, as small a number as only two individuals were allowed a license to publish news. And in Britain, the fixed costs of industrial presses created a barrier to entry even after the repeal of press taxes in 1855. Those limited to traditional methods struggled to match the volume of output of their more technically advanced and better-endowed competitors.

The prevalence of barriers to the flow of information in the Dutch Republic and early modern Britain is perhaps not so surprising since similar ones still exist in the US today. Nevertheless, shared features in communications control mechanisms show how bounds on information can exist under relatively less-centralized polyarchy. The costs of information dissemination especially allowed investor blocs in each example to wield disproportionate influence over how and what news circulates.

In all three cases, bounds on information led to policy lock-in by enabling institutional capture by select investor coalitions. Eventually, however, rent-seeking by the dominant investor bloc becomes intolerable to other investors. Such behavior creates economic distortions that limit profit opportunities—not least to new investors emerging in the natural course of technological change. Decay in fiscal-militarism, for example, has coincided with the scarcity and hoarding of real commodities such as corn or oil. The decay of market organization, on the other hand, has coincided with monetary hoarding. In response to every episode of decay, a new coalition of investors coalesced in favor of the alternate regime. The interchange of these two regimes has indeed characterized global development over the past 500 years. But as the next two chapters will show, the principal cause behind the transition from fiscal-militarism to market organization is not internal but instead the ever-changing relationship of a state to the world at large.

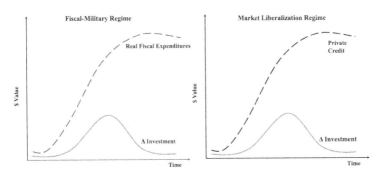

*Figure 3.2*

**Figure 3.2** offers stylized representations of each regime, which initially revives investment but ultimately gives way to rent-seeking and stagnation.

# 4

# GLOBAL INVESTMENT

I nvestment transcends national boundaries when investors lend resources to foreigners or directly employ their labor or local resources. When technological disparities exist between countries, purchasing power also transcends boundaries, and investors in the more developed nation can wield inordinate influence in foreign markets. As mentioned earlier, the term *international trade* inadequately describes the commercial exchange between inhabitants of two different jurisdictions When residents of one nation have monopsony power over the residents of another, markets are more *global* than international. States, then, play a role subsidiary to multinational enterprises.[1]

A familiar characterization for the process by which investors of one country organize production abroad is *globalization*. The phenomenon of globalization has existed for more than eight centuries. As mentioned, Venetian and Hanseatic (North German) traders established operations in England as far back as the thirteenth century. Four hundred years later, Dutch traders reached every inhabited continent.

As with domestic investment, the search for profits fuels globalization. Carrying market organization abroad creates profit opportunities in three ways. First, cheaper labor produces an incentive to outsource production. Second, foreign geographies may possess resource inputs unavailable at home. And, of course, foreign economies offer an enlarged scope for sales.

The conventional narrative represents trade as mutual barter between countries maximizing comparative advantage. It overlooks the fact that investors belonging to one country can wield disproportionate market power in global exchange. The difference between these narratives is behind the apparent inconsistencies in macroeconomic phenomena across nations.

In the mainstream view, one country's current account surplus funds another country's deficit. Since the current account balance is equal to domestic savings minus domestic investment, this view amounts to the international version of the doctrine of loanable funds. During the 2000s, for example, monetary authorities attributed the US current account deficit to a "global savings glut"; excess savings in the foreign sector flowed into the US Treasury and depressed interest rates.[2] Proponents of this hypothesis claimed that America was vulnerable to a potential withdrawal of savings by foreigners, who, at some point, would be unwilling to fund persistent external deficits. Again, such a line of argumentation parallels similar claims about the US fiscal deficit.

Yet the United States has maintained an external deficit for almost thirty years—a period that has coincided with disruptive bouts of strong dollar demand. Furthermore, the bulk of gross financing flows have demonstrated little correspondence to trade flows.[3] Even more revealing, gross financial flows have often originated from the United States—only to find their way back.[4]

Trade, indeed, falls well short of explaining global economic developments. Data from the Bank of International Settlements shows that trade alone cannot explain daily currency turnover for many countries. Turnover of the US dollar, for example, has averaged as much as one hundred times trade volume.[5] More generally, the US dollar has had a disproportionate role in global exchange.[6]

As is the case for the domestic economy, movements in the market for financial assets drive real flows (trade) at the international level. As investment rises at the global level, so too does savings, to match its increase. With ready access to financing, American firms can fulfill their investment plans without depending on a prior supply of external savings. As a result, the US current account balance—though not necessarily that of other nations—emerges as an epiphenomenal displacement of investment activity in the foreign sphere.

## Dollar Dominance

In other words, the causal chain of external financial flows from the United States starts with domestic entities and their investment whims. To repeat, developmental differences between the United States and the rest of the world confer disproportionate purchasing power on American firms. As a result, residents in other countries become willing holders of dollar-denominated financial assets, such as those that may fund the purchase of imports or foreign assets.

It's worth emphasizing that this property is not the result of a mutual agreement among all countries to assign a privileged role to the dollar. Instead, it stems from the differences in the productive capacity of the United States and other countries. An obscure but illuminating example is that of the South African Common Monetary Area. Namibia, Swaziland, Lesotho, and Botswana have all pegged their exchange rates to the notoriously volatile South African rand. Over the past decade, the rand has lost more than 60 percent of its value against the US dollar. Despite this, the satellites have struggled to maintain adequate rand reserves. An end to the peg today would likely cause the smaller currencies to depreciate against the already weak South African currency.

Why have the satellites struggled to acquire rand even as it depreciates against the dollar? An obvious explanation is that their own economic problems are worse than South Africa's. But this reason ignores the nature of their dependence on the economy of their larger neighbor. A telling fact is that South African financial institutions have majority stakes in satellite financial systems.[7] If they believe South Africa's troubles will disproportionately affect the satellites, then investment in the latter countries will be wanting. Rand scarcity will then prevail in South Africa's economic periphery.

In the preceding case, South African investors—and foreign ones more generally—have recourse to the US dollar. Hence, prolonged weakness in the South African economy is consistent with rand depreciation. But American investors, who dominate global economic activity, lack such an alternative when the US economy struggles; all other economies depend on *their* investment expectations.

The dollar thus holds the dominant position in the hierarchy of money.[8] Some countries, like South Africa, may have their own monetary areas with extensive "offshore" use of their currencies. But all such areas are enveloped by the global dollar umbrella. This property is why the observed macroeconomic constraints of less-developed countries do not apply to the United States. It also explains why America has sustained a current account deficit for a length of time unavailable to all other nations.

On the other hand, foreign money carries risks relative to the dollar. The outsized influence of the United States on the global economy makes foreign profits dependent on the US business cycle. To the extent that foreign profits govern the desirability of assets denominated in foreign currency, the value of foreign currency becomes tied to the animal spirits of American investors. When panic among the latter leads to expectations of lower profits outside of the United States, investors eschew the risk of foreign money for the safety of the US dollar.

Alternatively stated, foreign currencies do not have zero

elasticity of substitution. When their value rises, investors become tempted to book gains in US dollars. Further, other countries' currencies offer poor insurance against adverse economic conditions—when US demand is weak. This property also makes foreign currencies, especially in underdeveloped economies, subject to trapeze leaps—violent movements in price.

Less developed nations, through their dependence on imports, face more binding supply inelasticities in key goods. When their currencies depreciate, import prices rise and exert inflationary pressure. As a result, an adverse feedback loop develops, with inflation causing further depreciation.

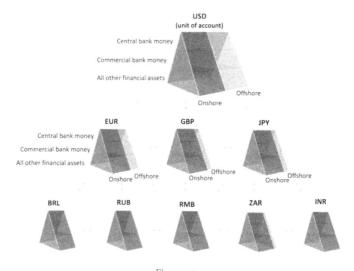

*Figure 4.1*

**Figure 4.1** shows the principal monetary areas in the global economy. Money denominated in each currency (unit of account) is depicted as a pyramid with central bank liabilities, the safest asset, at the top of the hierarchy. Many currencies, like the South African rand, find offshore use. But their monetary areas serve as mere appendages to a global dollar-backed financial system. **Source of image**: Steffen Murau, Joe Rini, and Armin Haas, "The Evolution of the Offshore US-Dollar

System: Past, Present and Four Possible Futures," *Journal of Institutional Economics* 16, no. 6 (2020): 767–83.

---

America's relative position in the global economy, however, inhibits such a feedback mechanism. First, supply constraints are far less binding. More importantly, weaker American demand would cause global prices to fall. A second-order impact would also occur as weaker US demand would cause demand in other countries to decline.

It's instructive to examine notable historical episodes of dollar depreciation. In the past fifty years, five episodes of prolonged dollar "weakness" have occurred: 1971–73, 1975–79, 1985–92, and 2002–08. During these periods, foreign financial investments outperformed American ones.[9] Yet none of these episodes coincided with the contraction of output in the United States. Instead, each cycle coincided with economic expansion in the US. And the dollar appreciated during the recessions that marked the end of each episode.

Not only that, but in each of these episodes, the US current account deficit widened as imports grew. The deficit only narrowed when demand—and, as a result, imports—declined. A narrower external gap therefore coincided with dollar strength. This phenomenon is the opposite of what one would expect in a currency crisis precipitated by a panic-driven flight of investment from the United States—typical of crises in less-developed nations.

The evolution of the external position of the United States has tracked the changes in its peculiar economic relationship with the rest of the world. It has also exhibited a pattern of change similar to what was seen in the external balances of the country's predecessors in global hegemony. With a technological lead, production in each state was able to extend beyond national boundaries. A marked deterioration in the trade balance occurred, but the balance of services—and more notably, foreign investment income—increased.

In the Dutch Republic and early modern Britain, service and income balances more than offset trade balances to produce current account surpluses.[10] But these surpluses resulted from strict adherence to the gold standard. In the case of the United States, a floating exchange rate regime has permitted persistent deficits in the current account. Nevertheless, the United States has demonstrated a confounding ability to increase the net income it derives from investment abroad despite a concurrent rise in liabilities owed to foreigners.[11] No other country has matched the United States' outsized returns on its foreign investments.[12] This peculiarity becomes less surprising, however, when one sees America's rentier empire, like those of the Dutch Republic and Britain in its heyday, as a particular stage of its economic development.

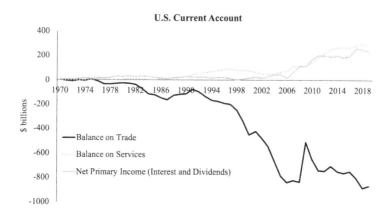

*Figure 4.2*

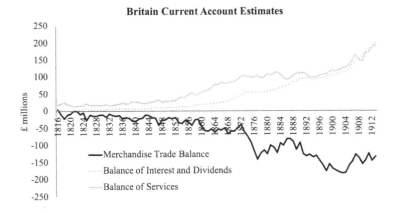

**Figures 4.2 and 4.3** show how the components of the U.S. current account have followed a similar trajectory to those of the British current account in the 19th century. After each country attained technological primacy, its residents expanded their activities in the foreign sphere. Increasing receipts on services abroad, rising investment income, and a declining trade balance characterized both periods of globalization. **Sources**: Albert H. Imlah, "British Balance of Payments and Export of Capital, 1816–1913," *Economic History Review*, 5 (1952): 208–39; U.S. Census Bureau and U.S. Bureau of Economic Analysis, retrieved from FRED, Federal Reserve Bank of St. Louis.

## Global Finance in the Era of Dutch Hegemony

During the seventeenth century, the Dutch came to derive a sizable portion of their external receipts from "invisible earnings" related to shipping and banking services to other nations.[13] The Bank of Amsterdam, in particular, became known as a source of finance and a secure haven for the store of wealth, and the bank's bill of exchange—a financial instrument similar to a check or promissory note—became universally recognized.[14]

Like the United States today, the relative economic advancement of the United Provinces conferred certain monetary privileges. While the rest of Europe struggled to maintain adequate metals reserves, the Dutch Republic served as a destination for fleeing money. Contemporaries were aware of this phenomenon and launched spiteful tirades against "the intrusions of Dutch capitalism,"[15] asking, "What masses of money and gold have they, against the laws of the realm, transported out of it?"[16]

Though Dutch merchants engaged in "heavy export of silver in coin and plate," confusion reigned as to whether the benefits they brought outweighed the costs. Another observer remarked:

> I confess it hath supplied the necessities of merchants, and helped to drive trade. But my query is this. . . Have they not lived by our trade, and the merchant adventurers, and soaked the kingdom of as many times principal as they have practised this usury many times ten years, and in the end drawn or carried all away?[17]

One English economic philosopher, Gerard de Malynes, had, by the early 1600s, identified the leading role of speculative flows. Malynes—"a fanatic believer in conspiracy theories" —attributed exchange rate movements to "the tricks of bankers rather than the movement of exports and imports."[18] But Malynes cannot be disregarded for the conspiratorial nature of his views. He not only devised a deductive system of causal macroeconomic relationships but was also far ahead of his time in attributing England's economic troubles to a single cause: the international money market.[19]

Perhaps his own experience trading in Dutch financial markets informed his views.[20] Malynes was aware that bullion tended to gravitate toward certain locales "'where our money concurring with the monies of other countries causes plenty."[21] His allegory *St. George for England* could well describe developing-world exchange-rate crises. Malynes asserted that exchange rate speculation causes "a great part of our wealth to be imagined" and therefore "causes us to spend far above our revenues." The result is that the speculator "carries out our treasure in bullion and money, impoverishing our commonwealth."

Such behavior is familiar to modern times. Speculative hot money flowing from American investors into less-developed countries can lead to sharp increases in those countries' exchange rates. Such exchange rate appreciation can create illusory perceptions of increased purchasing power that raise import demand and, eventually, lead to a drain on foreign reserves.

As the seventeenth century progressed, more countries came to blame their monetary troubles on Dutch speculative activities. "English and French writers in this century were prone to credit the Dutch with devilish ingenuity in drawing away their currencies by manipulation of exchange."[22] England's ambassador wrote to Charles II in 1668 that Dutch merchants were funding the king's usurious lenders. "Encouraged by the great interest they gain there in lieu of [the gain that is] so small here" the latter supplied funds to English bankers.[23]

Dutch investment activity indeed had a profound effect on Europe's money supply in the late sixteenth and seventeenth centuries. Merchants would supply bullion when organizing trade in European outposts. Foreign mints—often operated by the Dutch themselves—would then coin the metal for local needs. In times of economic panic, however, merchants would be less willing to provide bullion for domestic minting. Mints would then have to debase coins by reducing their precious metals content and using substitutes such as copper.

The international investment boom from 1590 to 1610 is illustrative. These years coincided with a rush to establish new routes to Asia. Dutch investors competed to establish rival East India ventures in England, Scotland, France, Denmark, and Tuscany.[24] A more general extension of Dutch economic involvement abroad also occurred in India, Southeast Asia, and Japan.

But the mania ended in a pan-European currency crisis. As Dutch merchants repatriated bullion to Amsterdam, peripheral economies could not maintain an adequate supply of money. The ensuing debasement was recognized as the "Kipper und Wipper" crisis in Germany and "the rising of the moneys" in England.

Charles Kindleberger dates this crisis as lasting from 1619 to 1623, but evidence suggests that it started much earlier.[25] A broadsheet of coin values in various German cities shows that coin depreciations started as early as 1615 and then declined more aggressively.[26] Spain, after ten years of monetary stability, coined five million ducats between 1617 and 1619 and a further five million in 1621.[27] Likewise, the sterling's value also declined in the period from 1618 to 1622, albeit more mildly.[28]

Data from the Bank of Amsterdam provides evidence for the path of financial flight. Its metals stock fell from 1.4 million florins in 1611 to a low of 640,000 in 1614. By 1618, however, metals holdings recovered to 2.2 million florins and rose above 3 million by the middle of the next decade.[29] The severity of bullion outflows was enough to cause English officials in 1618 to arrest a group of Dutch merchants, accusing them of siphoning £7 million in coin abroad.[30]

In contrast to the rest of Europe, the value of coins minted at the Bank of Amsterdam remained stable, and that price stability would endure until the end of the next century. Although a flood of debased money did enter the circulating coinage of the Dutch Republic, deposits at the Bank of Amsterdam remained unaffected since it minted its own unique coins.

## International Financial Flows in the Victorian Era

Given the absence of records, information about Dutch external accounts comes from secondary and anecdotal sources. In the case of Victorian Britain, however, improvements in data collection have enabled the construction of reasonable estimates.[31] Imputed data shows its trade balance declining from a neutral position in 1821 to a deficit of –£92 million by 1890.[32] Yet over the same period, the balance of interests and dividends grew from a negligible balance to £94 million—enough to offset the trade balance.[33]

In Britain, like the Dutch Republic, demand to invest in the foreign sector prompted gold outflows, with investors frequently borrowing domestic bullion in order to re-lend it abroad. In fact, directors of the Bank of England, which was originally a private monopoly, participated in this trade in the early part of the nineteenth century. Before the Panic of 1825, for example, they loaned gold—a "useless asset" given the opportunity costs of owning it—at 3.5 percent to Nathan Rothschild, who re-invested it abroad at higher rates.[34] In 1838, the Bank directly sent £1 million to earn higher rates in the United States.[35]

But when lending to Belgium and France led to further outflows of gold the following year, directors panicked and raised the bank rate to a record-high 6 percent.[36] Indeed, such drains prompted anxieties about price stability—specifically, the Bank's ability to meet calls on its notes—on multiple occasions. In response, Bank of England officials would sharply raise the discount rate in order to bring gold deposits back.[37]

Many have attributed bullion outflows to the trade channel and, more specifically, to poor harvests.[38] But evidence points to the financial channel, with speculation in foreign markets as the cause of "external drains." Bank of England balance sheet data shows that bullion outflows had a procyclical character. They flowed out of the Bank as the appetite for risk increased and flowed back during times of panic. Relative peaks in the

Bank's holdings in 1821, 1833, 1844, 1852, and 1859 marked the end of periods of risk aversion and the beginning of new speculative cycles.[39] Like the United States in the modern era, England was never at risk of a serious foreign-exchange crisis in the nineteenth century, and convertibility risks only appeared during moments when animal spirits ran high. Gold holdings were low precisely when exuberance lured British investors to more risky foreign ventures.

This phenomenon also explains why the Bank of England's interest rate policy was often volatile. In one moment, the opportunity cost of idle gold deposits could prompt directors to lower the discount rate. In the next, dwindling bullion reserves could lead to a sharp policy reversal. Evidence from the London money market also shows that the transmission mechanism for economic shocks ran from British financial markets to the rest of the world.[40] Similar to Bank of Amsterdam bills two centuries earlier, bills of exchange issued by British multinational banks had come to finance 90 percent of the world's trade credit.[41]

Most Victorian-era economists explained international capital flows using classical-school notions of equilibrium. An alternative explanation was offered by Thomas Attwood of the Birmingham School—a critic of the gold standard—in the early nineteenth century. More than one hundred years before Keynes, Attwood saw demand deficiency as a more pressing problem than monetary instability.[42] He attributed post-Napoleonic war deflation to money, which, he argued, "stagnates in inert masses."[43] This led Attwood to call for redistributive policies that would raise domestic consumption. His own links to the manufacturing industry, which, in his view, was affected by "underconsumption," undoubtedly colored his views.[44]

Attwood also recognized Britain's unique position in the global economy. He argued that weak demand and risk aversion in England caused instability abroad: "We have drained Europe of her bullion, and then we gravely wonder that there should be foreign distress."[45] He also implied the existence of a demand multiplier for trade, claiming, "There is no way of increasing our foreign exports, but by increasing our own internal consumption of foreign imports."[46]

Attwood's ideas, however, were ignored for the rest of the century. Despite the start of a long depression after 1873, the British government remained committed to its gold peg given the extensive rents it derived from a global sterling standard in which it was the "banker, moneylender, insurer, shipper and wholesaler to the world at large."[47] Before US ascendance, the pound remained the world's currency, circulating as freely outside Britain as it did within it.[48]

Sterling dominance was evident in the aftermath of the Panic of 1873. Several countries, including the United States and those in the Latin Monetary Union, were forced to adopt a gold standard to preserve the value of their currencies against the pound. A popular narrative has mistakenly attributed these actions to the beginning of a new era of globalization that lasted from 1873 to 1914. Instead, trade had peaked at the *beginning* of that period, following the end of a British frenzy for investment in the foreign sector.[49] The end of this mania led to a money supply overhang and gold outflows from Britain's economic peripheries, which forced them to redouble their commitment to price stability—not unlike the renewed commitments to austerity many governments made following the currency crises of 2011–12.[50] A revealing fact is that while other countries struggled to maintain their gold reserves, those at the Bank of England grew from £18 million in 1869 to a new record of £32 million by 1879.[51] Unfortunately, the inflexibility of Britain's financial empire would ultimately set the world down a grim trajectory.

| | 1870-1876 | 1877-1886 | 1887-1896 | 1897-1909 | 1910-1913 |
|---|---|---|---|---|---|
| Return on non-domestic Equities minus return on domestic equities | -31% | 81% | -37% | 170% | -17% |
| Net change in Bank of England holdings of gold | £7 million | -£3.8 million | £16 million | -£3.4 million | £6.1 million |

*Table 4.1*

| | 1976-1980 | 1980-1985 | 1985-1992 | 1992-2002 | 2002-2008 | 2008-Dec. 2020 |
|---|---|---|---|---|---|---|
| Return on non-domestic Equities minus return on domestic equities | 30% | -17% | 111% | -143% | 67% | -157% |
| Change in the U.S. Dollar Index | -18% | 79% | -45% | 40% | -34% | 20% |

*Table 4.2*

**Tables 4.1 and 4.2** demonstrate how the financial channel (through expected returns to investment abroad), rather than trade, drives the global movement of money. During British hegemony, the poor relative performance of foreign equities caused bullion to flow back to London. Poor performance in non-U.S. markets today increases the demand for dollar-denominated assets (causing dollar appreciation). **Source**: Michael Edelstein, "Realized Rates of Return on UK Home and Overseas Portfolio Investment in the Age of High Imperialism," *Explorations in Economic History* 13, no. 3 (1976): 283–29.

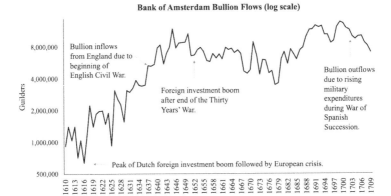

*Figure 4.4*

**Figure 4.4** illustrates how in the Dutch Republic, too, bullion flows corresponded to Dutch speculative appetite for foreign investment. Risk aversion led both domestic and foreign bullion to flow back to the Bank of Amsterdam (with the exception of the French invasion of 1673). **Source**: Johannes Gerard Van Dillen, *History of the Principal Public Banks* (London: Cass, 1964), 117.

# 5

## THE IRON CHAINS OF HISTORY

hen Friedrich List published his critique of Adam Smith, David Ricardo, and the classical school in 1841, America was reeling from the effects of a panic-driven external drain. Speculative financial flows from Anglo-American banks had earlier fueled a land bubble, which culminated in the Panic of 1837. The episode caused List, who had lived in the United States, to grow only more convinced that free-trade doctrine amounted to British propaganda.

List's *National System* argued that unregulated trade allowed Britain to exploit its hegemonic position in the world economy. Echoing Malynes' comments about the Dutch two centuries earlier, he compared England to "the rich banker who, without having a thaler in his pocket, can draw for any sum he pleases on neighboring or more distant business connections."[1] Its trading partners, on the other hand, were like the poor man "who is drawn upon if the rich man gets into difficulty; who can therefore not even call what is actually in his hands, his own."[2]

List also pointed out that Britain, two hundred years earlier, was in a position not dissimilar to the countries on its economic periphery. He placed it within a lineage of hegemony, starting with the Italian city-states, and asserted that each power owed its success to restrictions on foreign commerce. For example, the "Hansards" (the Hanseatic League), whom he claimed succeeded the Venetians, had limited trade to their own vessels. The Dutch then emulated the Hansards, and the English continued the tradition with the Navigation Acts in the seventeenth and eighteenth centuries. But once a nation achieved a leading position, according to List, it embraced free trade.

List's *National System* inspired nineteenth-century nationalists who sought to protect their native countries from foreign powers. It also justified imperialism by arguing that the acquisition of colonial markets was necessary for development. List quoted Montesquieu as saying, "A nation which has fallen into slavery strives to retain what it possesses than to acquire more."[3] He further asserted that "primitive" societies needed initial development from more advanced ones before they could pursue their own nationhood.

Thus, in addition to making a case for protectionism, List posited a life cycle of nations. Economic historians have adapted this idea over time. Countries transition through peripheral, semi-peripheral, and core status.[4] Alternatively, their economies start in relative backwardness, accelerate, and then undergo relative decline. In the first phase, a country with a significant technological lag relies on foreign investment. In the next phase—the "takeoff" phase—non-commodity sectors, and, typically, the export sector, grow. And finally, in the mature phase, a sizable financial sector emerges and invests in new underdeveloped nations.

The economic historian Charles Kindleberger grouped these theories under the umbrella of "s-curve" cycles.[5] By his own admission, the s-curve is an imperfect descriptive tool, since considerable differences mark individual cases of country development. The two principal sources of variation are the pace of growth and a country's geographical reach. Still, enough common patterns exist to make the s-curve a convenient way of encapsulating development.

While Dutch, English, and American development all fit a

protracted s-curve, modern times have offered examples of more accelerated growth. After the Second World War, Japan produced a growth miracle with rapid export-led industrialization. Once this phase ended, its economy gave way to a financial bubble that saw the value of the land under the emperor's palace match the value of California's total real estate.

Korea followed Japan's sequencing of export-led growth and financialization, and then China also followed suit, at a much larger scale. Though smaller in size, the economies of post-Communist Central Europe—Poland, Hungary, the Czech Republic, and Slovakia—have also conformed to this pattern.[6] Manufacturing exports accelerated there, only to give way to a domestic credit boom. China is now in the middle of its own financial expansion. And the central European countries and Korea contend with the aftermath of theirs.

### Technological Diffusion through Foreign Investment

In the beginning stage of the national cycle, foreign investors invest in an underdeveloped geographic area possessing an abundant commodity or inexpensive labor. That is, they seek to exploit a given locale's comparative advantage. Early periods in the Dutch Republic, early modern England, and the United States over the past century all serve as examples. In the medieval era, urban growth in Flanders led to increased demand for energy in the form of peat. Entrepreneurs set up colonies in the Northern Netherlands to dig the resource and export it back to the cities.[7] English wool attracted Italian and Hanseatic merchants. After Elizabeth I (r. 1558–1603) expelled the latter, unfinished cloth became the country's principal export to the Dutch Republic, which processed it into finished draperies. And Americans exported a variety of agricultural staples (tobacco, indigo) before they began shipping cotton to England.

Foreign investment, in each of these cases, prompted technological diffusion from the more developed to the less developed economy. Flemish investors introduced several building techniques—especially in digging, draining, and transport—that the Dutch Republic's engineers would later refine.[8] It was also the Flemish who brought windmill technology, often identified with the technological primacy of the Netherlands.[9] Ships such as the herring bus and carvel—the golden geese of Dutch shipping—had also been invented in other countries.[10]

By the seventeenth century, Dutch investors began exporting their own iterations of this technology. Nowhere would technical spillovers from the Republic prove more consequential than in England, where agricultural productivity increased after 1600.[11] Evidence points to Dutch innovations as a source of the latter phenomenon. Large landowners invited Dutch engineers to drain and reclaim fens, and English farmers also adopted tools such as the Dutch plow. New practices in growing fodder, too, came from the Netherlands.[12] Indeed, as has been the case throughout history, relieving agricultural bottlenecks was paramount to England's economic progress.

In addition to increasing the supply of food, these methods helped meet wool demand from England's growing textile industry.[13] But English textile development itself owed much to technological diffusion from the United Provinces. By the second half of the seventeenth century, the Dutch loom found its way to Manchester from London, as did the Dutch ribbon frame, which improved the speed of silk-ribbon weaving.[14]

Such devices circulated in the countryside under a putting-out system already in existence in the United Provinces. Central to the system's operation was the credit provided by London merchants, who themselves, either directly or indirectly, relied on Dutch financial backing. Dutch finance flowed to English goldsmith bankers during the Restoration (the return of the Stuart monarchy, 1660–89), and, even earlier, London merchants tapped the Amsterdam money market to lend to James I (King of Scotland as James VI from 1567; King of England, Scotland, and Ireland 1603–25).[15] Early English companies undertaking agricultural improvements in the early seventeenth century also derived their financing from Dutch investors.[16]

Two centuries worth of English innovations in technical knowledge inherited from the Dutch found their way to America. As is well known, Samuel Slater seeded the textile revolution in the early years of independence. New techniques in canal building, which fueled an investment boom in England, also reached the United States in the 1790s.[17] In the northern states, canal investment heralded the beginnings of public-private partnerships, which served as an organizational template for railroad construction later on.

Fittingly, both Dutch and English investors had a stake in America's first canals.[18] Relative underdevelopment would keep the United States dependent on foreign finance, particularly England's, until 1900. Even after independence, English lending to Southern planters was so extensive that Madison remarked that Britain's monopoly in Virginia was as complete as it had ever been.[19]

This claim had a special irony since aggrieved indebted planters had helped instigate the American War of Independence. But the new country's dependence on external investment kept London creditors whole under the Jay Treaty of 1794. The clause would continue to be a source of tension between Alexander Hamilton, who supported its insertion, and Thomas Jefferson, who aligned with the planters opposing it.

### The Challenges of Development

Hamilton was famously no advocate of unregulated trade. His Report on Manufactures argued for protections on infant industries and inspired the ideas of Friedrich List. Early nineteenth-century protectionists like Hamilton and List believed that higher-productivity competitors in England could stifle fledgling manufacturers who lacked the same cost advantages. Even John Stuart Mill, one of the fathers of economic liberalism, conceded this argument: "The superiority of one country over another in a branch of production, often arises from having begun it sooner."[20]

A more general problem with open trade is that it can produce a temporal tradeoff. On the one hand, foreign investors serve as an immediate source of foreign exchange, necessary to import goods and equipment unavailable at home. On the other hand, the goals of foreign investors can be at odds with long-term development.

The so-called "natural resource curse" illustrates this catch-22. Countries with large commodity endowments tend to be developmental laggards. Their comparative advantage offers a ready means to acquire items not produced at home. By importing certain goods, particularly manufacturing and industrial products, a country has less incentive to develop domestic output in those categories. Proponents of free trade dismiss this concern by arguing that producing goods in globally uncompetitive categories is inefficient.

But investment in certain sectors—namely manufacturing —can have favorable long-run effects, despite seeming suboptimal in the immediate future. They produce positive externalities—through "learning-by-doing" effects and knowledge spillovers—on broader industry.[21] Growth can become self-sustaining if such dynamic sectors achieve enough of a share of economic output. Relative technological progress becomes especially possible if this process helps produce new and diverse items for export. As the export sector diversifies, foreign exchange and imported inputs become less scarce. In turn, opportunities for reinvestment into dynamic industries expand and lead to the accelerating growth characteristic of the second or "catch-up" phase of the s-curve.

Learning effects and knowledge do not easily spill over across borders.[22] For this reason, the relative development of countries relying on resource exports can stagnate. Furthermore, investment in the resource sector, like any other sector, is prone to violent animal spirits and, as a result, overinvestment. If foreign exchange is scarce, malinvestment in the resource sector siphons away funds that could otherwise be used to develop dynamic industries.

Open capital markets compound the challenges to growth posed by unregulated trade in goods. Foreign financial flows offer a ready source of foreign exchange but also are prone to considerable volatility and "irrational exuberance."[23] These "hot money" inflows and outflows can create macroeconomic instability that is harmful to long-run development.[24]

International financing also tends to be procyclical. It may only be available, often in a predatory form, when exuberance in capital markets is high. As a result, a country can become burdened with servicing foreign debt claims predicated on unrealistic expectations.

Recall that economists have noted the idiosyncrasy of Argentina's recurring defaults and bouts of inflation. One reason such problems have seemed perplexing is that Argentina possesses abundant natural resources. But instead of being at odds with a long history of economic challenges, this fact helps explain them. Additionally, Argentina has actively participated in international capital markets since the 1820s. Its vulnerability to the resource curse, together with its long historical exposure to volatile financial flows, makes its record of eight defaults over two hundred years less surprising.

Given its developmental success and extreme monetary stability, Japan—the other economic anomaly—offers a stark contrast. But examining Japan's more distant history shows that it once faced problems similar to Argentina's. In the early seventeenth century, Japan integrated into the global economy as a vital source of silver—coincidentally *argentum* in Latin— for Dutch traders.

Japan's silver resources were a mixed blessing, however. Historical records show that Japan began to experience extreme outflows of silver in the 1640s. Amid a shortage of bullion, Japanese authorities used sumptuary laws to restrict the import of foreign luxury goods.[25] Monetary struggles persisted, and the government issued a ban on silver exports in

1668.[26] Further price regulations in 1672 on the export price of gold trade coins combined with their degrading quality led to the emergence of a parallel exchange rate.[27] Following a ban on gold exports in 1685, officials relented and debased domestic coin in 1695.

Japan's experience with monetary instability did not end there. Its re-opening of international trade in the 1850s precipitated a massive outflow of gold.[28] It also owns the distinction of being the first country to break the international gold standard following the onset of the Great Depression.

## The "Iron Chains of History"

Recurring crises in the developing world have sparked renewed interest in state industrial intervention. Its proponents point to the successes of the East Asian economies that employed industrial protections and capital controls.[29] They also point to the role intervention played in the historical development of the United States, despite its strong advocacy of free trade over the past forty years.

As I discussed earlier, those who champion active state industrial policies are not wrong to point out how free trade has adversely affected less-developed countries. But they exaggerate the possibilities of deliberate, and more importantly, benevolent state agency in development. Instead, the life cycle of nations is subject to strong path dependence. Historical context has severely constrained the developmental options available to societies. The role of history also offers strong reasons to doubt the efficacy and appropriateness of policies a government pursues unilaterally. In other words, arguments for intervention too often ignore the fact that states do not exist in a vacuum.

Path dependence in development manifests in several ways. First, industrial policy requires the presence of a formidable investment bloc that favors its implementation. Such a bloc can take a long time to emerge and only does so through technological progress and its diffusion. Second, technological progress itself depends on features arising from historical accident. Two of the most important have been immigration and the developmental status of neighboring countries, which depends on geography.[30] Lastly, the state of global aggregate demand—influenced by dominant investor blocs in advanced nations—has, historically, imposed a severe constraint on developmental possibilities for less-advanced societies.

Take the case of England. Many historians attribute its development to protectionist policies implemented after the Restoration. But its government attempted such schemes much earlier, only to find disastrous results. The most notable was the 1614 Cockayne Project. It sought to establish a domestic cloth-dyeing industry that could compete with the Dutch Republic's own, but could not overcome its cost disadvantages and led the Dutch to ban cloth imports from England.[31]

Early industrial policies in the United States likewise had mixed results. The Embargo Act of 1807 (in which the young American government banned all foreign trade) seems to have given an impetus to fledgling manufacturers. But its role in seeding industrial enterprise is difficult to extricate from other factors, such as the skills threshold Americans had attained by this point.[32] Further tariffs in 1816, 1824, and 1828 seem to have had little discernible impact.[33]

Governments will fail to adopt protectionist schemes if these programs lack the backing of a politically influential investor bloc. Since such a group may only arise after sufficient technological progress, industrial policy, historically, is more likely to have accelerated than seeded development. In England, the outport (non-London) shipping interests that supported the "old colonial system" of protections had emerged well before the Navigation Acts, which restricted importation transport to British vessels.[34] And, in the United States after the Civil War, the manufacturers constituting the powerful tariff interest had already established a significant presence in the economy.[35]

In addition to tariffs, many, like List, have viewed immigration policy as an example of how active state intervention can fuel industrial progress. An instance that informs such views is the role of Huguenot immigrants in England's development. Fleeing France, they brought a host of new techniques in the 1680s: silk weaving, arms manufacturing, glass blowing, and papermaking.[36] In turn, demand from silk weavers prompted the construction of the first water-powered mill.[37] Likewise, the operations of arms makers who settled in the provinces were critical to English industrial expansion.[38] And later, in the United States, too, Huguenot immigrants—most notably the Du Ponts—helped seed American industry.

Regarding immigration policy, the line separating historical accident from deliberate state action is also blurred. Although England extended tolerance to French Huguenots in the 1680s, their influx was also the product of circumstances that led to greater intolerance within France. Similarly, the Naturalization Act of 1790 was well in place in the United States before the turmoil of 1848 caused Germans like the Bausch and Steinway families to bring their technical expertise to the US.

Finally, the luck of geography has had considerable influence on development.[39] The concentration of modern East Asian growth miracles in one region is no coincidence.[40] As Japan moved up the technical frontier, the Asian "tigers" benefited from the migration of lower-productivity manufacturing. China was next in line, and, as its economy matures, Vietnam now follows. The same phenomenon was present in Europe, which saw manufacturers move from more developed Western countries to Central Europe by the late Nineties and early 2000s.[41] None of the economies in the latter region pursued intervention as aggressively as their Asian peers, yet they, too, managed to achieve rare developmental success.

## The Role of External Demand

Belgium, the second country to industrialize after Britain, also owed much to its favorable geographic position. The Southern Habsburg Netherlands (which evolved into Belgium) had a developmental advantage over their Northern counterparts at the start of the sixteenth century: they manufactured cloth, weapons, and nails, while also mining abundant iron, coal, and lead deposits.[42] But the wars of religion between the rebelling Northern provinces and Spain had destroyed productive capacity in the southern territories until outsourcing from the Dutch Republic fueled its revival in the second half of the seventeenth century.[43] Belgium's proximity to England also allowed it to access the new technologies emerging in the 1700s —the Newcomen atmospheric engine in 1720, a variety of agricultural techniques, and, later on, new textile machinery.[44] Yet as peripheries of London and Amsterdam, the Belgian cities suffered from frequent financial outflows and a scarcity of investment.[45]

After the turn of the nineteenth century, an unexpected ingredient allowed the Southern Netherlands to re-take their technological lead over their siblings in the north: demand. The invasion of the French Army during the Revolutionary Wars opened a vast new market to Belgian industry. With privileged access to French territorial holdings, it became a key supplier for Napoleon.[46] Later on, industrial progress, unlocked by war demand, eventually spilled over into steel manufacturing and the construction of railroad engines, which grew to rival their British counterparts.[47] Following the stylized s-curve pattern, relative advancement facilitated the rise of a stable banking sector (though it did suffer the growing pains of a bubble in the 1830s) that made Belgium a secondary financial center during that century.[48]

Strong external demand has been the secret to the success of many, more modern "economic miracles." Most of these cases benefited from the Cold War Keynesianism of America and its allies. American military spending in East Asia created favorable external demand conditions for Japanese and Korean industrialization. Singapore, too, received considerable stimulus from the British bases that maintained their presence after its independence.

England and the United States also saw the military spending of allies stimulate their development. War with France in the late seventeenth century ended Dutch parsimony.[49] Dutch demand consequently provided a significant tailwind to English exports.[50] And America benefited from an unprecedented surge in exports when Britain went to war with Germany. By forcing it to abandon its century-long gold peg, the First World War helped remove Britain's fiscal straitjacket.

The effects external demand had on their export sectors allowed England and the United States each to eclipse their predecessors. England did not experience another balance-of-payments crisis after 1672 (at least until after 1940). Similarly, America did not have to worry about foreign reserves after 1920. Of course, although robust external demand was critical to the relative ascendance of both countries, it came at an immense price.

External demand conditions have also constrained development through the collective effects of interventionism. The desire of all countries to grow exports at the same time creates a paradoxical outcome.[51] The Great Depression offers a salient example: competitive devaluation and tariffs only weakened global demand, creating an environment even less conducive to growth. Development is thus subject to a collective action problem in which not all countries can simultaneously pursue protectionism.

## Cooperation and Conflict

To a significant extent, the debate on the efficacy of state intervention is a false one. The public-private distinction clouds the overwhelming influence investor blocs have on policy. As Polanyi argued, markets—like those of nineteenth-century England and post-1970s America—are creations of the state. And as I argued in Chapter 3, they depend on institutions formed at the behest of select investor factions.

Countries where authority has been relatively more central-ized perhaps offer the best historical examples of how markets function as a state-imposed instrument for development. The similarities between three cases, in particular, are worth exam-ining: France in the first two-thirds of the seventeenth century, Germany from 1806 to 1870, and China after the death of Mao. In each case, the state employed market, or market-like, institu-tions as a growth strategy. Furthermore, such policies had the deliberate aim of pursuing economic advancement through trade with more developed peers. Alternatively stated, markets served as a mechanism for strategic cooperation.

Even before promulgating the Edict of Nantes (the 1598 order protecting both local and visiting Protestants), Henry IV of France (r. 1589–1610)—inheriting a country scarred by reli-gious wars—recruited Dutch engineers for land reclamation projects.[52] Henry further encouraged the application of new Huguenot agricultural techniques—possibly derived through intellectual exchange with the Dutch in Geneva—to develop commercial agriculture.[53] A succession of state ministers—Richelieu, Mazarin, and Colbert—continued to carry out a series of changes to introduce more flexible commerce. Inviting Dutch manufacturers and merchants to set up commercial operations became a central policy.[54] Like Henry IV, Richelieu "encouraged Dutch investments and services and even toler-ated the purchase of Dutch-built ships" to revive France's econ-omy.[55] Dutch merchants, in turn, invested heavily in French production, which could produce, among other items, cheap wines to sell back home.[56] Under Mazarin, the Dutch erected a cloth manufactory and sugar refineries.[57] Colbert, whose agenda went the furthest, attracted Dutch shipwrights to the Royal Naval Yards.[58] He also created the Five Great Farms, a no-tariff zone that historians have called "one of the largest free-trade areas in Europe."[59]

The Dutch also offered a critical service to the French state: international finance.[60] Dutch bankers drew bills of credit on their contacts in Amsterdam on behalf of Versailles. They also likely funneled Louis XIV's extensive foreign bribes, in addition to providing a foreign haven to funds stolen by the state ministers.[61]

Two hundred years later, the German states, led by the Prussian monarchy, turned to market institutions to catch up to their industrializing peers in Europe. After being defeated by Napoleon in 1806, the German states freed labor and land markets to stimulate the growth of commercial agriculture.[62] After 1848, they began relaxing a strict system of patents, privileges, export permissions, and controls on foreign firms.[63] Under *Gewerbefreiheit*, or freedom of establishment, occupational choices became more flexible, the banking system expanded, and foreign investment flowed in from earlier industrializers like France and Belgium.[64]

The most important new policy, however, was freer trade. Estimates show an acceleration in exports, beginning in the 1840s, that coincides with trade liberalization throughout Europe.[65] This process was already underway earlier when Britain in the 1820s began outsourcing agricultural production to Eastern Prussia. Agricultural receipts in the East, in turn, stimulated demand for manufactures in Western Germany in addition to railroad investment.[66] And as a result, Germany began exporting textiles and iron after 1850.[67] Finally, a financial asset and property boom emerged as the German economy reached relative maturity around 1870.[68]

From the rise of Deng Xiaoping in 1978 to its WTO accession in 2001, China has followed a similar trajectory. After the failure of agricultural collectivization, the government introduced greater individual rights and market liberalization to farming.[69] To attract foreign direct investment, it also created special economic zones that offered tax breaks and lighter regulations to foreign firms.[70] Like the Belgians and French in the nineteenth century, Japan and the Asian Tigers (Hong Kong, Singapore, South Korea, and Taiwan) moved lower value-added manufacturing to these areas, with US firms following soon after.[71]

More centralized authority allowed the governments of France, Germany, and China in these eras to pursue the expedients necessary to attract foreign investors, who took advantage of a sizable and inexpensive labor force. They were thus well positioned to capture the migration of production from more advanced nations. Worth mentioning is that although authority was more concentrated in all three cases, investor blocs were still present. The counterparts to private investors in these cases were competing factions of bureaucrats with differing economic visions. Under resource constraints, the stakes for the failure and success of these visions are high. Privileges or outright wealth can accrue to those bureaucrats who lead successful development, while the success of a rival can bring demotion or even death. France's state ministers, German officials, and now, Chinese authorities, all acquired sizable fortunes during periods of economic reforms.[72]

All but the most draconian policies, however, will fail to overcome weak external demand. Once demand deficiency becomes severe enough, the appeal of cooperation will wither. In the past, the failure of cooperative trade has given way to autarky, which is often accompanied by war. Among the most notorious examples, of course, is the Soviet Union under Stalin when, after the failure of the New Economic Program of the 1920s, it looked inward. By the start of the Second World War, its merchandise exports amounted to a paltry 0.5 percent of output.[73] But "forced saving"—the repression of spending on consumption goods—and the continual reinvestment of inputs, especially in armaments production, spurred industrial expansion.[74] And the use of those arms to expand the Communist bloc during the 1940s, in turn, made more inputs available.[75]

Autarky also fits English colonialism after 1650 and American imperialism after 1850. After the failure of free trade in each respective era, the latter two turned toward growing their internal, albeit market-driven, economies. The use of force, as is well known, facilitated the acquisitions of new territories, allowing both countries to exploit economies of scale in various realms of production. Until their own embrace of free trade, forced savings, by use of duties and tariffs, subsidized dynamic sectors. And as was already evident in the English munitions trade of the 1700s, war stimulated the arms industry, which had spillover effects on other activities.

England's foray into autarkic development began when Cromwell, amid struggling finances and capital flight, grew the size of the navy and wrested control of Jamaica from Spain.[76] For more than a century afterward, war and slavery would subsidize the expansion of manufacturing, shipping, and colonial commodity production. Ironically, America's embrace of the potential of its internal market began with the abolition of slavery. The US Civil War provided a push to nascent mining and steel operations, albeit at the expense of repressed consumption (and, of course, the lives lost).[77] More importantly, the South's links to Britain were severed, and it was more deeply integrated into northern and western markets. Later, the territories consolidated after the last American Indian Wars, and after the Spanish-American War, increased the scale of the US economy. Of course, both English colonialism and US imperialism occurred in eras in which other countries, following the demise of global free trade arrangements, pursued similar initiatives.

## Decentralized Authority and Hegemony

Rapid growth in centralized states like the Soviet Union, the Asian Tigers, and now China, has elicited awe among observers.[78] Their predecessors, France and Germany, inspired similar fear and astonishment. Indeed, such societies have demonstrated an overwhelming advantage over more decentralized polyarchies in their ability to develop over *short* periods.

When the Dutch Republic and its hegemonic successor Britain stagnated, their larger, more centralized rivals seemed poised to pass them on the frontier of technological innovation. Louis XIV, for example, did not have unfounded confidence when he invaded the Dutch Republic in 1672. Likewise, Germany managed to narrow its gap to Britain by the end of the nineteenth century. Today, significant hysteria, manifesting in both anxiety and praise, has accompanied China's speedy ascent.

And yet the Dutch Republic and early modern Britain were each succeeded in hegemonic roles by a less centralized state. Furthermore, all three hegemonies had protracted developmental paths as the borders between the independent states constituting them took time to dissolve. Even England was, for a long time, an unwieldy union of fairly autonomous regions. Not only did these include Scotland, Ireland, and Wales, but also London and the counties.

A natural question to ask is why relatively more polyarchal states tend to occupy the forefront of the frontier of technological innovation. But this question rests on the false premise that nation-states shape technological change. In fact, the causality runs in the opposite direction. Countries are vehicles, albeit highly flawed ones, for harnessing technological change. They offer not only a means for cooperation but also a means for conflict. Furthermore, debating the economic merits of centralized authority falsely assumes that states are fixed entities. Instead, endogenous economic change subjects their institutions, inhabitants, and geographies to continuous flux in a process that reveals the flaws of viewing the world through the prism of the nation-state.

Greater decentralization emerges as society learns to accommodate cooperation among greater numbers without the frictions imposed by borders. In a sense, decentralized organization itself is a novel technology subject to improvement over time. America in the twentieth century was a different nation than the sum of its constituent elements two hundred years earlier. The same can be said for Britain in the nineteenth century.

The evolution of the world since Dutch primacy shows that societies, on their own, possess limited agency in their economic advancement. Their relative development is instead subject to the tides of cooperation and conflict between nations. This process forges new states, expands existing ones, and rips apart old ones. And underlying this phenomenon, too, is a process of technological progress and its diffusion—a process on which the very existence of nations imposes limits.

# 6

# PIRATE EMPIRE

I n 1598, England's ambassador to the Dutch Republic—the United Provinces of the Netherlands—marveled at the loose political structure of the ten-year-old state:

> Their state (unlike that of ancient Rome or modern-day Venice) is without a head, which directs and commands all other members of the body, but is made up of equal members. . . Not only the least important province, but even the smallest town, claims to possess a certain form of sovereignty, and wishes just as much say as the greatest.[1]

The union of this confederation of provinces and towns had little precedent in Europe. Even more remarkable is that the Dutch Republic was the world's most powerful nation for much of the seventeenth century.

The era of Dutch hegemony, the Netherlands' "Golden Age," is the period between 1566, the year of the Dutch Revolt, when the Northern Netherlands successfully threw off Spanish rule, and 1688, when outbreak of the Nine Years' War marked the beginning of a long period of decline. Before the Dutch Revolt, the northern provinces had been part of the Burgundian Netherlands. The latter included the commercial centers of Bruges and Antwerp. Many of the Republic's polyarchal institutions came from its former parent, whose cities originally established peat-digging colonies in the north. Its most important institution was the States General, an assembly of provincial representatives.

Concern for property rights underpinned Burgundy's political arrangements. Its States General negotiated regular taxes with the Duke and extraordinary taxes that were subject to refusal. A constitutional charter of 1477, known as the Great Privilege, ratified the States General's ability to limit the Duke's fiscal powers.

But when possession of the Netherlands passed to the Habsburgs in the sixteenth century, Charles V (r. 1519–56) and later his son Philip II (1556–98) sought to undo these limitations. By 1650, the Northern Dutch towns had developed a formidable commercial presence, not least in shipbuilding and navigation. Their wealth offered a compelling source of funds for Habsburg military campaigns during the Counter-Reformation.

It's not difficult to see why Holland and its sister provinces began revolting in 1566. A debt default by the Habsburg state in 1557 had severely damaged key financial centers in Burgundy, Italy, and the German states.[2] Dutch nobles, too, were in debt and therefore could not afford to relinquish precious funds.[3]

Under the 1579 Union of Utrecht, the Northern Provinces formed their own States General. Within the assembly, Holland, the largest province, commanded disproportionate power. It derived considerable influence from its large economic base, which made an outsized contribution to tax revenues. This gave Holland effective control over fiscal affairs; the Union of Utrecht stipulated unanimous agreement among the seven provinces for any decisions to alter revenues.

The new head of state was known as the *stadtholder*. Although the provincial assemblies selected him, the position stayed within the House of Orange, making the title quasi-monarchical. As the leader of the military, the stadtholder needed to request funds from the States General. This feature often made his power secondary to that of Holland's Grand Pensionary, who headed its provincial assembly.

Holland's own interests were by no means uniform. Although Amsterdam, the largest city, became the seat of global commerce, it was often at odds with other cities in the province, such as Leiden and Haarlem. Competing economic interests, not only within Holland but throughout the Republic, were responsible for the rivalry between towns.

Indeed, local politics was oligarchical and became more so over time. The town councils, known as the *vroedschap,* governed each city under a closed patrimonial body in which regents selected their successors. These regents, in turn, sent representatives to the larger assemblies. Wealth was the foremost qualification for membership, and councils often selected members for their extensive commercial links, in addition to the expertise they brought to committees. The importance of such committees stemmed from towns' historical role as closed corporations with competing guild regulations. In large cities such as Amsterdam, commercial affiliations within the council were diverse and subject to change.

## Investment Blocs in the Dutch Republic

This diversity of commercial interests naturally created political investment blocs. Historians often depict the Dutch Republic's history as a conflict between an Orangist party—loyal to the church and stadtholder—and a republican party favoring religious toleration and provincialism. But political developments throughout the Dutch Golden Age strongly correspond to coalitional changes among the regents themselves. Issues of identity concerning nation and religion were secondary to the economic ends of these factions.

Seventeenth-century Dutch politics offered the purest distillation of Ferguson's investment theory of party competition. Those in charge ruled, with little accountability, on behalf of commercial interests. Key political events during the Republic's hegemony thus had a direct link to changes in investor coalitions. And the issues that created bitter disputes among the regents are familiar ones: military spending, debt, taxes, and tariffs.

Given the Dutch Republic's size relative to the rest of Europe, foreign policy was the most important concern. The Republic's eighty-year conflict with Spain (1568–1648) showed that war could be immensely profitable. According to one estimate, the weapons industry accounted for 5 percent of the Dutch gross national product during this period.[4]

Peace, on the other hand, could free access to lucrative foreign markets. The Catholic powers, after all, possessed the largest populations in Europe. Many regents also had pre-existing trading relationships with the Spanish provinces, as was developed with the Cadiz wool trade, for example. Dutch merchants were indeed notorious double dealers and continued trading with enemies during war.[5] Of course, regents had to weigh the potential benefits of military aggression against the prospect of increased taxation. After all, profligate military expenditure had been the principal reason for their separation from the Habsburgs.

During the seventeenth century, the Dutch Republic's economic relationship with the rest of the world underwent notable change. As a result, foreign policy preferences changed too. In earlier centuries, when the Netherlands were a developmental laggard, city guilds implemented protections to stave off competition from more advanced regions. But as the Dutch moved to the cutting edge of technological innovation, the sectors interested in free trade became more influential.

Technical advances allowed the Northern Dutch provinces to climb the ladder to higher value-added processing such as oil-pressing, sawmilling, or tobacco processing; or higher value-added consumer goods, such as tobacco pipes, paper, and imitations of East Asian products.[6] The last item became especially important as demand increased in Europe for colored textiles such as printed calicoes. More liberal trade relations offered an opportunity to expand the markets for these goods, especially when no other countries possessed the sophistication to compete.

The financial advantages that accompanied technological advancement were another source of foreign policy shifts. As Amsterdam became the world's monetary center, its merchants gained access to cheap finance, which allowed them to reap the benefits of scale enterprise. In the textile industry, for example, Dutch merchants gradually consolidated the production chain. They then proceeded to move it to the lower-wage countryside, or even out of the country itself.[7] This process eventually gave way to the "deindustrialization" of manufacturing towns, which had ceased to become competitive.[8] Over time, advocates of the old "closed city" guilds clashed with the narrower interests favoring the new "open city" putting-out system.

## Seventeenth-Century Globalization and the Dutch Invisible Empire

During the Golden Age, wealth increasingly accumulated in the hands of the mercantile elite of the province of Holland, and more specifically of Amsterdam. By 1672, Dutch regents had managed to keep the position of *stadtholder* unfilled for twenty years. Over the same period, they had also launched the first modern attack on guild power.[9]

But in no other respect were Dutch merchants more notable than the extent to which their commercial activities ensnared the rest of the world. Wherever they landed, the economic life of that society became, as Violet Barbour has described it, "honeycombed by Dutch enterprise and many of their most valuable resources were appropriated by the invaders."[10] In the seventeenth century, they were involved in a range of activities in Europe: shipping, engineering, mining, financial services, and munitions manufacturing among others.[11]

Their activities abroad were often less than scrupulous. Prefiguring England's later activities in Asia, the Dutch introduced opium to the Javanese islands. There, Dutch East India officials also carried out a grizzly massacre of English rivals in 1623. And, of course, bulk-shipping advances found a lucrative application in transporting slaves across the Atlantic.

Yet governments could not fully extricate themselves from "the tentacles of Dutch capitalism" even when they tried.[12] Dutch economic influence was so powerful that such efforts would often prompt resistance from local enterprises. The Republic's economy acted as a demand sink—a reliable export destination—for the European periphery, which sold goods to its residents. In times of war, this consideration seriously constrained the actions of enemy combatants, who feared that any economic ruin brought upon the Dutch would only bring disaster to their own economies.[13]

By 1650, the Dutch Republic's estimated per capita GDP was nearly double that of the Italian city-states, and nearly triple that of England.[14] A century earlier, it had barely caught up to the city-states, which were in relative decline. Foreshadowing what would later occur in Victorian Britain and the United States, Dutch society became extremely unequal, with 1 percent of the population eventually monopolizing half of Amsterdam's wealth.[15] The beneficiaries of this process combined to form powerful associations known as *partenrederij*—predecessors of the British "Finance Company" and American private equity firms—which controlled a host of activities. Trading voyages, whaling expeditions, and the Norwegian timber trade were some of the functions these proto-conglomerates undertook.[16]

As their fortunes rose, Dutch merchants grew to "prefer speculative trading in commodities and company shares, and investment in public loans and annuities."[17] *Sociétés anonymes*, anonymous associations, would corner markets for important staples through trading monopolies and price-fixing rings. Whale products, Italian silks, gunpowder, sugar, and copper are just some of the 230 commodities affected in the first half of the seventeenth century.[18] That number doubled in the second half. Speculative hoarding became so extreme that it caused a shortage of grain in France and other European nations.[19]

General financial hoarding also caused Dutch interest rates to gradually fall for most of the century, a phenomenon symptomatic of demand deficiency. Rough estimates suggest that money velocity collapsed in the eighteenth century alongside the growth of Amsterdam's financial market.[20] Since interest rates were already in decline, however, and financialization well underway, velocity likely started falling earlier. After the 1660s, a collapse in real investment was evident, and aggregate demand weakened to such an extent that stagnation may be "too soft a term," as Jan de Vries and Ad van der Woude put it.[21]

Historians seem to take for granted that trade balances regulated the international flow of a fixed supply of global savings. This view implies that savings acquired from foreign trade—in the form of bullion—causally drove Dutch economic output. But evidence suggests that economic output in the Republic was demand-determined, fluctuating with the investment decisions of Dutch merchants. Additionally, early Dutch business cycles likely affected the global economy, not just that of the Republic.

The Bank of Amsterdam bills market was the main transmission mechanism of international financial shocks. Created in 1609, the bank had strict controls on the quality of coins it would hold in deposits, which were fully backed by reserves. In other words, the bank did not allow overdrafts. Its principal instrument was the bill of exchange, which gave its holder claims to the physical gold deposits of its original drawer. Because of their sheer purchasing power, Dutch merchants could make international payments in their own bill of exchange—a privilege other countries struggled to replicate.[22] Indeed, this was an early manifestation of the "exorbitant privilege" later possessed by Britain and the United States.

Although foreigners had accounts at the Bank of Amsterdam, local Dutch agents largely intermediated cross-border finance.[23] These agents would act as "paymasters" for foreign governments and remit *monnaye de Hollande* to Amsterdam. Similar agents would serve as conduits for British credit to America in the early nineteenth century.[24]

And although the international monetary standard was based on bullion, Keynesian effective demand still prevailed at the global level. During periods of international financial instability, money flowed back to the Republic. Only the amount needed for domestic commercial purposes circulated while merchants melted down the rest for deposit at the Bank of Amsterdam.

Domestic prices were extraordinarily stable. In the hundred years since the Republic's founding, the value of the Dutch guilder in terms of gold declined only 40 percent—a little more than 0.3 percent per annum.[25] Most other European countries, on the other hand, experienced significant inflation over the same period. Dutch merchants' outsized purchasing power backed an international financial architecture in which money gravitated back to the Republic during times of uncertainty instead of flowing out.

Interestingly, most of the guilder's depreciation against gold during the Dutch Golden Age happened before 1645. From that point on, its gold value—0.74 grams per guilder—was stable for an entire century. The stark difference in price stability before and after the mid-century mark corresponds to two distinct political regimes: fiscal-militarism and free trade.

## The Dutch Fiscal-Military Complex

During the Eighty Years' War against Spain (1568–1648), a sizable fiscal-military complex came to have a considerable impact on Dutch economic output. The first bout of conflict, after the 1566 revolt, birthed a new economy predicated on military expenditures. Following a period of peace from 1609 to 1621, the second bout of conflict—part of the larger Thirty Years' War in Europe (1618–38)—saw its entrenchment and

subsequent decay. By the 1640s, the Dutch army was the country's largest employer, and more than 40 percent of the Republic's budget went to pay soldiers.[26] Regular expenditures on
these forces, in addition to spending on garrison towns and
naval boards, supported aggregate demand by redistributing
income from Holland's main towns to provincial areas.

Given the extent to which employment in the Republic was
seasonal, regular annual pay to soldiers amounted to a transfer
to the local garrison towns that housed them. Where these
towns were situated, local industries such as brewing, agriculture, housing, construction, and, to a lesser extent, textiles,
prospered. Town regents—looking to benefit from the propi-
tious effects that garrisons had on public revenues—often
requested their enlargement.[27]

Naval boards also stimulated employment by issuing contracts
for ship construction and repair. These boards effectively operated
as autonomous bodies, controlling local customs duties.[28] Often
developing strong links with local regents, they outfitted private
vessels for military combat, allowing the Dutch to expand naval
capacity. By the beginning of the seventeenth century, they began
to offer considerable subsidies, directly through finance and indirectly through protection, to fisheries and the Dutch East India
Company (the *Vereenigde Oostindische Compagnie*, VOC).[29] Finally,
the geographic dispersion of naval boards led to the redistribution
of fiscal revenues. Subsidies to Rotterdam's board, for example,
allowed it to grow into a major city.[30]

Intense privateering fostered close connections between
naval and commercial interests. State-sanctioned piracy was so
extensive, however, that a blurred line separated naval units
and plundering outfits. In 1572, for example, privateers called
"Sea Beggars" helped deliver a decisive victory against Spain.[31]

Between 1587 and 1596, the number of large warships in the
Dutch navy doubled.[32] A need for ships that could carry heavy
artillery helped spawn new vessels able to store bulk cargoes
and stay at sea for up to half a year.[33] Indeed, naval activity

early in the war was an important source of the innovations contributing to the Republic's maritime supremacy.

By the turn of the seventeenth century, breakthroughs in navigation—mapping new routes, estimating endpoints, and confirming those estimates—enabled the Dutch to become leaders in long-distance sailing.[34] Previously, Dutch shipping had been limited to intra-European bulk freightage, carrying staples such as grain, timber, salt, and fish. With improved access to the New World and Asia, trading in such scarcer items as tobacco, silk, and spices increased. New commodities from long-distance trade also sparked the production of highly specialized items such as dyes, ceramics, patterned silks, and tapestries.

Dutch investment abroad also started to spread into the new century, carrying new techniques to other countries.[35] Among these were innovative agricultural, engineering, and cloth-making practices.[36] Dutch merchants also began to engage in significant cross-border financial operations. From financing Sweden's copper mines to operating mints for the Polish Crown, and providing initial equity for the new Bank of Hamburg, they offered a range of banking services to foreign governments.[37]

The VOC's exclusiveness, an enduring source of tension, also led numerous entrepreneurs to bring navigation techniques abroad in attempts to build similar monopolies elsewhere. The early decades of the seventeenth century coincided with Dutch efforts to create Danish, French, Scottish, and Tuscan East India Companies; Republic merchants also helped finance the English East India trade on the Indian subcontinent.[38]

Booming foreign investment coincided with favorable economic conditions at home. Eventually, domestic financial conditions became loose, causing authorities to curb credit expansion by cashier banks in 1609. Exuberant animal spirits gave way to bust around 1615, and, as a consequence, the

Republic experienced a serious slump, second only in that century to the long depression of 1670.[39]

Economic activity would not recover until the next decade, and commerce with mainland Europe remained weak for twenty years. Yet, as difficult as the end of the boom was on the Dutch economy, it had a calamitous effect on the rest of Europe. Some historians describe the start of the period as the Trade Depression of the 1620s. Sound toll registers—records of ships passing through the strait between Denmark and Sweden—confirm a decline in European commerce.[40] Dutch trade to the Baltic region suffered while English exports to the German region, Poland, and the Baltic States declined by as much as 50 percent; French trade with the Levant also halved.[41]

Although incomplete, records show that the VOC stock price fell by 50 percent between 1614 and 1617.[42] When economic distress reached the domestic economy in 1616, riots erupted in the manufacturing towns. Dutch textiles were notably facing competitive pressures from the Southern Netherlands, whose production was recovering during peace.[43] A dispute between hardline and liberal factions of the clergy simultaneously led to religious riots, which regents tied to the Indies trades and used to oust Grand Pensionary Johann Oldenbarnevelt in 1618. Oldenbarnevelt, who had lobbied for peace in 1609, attempted to lead Holland's secession but was arrested and executed. The events allowed the stadtholder to consolidate political power and help the Orangist war party gain control of Amsterdam's council.[44]

Though war with Counter-Reformation forces returned, the Dutch economy recovered from the trade depression with a new speculative boom beginning around 1630. Demand for food and agricultural provisions in Germany, where war was most intense, initiated the business cycle. With war disrupting the usual supply chains, such as those from the Baltic, an opportunity arose to feed the large armies warring in central Europe.[45] Agricultural demand gave local investors an incentive to make land more arable for farming. As remains the case today, a sizable portion of Dutch land was below sea level.

Around the same time, a technological breakthrough occurred. Since the sixteenth century, Dutch engineers increasingly applied windmill technology to poldering—the process by which they drained wet areas to make artificial tracts of land, or polders, suitable for agriculture. Size constraints, however, limited pumping capacity since the entire windmill had to be rotated.[46] Slow innovations, like mills that only required their cap to turn into the wind, began to increase capacity. As a result, engineers gained the ability to drain bodies of water the size of small lakes. By 1624, they learned to line up windmills to pump water in concert and could drain lakes as deep as 4.5 meters. Another development arrived in 1630 when engineers replaced the paddle wheel with the Archimedes screw.

Unprecedented and unmatched land reclamation activity took place in the first half of the seventeenth century, especially between 1610 and 1640.[47] One-half, or 125,000 hectares, of all of the land transformed between 1500 and 1800 was poldered during this single period.[48] Speculators invested ten million guilders, more than the amount put into the Dutch East India Company, into agricultural projects.[49] A persistent rise in farm rents, which increased into the 1650s, fueled the speculative activity.[50]

Simultaneously, new methods of organization emerged for supplying agricultural products. Capital investment in buildings and equipment transformed farms while barn storage expanded with new dairies and cooling cellars. Weekly markets opened near cities, whose growth provided a significant source of demand, especially for processing and exporting farm output.[51] A desire to improve the movement of goods in urban areas also led to a boom in canal construction.[52]

In addition to its effects on agriculture, the Thirty Years' War rekindled growth in the fiscal-military apparatus which had paused during the Twelve Years' Truce (1609–21). Conflict helped the Republic's arms dealers enlarge their fortunes. For example, in 1624, Louis de Geer and the Trip brothers—the most prominent merchants of war—organized a joint venture capitalized at 72,000 guilders. Just two years later, it had grown almost sixfold, to 400,000 guilders.[53]

Ironically, the fiscal-military complex became troubled not long after the Orangists gained political control. Whereas military expenditures had been only three million guilders per year around 1590, they jumped to fourteen million in 1621.[54] In 1624, tax riots erupted as taxation primarily consisted of excises on ordinary citizens. A year later, the deficit swelled to one of its widest marks in the century.[55] Five years later, some provinces faced budgetary crises and had to be bailed out by the West India Company, which in turn suffered its own financial difficulties the following year.[56] Given the circumstances, the States General had to enact wealth levies and debate the necessity of forced loans almost every year from 1626 to 1635.[57]

Holland's regents were less than pleased with the state of fiscal affairs. Despite having less than half the total population, the province had to contribute 60 percent of revenues.[58] And prolonged war caused its stock of debt to rise steeply.[59] Also troubling was the growing debasement of coinage by other provinces—a practice Holland avoided.[60]

The Bank of Amsterdam, too, experienced financial strain. Lending to the Dutch East India Company—a practice that only began after Oldenbarnevelt's execution—grew from 97,000 guilders in 1620 to 1 million guilders in 1629. By this latter year, deposit coverage at the Bank of Amsterdam fell to 50 percent.[61]

Republican regents in Amsterdam (and Holland more generally) used the dire condition of public spending to wrest back control from the hawks.[62] The new stadtholder Frederick Henry, who assumed power in 1625, had to adopt a more conciliatory approach from the start of his tenure. Against the wishes of hardline Calvinists, he took a more tolerant stance toward religious freedom and sought compromises with the republican faction.

By the 1640s, decay in the Dutch war regime was visible. Corruption and fraud emerged in the admiralty boards, which began collaborating with local merchants to underreport customs duties.[63] Holland threatened to withhold funding for troops if naval management did not improve.[64] Amsterdam merchants, growing ever wealthier, also discovered that hiring privateers proved to be more effective in protecting Dutch ships; the necessity of a stadtholder-administered navy came increasingly under question.

The West India Company's dismal performance delivered an added blow to the hawks. Its share price collapsed from 200 florin in 1629 to 50 by 1645. It also came close to bankruptcy in 1636, prompting the States General to open its trade to all shareholders. By 1648, all Dutch merchants were allowed to trade in the West Indies.[65]

*Figure 6.1*

*Figure 6.2*

*Figure 6.3*

**Figures 6.1, 6.2, and 6.3** show how fiscal policy and prices evolved alongside Dutch political institutions. The Eighty Years' War with Spain birthed a fiscal-military regime whose expenditures on fortifications redistributed income from Holland to the other provinces. The effect of war spending is evident in the growth of wages and the diminishing gold content of the guilder. Fiscal austerity after the 1630s arrested wage growth and led to an extended period of price stability. Source: Marjolein 't Hart, *The Dutch Wars of Independence: Warfare and*

*Commerce in the Netherlands 1570–1680* (New York: Routledge, 2014), 93; Jan Luiten Van Zanden, "Prices and Wages and the Cost of Living in the Western Part of the Netherlands, 1450–1800," International Institute of Social History, accessed January 29, 2021, http://www.iisg.nl/hpw/brenv.php; Jan de Vries and Ad van der Woude, *The First Modern Economy: Success, Failure, and Perseverance of the Dutch Economy, 1500–1815* (Cambridge: Cambridge University Press, 2010), 85.

## The Era of "Free Trade"

Coalitional dynamics shifted further in favor of peace. Talks to end the war had begun as early as the late 1630s. A contemporary pamphlet reflected changing sentiment, stating an observer's opinion that "for every one grown rich through piracy or illicit trade, a hundred others have been made poorer." The pamphleteer, notes the historian Craig Harline, further listed "the various taxes, convoy charges, and armament expenses that businessmen were obliged to pay during the war."[66] It is worth emphasizing here that this critic deliberately alludes to the burdens on *businessmen*. Continued war was not undesirable for moral reasons, but rather because of its mounting onerousness to segments of the wealthy.

Perhaps more than the costs of war, growth in the number of political groups benefiting from peace caused a change in political winds. Among these were holders of the sizable debt issued during the war. Undoubtedly, price stability and reduced expenditures supported the value of their holdings. It is likely no coincidence that a fictional debate about foreign policy portrayed in a well-circulated 1639 political pamphlet featured "the government bondholder" as a central character.[67] In the pamphlet, which features a policy debate on naval expenditure, the bondholder is inclined to believe that Dutch ships have sufficient protection.[68]

Peace also favored Dutch merchants involved in the nascent triangular trade. These individuals had found a sinister yet profitable application of bulk shipping in helping other countries transport slaves. The Dutch also applied the new windmill designs mentioned earlier to processing colonial sugar and tobacco. Whereas only three sugar refineries existed in 1607, forty were in operation by 1650.[69]

All the while, some merchants had still managed to carry on trade with Spain. Oddly, their importance to Spain had only grown in the second phase of the war.[70] One reason may have been innovations in Dutch textile manufacturing that increased the demand for Spanish wool.[71] By the time the Treaty of Munster made peace official in 1648, the Dutch had managed to fully capture trade on the Iberian Peninsula.[72]

A more general development was that the purchasing power of Dutch merchants had only become stronger by mid-century. Such financial strength, *global* in scale, enabled them to vertically integrate textile production and move its components where costs were lowest.[73] It also helped acquire monopolies in a range of goods, such as Venetian mercury, Caribbean sugar, Russian caviar, and marble from Genoa—monopolies that could offer reliable profits of up to 40 percent per year.[74] Dutch merchants' ability to assume financing costs and selling risks also made them compelling trade partners.[75]

Relative technical advancement, of course, was the source of Dutch purchasing power. Its application abroad through foreign investment offered sizable profits. After 1650, "the outflow of technology reached a truly massive scale and large geographical sweep."[76] Consequently, deposits at the Bank of Amsterdam fell from their peak in 1645 and did not recover this level until 1690.

## Dutch Financialization

Following peace with Spain in 1648, Holland's regents, concerned about the Province's deficit, began implementing budgetary austerity through cuts to military expenditures.[77] In response, the new stadtholder William II, who succeeded his father in 1647, invaded Amsterdam three years later and jailed the city's regents. A quick compromise, however, limited military downsizing to only foreign troops; the imprisoned regents were released. That same year William II died and the States General left the stadtholder's seat unfilled, even though his son was born only eight days later.[78]

Holland's regents had already questioned the necessity of the stadtholder, and the shock of William II's actions sealed their decision. A twenty-year period of stadtholder-less rule began in which the republican regents, led by Grand Pensionary Johan de Witt, dominated the States General. Among his strongest supporters were regents, like his in-laws, who had strong commercial ties to Spain.[79]

De Witt continued to push austerity policies. Garrison towns naturally suffered as they lost subsidized demand. Likewise, fortifications in the New World were neglected, which led to the loss of Brazilian outposts and, later, New Amsterdam (now New York). But de Witt achieved his goal as Holland's indebtedness, which had been rising continuously, stabilized.[80] Debt yields fell from 5 to 4 percent by the early 1660s, while those on other obligations continued to fall even lower.[81]

Although the decline in borrowing costs seems a welcome result of more budgetary discipline, interest rates had already fallen significantly from 8 percent in 1600. Furthermore, consumer prices had risen only 1 percent annually over the first half of the century, while gold deposits at the Bank of Amsterdam had grown tenfold.[82] This macroeconomic path is not what one would expect in times of fiscal excess. Instead, demand deficiency was likely already present by the beginning of the stadtholder-less years, which only worsened it.

That demand deficiency coincided with an increasing concentration of wealth is no coincidence. Economic inequality gave way to hoarding and greater demand for financial assets. Such behavior accelerated after 1650. As mentioned, the second half of the century saw greater speculative activity through commodity futures and options in addition to the formation of cartels and price-fixing schemes.[83]

Hoarding of "safe" government securities raised their price to the extent that they became virtually indistinguishable from cash.[84] An English diplomat observed in 1673 that "whoever has a bill of any publique debt, has so much ready money in his coffers, being paid certainly at call, without charge, or trouble."[85] Foreigners marveled at the "elasticity" of Dutch finance in meeting the government's spending demands.[86]

Among the most important stores of wealth for rising fortunes was property. Already in 1639, one pamphlet reminisced about times when merchants "didn't think of buying up lands and castles" and instead "reinvested profits in their businesses."[87] Such behavior eventually led to a bubble, especially in the cities. By the end of the 1640s, financial flows into property markets had grown to "speculative proportions."[88] The Herengracht index shows that property prices in Amsterdam rose two and a half times between 1639 and 1660, and 60 percent in the short period of 1655 to 1660.[89] While construction data from the period is lacking, activity can be imputed from taxes on building materials, which show a multi-century peak near 1660.[90] Housing rent data, which plunged in the following decade, also suggests oversupply.[91]

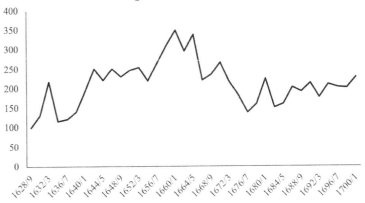

**Housing Prices in Amsterdam (Index = 100)**

*Figure 6.4*

**Figure 6.4** shows that Amsterdam experienced a speculative boom in property prices in the middle of the 17th century. The Dutch property bubble occurred during the more general financialization of the Republic's economy. **Source**: Piet Eichholtz, "A Long Run House Price Index: The Herengracht Index, 1628–1973," *Real Estate Economics* 25, no. 2 (1997): 175-92.

## The Stagnation of the Working Population

While the middle of the century brought greater prosperity to the Republic's merchants, the same cannot be said about other groups. The broad population grappled with the effects of "secular stagnation." This process was already underway in the 1630s when small traders and artisans lost their independence to merchant-entrepreneurs who possessed the resources to produce at mass scale.[92] Seasonal jobs became more difficult to hold as supplementary sources of earnings disappeared. Large-scale urban land ownership, for example, reduced peasant holdings, which provided a secondary source of income.[93] Similarly, land reclamation removed opportunities for inland fishing. The transformation of labor thus left inhabitants of rural areas increasingly exposed to long bouts of unemployment.[94]

The low-skilled employment that emerged as a substitute for this general squeeze was inferior in quality and more precarious. Those who previously been subsistence farmers on household plots had to sacrifice their autonomy by becoming wage laborers on commercial farms. And unsteady construction work in reclamation projects replaced small-scale fishing. Likewise, as short-haul bulk freightage disappeared, maritime workers had to seek employment in riskier long-distance ventures. Furthermore, regressive excise taxes created a high-cost economic environment that forced those dispossessed into these less-advantageous sources of employment.[95]

Overcapacity began to emerge in the wake of deindustrialization and declining real investment at home. Brewing, for example, declined as competition from imported beverages increased and stimulus from garrison towns disappeared.[96] Land reclamation also slowed down after the end of the war. Farmland lost its appeal to urban investors, who preferred more certain returns on government bonds to the risky 3 to 4 percent on the former. By 1655, holders of farmland began selling their stakes to institutional investors, such as orphanages, as agricultural rents had become too low to justify continued ownership.[97] Farmers, who had devoted resources to fixed investment, especially in dairy, now found their holdings unprofitable amid stagnating and, later, falling agricultural prices.

In Leiden, the center of Dutch textile production, woolen cloth production peaked mid-century and declined sharply afterward.[98] The wool, linen, and cloth manufacturing that had prospered in the late sixteenth and early seventeenth centuries struggled to compete with the lower-cost countryside or, in certain cases, child labor.[99] Additionally, England, by 1650, finally learned to produce cheap woolens, which Dutch manufacturers substituted with more expensive cloth produced from the raw materials obtained through new monopolies in Spain and the Levant.[100] Yet such newer industries did not sufficiently offset excess capacity.

Leiden also happened to be the source of a "Great Stink" that was representative of the times. Sewage contaminated the local water supply as city officials, swayed by the textile industry, permitted overcrowding and degraded health standards. Eventually, "brackish" beer, brewed from dirty water, caused an outbreak of disease in 1669.[101]

The struggling industries' calls for protection went unheeded. Instead, Holland's regents weakened guild power by reducing the guilds' ability to restrict entry.[102] In newer trades, guild protections were absent. Where present, as Barbour tells it, "emphasis on guild charters was shifting from protection of craftsmen in a local market to control of employment and wages in the interests of employers competing in a world market."[103]

Available wage data shows a marked change in the middle of the seventeenth century. Whereas common wages grew 40 percent cumulatively between 1600 and 1640, they grew less than 10 percent in the forty years that followed.[104] In contrast, the salaries of occupations with greater prestige continued to climb.[105]

Reflecting on the Dutch Republic, Karl Marx claimed that "the people of Holland were more overworked, poorer, and more brutally oppressed than those of all the rest of Europe put together."[106] Though this could be an exaggeration, the seventeenth century was anything but a Golden Age for many Netherlanders. And one could hardly exaggerate the plight of the many migrant workers the Dutch employed, the Javanese captive to VOC opium, or the victims of the burgeoning slave trade.

## The Road Back to War

A long depression followed the end of the Dutch property
bubble. Depression had already been underway in agriculture,
which saw rents drop precipitously from the 1660s to the end of
the century.[107] The VOC's share price would barely surpass its
1650 peak in the rest of the century.[108] Consistent with worsening stagnation, Holland's interest rate would plunge further
to 3 percent. From the end of the 1660s, an "embarrassing
amount of capital" was struggling to find profitable
investment.[109]

Excess capacity in the Dutch Republic also coincided with a
decline in European trade. Toll registers from the Sound
between Denmark and Sweden show a collapse in passages by
1660, heralding the end of Dutch-led globalization. Though the
number of ships briefly recovered in the 1680s, the rate
remained depressed until 1720. The era of free trade that began
after Dutch-Spanish tensions subsided could not last under the
weight of falling demand caused by rapacious Dutch rentiers.

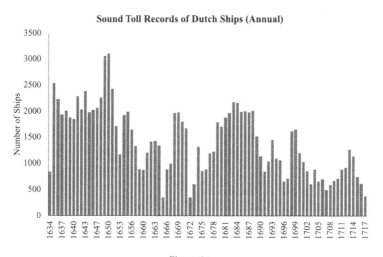

*Figure 6.5*

Figure **6.5** illustrates a long-term decline in the number of Dutch ships passing through the Danish Sound. The Sound Toll records proxy European trade cooperation, which declined after the mid-17th century. **Source**: The Sound Toll Registers Online, http://www.soundtoll.nl/index.php/en/over-het-project/str-online.

Few economies had benefited as much as France from cooperative trade relations with the Dutch. As argued in the previous chapter, Dutch merchants were indispensable to French development in the first half of the seventeenth century. This arrangement, though, produced mutual benefit. Dutch investors were drawn to the outsourcing opportunities France offered with cheaper production costs for items such as alcohol and salt.[110] But, amid stagnation, both countries began to adopt policies that viewed world trade as a zero-sum game.[111] French First Minister Colbert's tariffs in 1664 marked the beginning of an escalating trade war between the two nations.[112]

In Amsterdam, the failure of trade cooperation brought the more belligerent factions back to power. Like their counterparts in France and England, they saw colonial markets—principally slaves and sugar—as the scarce remaining sources of profit.[113] Skirmishes with Britain's Royal African Company in Western Africa, and intensifying competition with the English East India Company for the growing tea trade, bolstered their case for a more assertive military.[114] Regents could also no longer ignore that France had amassed the largest army in Europe and was encroaching on the Southern Netherlands. By the late 1660s, Amsterdam's hawks began allying with the Orangist-led industrial towns of Leiden and Haarlem, who sought retaliatory tariffs against France.[115]

Then in 1672, France, allied with England, launched an invasion of the United Provinces. The Amsterdam town council forced the resignation of de Witt, who was lynched by a mob soon afterward. The invasion allowed William III of the House of Orange to reclaim the mantle of stadtholder. After expelling the French, William and the Orangists undertook an expansion of the military.

Amsterdam's town council, however, still largely consisted of moderates. Amid rising absolutism elsewhere, they remained wary of the stadtholder's power. Already by 1676, the council became concerned with rising military expenditures, debt, and continued stagnation.[116] The following year, the republican faction returned to power and negotiated both peace and tariff reductions with France. Hostility between the two countries was renewed in the late 1680s, however, and ensnared Europe in two successive wars that lasted until 1714.

By the end of those wars, the Dutch Republic's relative decline had become apparent. One can easily blame the cause of these wars, as many historians have, on Louis XIV's territorial ambitions. But France's absolutism cannot be extricated from the conditions that enabled its rise. The benefits of Dutch commerce accrued to a narrow few—a fact unveiled by mid-century stagnation. Furthermore, the Republic's merchants cultivated and profited from France's ascendance. And both French and English mercantilism grew out of efforts to emulate the Dutch. In the end, the United Provinces succumbed to a monstrosity that reflected their own flaws.

# 7

# THE COUNTRY AND THE COURT

E ngland in 1600 was at the periphery of the global market, but by the close of the century, it would find itself on equal footing with the Dutch Republic. Initially, it confronted many of the classic economic problems that beleaguer less-developed economies: balance of payments pressures, persistent fiscal strains, prohibitive cost of capital, and a general lack of competitiveness. As much as 90 percent of England's export at the beginning of the century was unfinished cloth destined for Northern Europe; only a century earlier had it graduated from exporting wool.[1]

Yet its concentrated and low value-added external sector continued to make England highly susceptible to the vicissitudes of foreign demand. This vulnerability became apparent in the wake of the pan-European economic crisis that occurred at the end of the 1610s and preceded the Thirty Years' War on the continent. The fallout, combined with the growth of new economic interests, resulted in institutional changes that would set England on the path to overtaking the Dutch Republic.

At the start of the seventeenth century, England, like the Dutch Republic, had a greater degree of polyarchy than other societies in Europe. In addition to the Crown, approximately one hundred wealthy landowning families ruled over what was then an unwieldy territory and population, many times the size of Holland (though still smaller France and Spain). As the Magna Carta had stipulated much earlier, the king would call Parliament to authorize taxation but retained the power to dissolve it at will. To curb parliamentary power, the Stuart kings sought to avoid calling it altogether. Royal efforts to find extra-parliamentary sources of revenue would be the chief cause of the civil war that wracked the country in the 1640s.

The Crown's principal source of such revenue was its ability to grant monopoly trading rights both at home and abroad. Much of daily economic life—including housing, clothing, food, and leisure—were subject to such monopolies.[2] Power thus rested disproportionately in the hands of the Crown, its administrators, and its courtiers, all of whom were profitably engaged in the business of peddling privilege.

Few benefited from Crown privileges more than the mercantile oligarchy that controlled London, whose governance was organized under a grouping of livery companies (a type of guild) called the Corporation of London.[3] The Corporation consisted of two bodies: the twenty-six-member Aldermanic Court and the 237-member Common Council. Although the latter group was elected by freemen—individuals of a certain rank in livery companies—the former group dominated the Corporation.[4]

The most prominent London merchants were those who possessed foreign trading rights. Of these, the most important was the Company of Merchant Adventurers. Its members held exclusive privileges to buy England's staple—undyed cloth—at home and sell it abroad in European marts. Under the guild-like structure of the regulated company, the Adventurers' members operated independently, though like their domestic counterparts they were collectively protected from interlopers by the Crown.[5]

Merchants also helped influence the Crown's foreign policy. After two decades of war, James, like the peace party in

Holland, normalized relations with Spain immediately after gaining the throne. City merchants sought to open trade with the Iberian Peninsula, given the availability of consumer goods that they could import back to England.[6] In 1604, they attempted to form a Spanish Company, but Parliament ruled to keep trade in Spain open to all.

## Parliament and the Country

Parliament's dissolution of the Spanish Company underscores the enmity that existed between a sizable portion of the legislature and the merchants of the City (the financial center of London). The latter acquired fortunes that exceeded those of all but the largest landowners. Furthermore, courtier monopolists tended to be members of the Church of England, though some harbored Catholic sympathies.[7] Naturally, this placed them at odds with members of the Commons, several of whom were Puritan, came from outside the City, and did not depend on connections to the Court.

Conflicting economic interests between "country" and "court" grew to be a deeper source of rivalry than religion and social status. Economic change related to two key areas drove such divisions: agriculture and long-distance navigation. In both, technological spillovers from abroad played no small part.

Starting in the second half of the sixteenth century, England's landed gentry—both the lesser and the upper—experienced rising agricultural fortunes. One reason was a rise in general prices, likely an effect of war. In the century from 1540 to 1640, the price of wheat rose six times.[8] Another was the introduction of new farming practices from the Dutch Republic. Dutch agricultural tools, crop rotation methods, and dairy-farming innovations all found their way to England.[9] Third, as also occurred in the Republic, the growth of towns, a phenomenon itself fueled by cloth-making, created greater demand for food.[10]

The rising fortunes of English landowners offered a source of investment for a new form of economic organization that emerged in the late sixteenth century: the joint-stock company. In contrast to the merchant trading companies, joint-stock companies permitted passive ownership and had a governing board of directors. Passive investment opportunities in pirating ventures had already attracted England's gentry during the war with Spain. As was the case in the Dutch United Provinces, English privateering syndicates found immense profits in plundering Spanish galleons.[11] As long-distance navigation techniques reached England, the joint-stock enterprise offered a suitable commercial structure given the high capital requirements of far-off endeavors.

Two main types of joint-stock investing emerged in the early 1600s. One invested in companies trading in the East, like the East India and Levant Companies. Such enterprises attracted the more conservative City merchants who were looking for surer bets. As a standalone company, the East India initiative raised the largest sum of capital at £2.9 million, though independent privateering ventures still garnered the largest total investment at £4.4 million.[12]

The other invested in the New World of the Americas. Like those who started the Dutch West India Company, certain individuals, most notably Walter Raleigh, sought to establish colonial settlements as bases from which to carry out the plunder of Spanish ships.[13] American joint-stock investments were much smaller than Eastern ones, with £250,000 invested in Virginia offerings, £90,000 for Bermuda, £80,000 for Guiana, and far smaller sums for other well-known investments, such as Plymouth. These smaller sums reflect the more speculative nature of prospecting in the New World. As a result, they drew greater participation from the gentry than wealthier and more seasoned City merchants.[14] The former seemed more attracted to lottery-like payoffs than immediate profit. Expeditions like Raleigh's also had the patriotic luster of doubling as warfare against the Catholic menace of Spain.

The gentry's involvement in American joint-stock companies worsened foreign policy divisions, not least because half of those who invested in these ventures were members of the Commons.[15] Like their Dutch counterparts, England's political elite split between those who sought peace with Spain and those who favored a more belligerent stance. The Crown had a less-than-encouraging attitude toward colonial settlement, and in the early part of the century, its colonial policies fomented the lower house's antipathy toward the Crown.[16] James I's execution of Raleigh in 1618 to appease Spain, the dissolution of the Virginia Company in 1625, and the cessation of Canada to France by Charles I (r. 1625–49), are all examples.[17]

It was not a coincidence that the very foreign policy disputes that seized Dutch politics in 1618 also emerged in England. Before forming their West India Company, the Dutch twice sought to make it a joint venture with the English before James scuttled the proposal.[18] And just as their Dutch counterparts had, hardline Puritans attached Court accommodation of Spain to crypto-Catholicism.

### The Trade Depression

Between 1600 and 1610, membership in companies rose sevenfold.[19] But as a periphery of the global market, England could not grow sustainably without exports. None of the joint-stock companies would provide a contribution to export growth because most of them failed. Even the ones that became profitable—the East India and Levant Companies—made money by selling imported goods.[20] England's economic condition therefore remained tied to the health of the cloth trade.

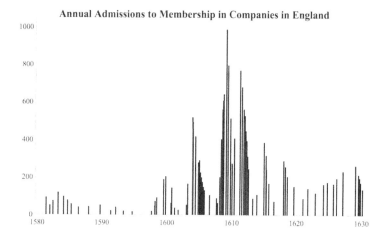

Figure 7.1

**Figure 7.1** shows annual admissions to companies in England. Membership soared during the Dutch-led foreign investment boom of the early 1600s. The subsequent bust produced an economic depression across Europe. **Source:** T. K. Rabb, *Enterprise and Empire: Merchant and Gentry Investment in the Expansion of England, 1575–1630* (Cambridge, MA: Harvard University Press, 1967), 127.

A favorable trade climate benefited exports of unfinished cloth from the beginning of James's reign in 1603 to 1614. Volumes grew 6 percent annually over this period until they reached a new peak.[21] Amid a healthy trade cycle, Crown revenues, and consequently the state's creditworthiness, remained stable despite James' large expenditures.[22] Crown borrowings were especially low in the first five years of this period.[23]

A serious textile depression emerged in 1616 as cloth customs fell by 25 percent. Conditions worsened in the ensuing years as a financial crisis spread throughout Europe.[24] By 1622, the worst year, textile exports troughed at 40 percent below their 1614 level.[25] According to the historian Barry Supple, "The economy, as it entered 1622, seemed doomed to a never-ending descent along a spiral of unemployment, idle capital, economic stagnancy and an unfavorable balance of trade."[26] England experienced a balance-of-payments crisis as complaints abounded in Parliament about a general "want of money" and its hoarding.[27]

As trade deteriorated after 1614, so too did the Crown's creditworthiness. It obtained a one-year loan from the London Corporation of £100,000 at 10 percent interest, which it did not repay for more than a decade.[28] The Corporation itself came under fiscal strain in the early 1620s and was unable (and unwilling) to meet further requests for loans until 1625. Interestingly, despite its fiscal struggles, the Crown did not seek recourse through currency debasement as other countries (aside from the Republic) did at the time. A near devaluation occurred in 1626 but was scuttled by Parliament.[29]

## Seeds of a New Economy

After Charles I succeeded his father in 1625, England's economy emerged from the worst period of the depression of the 1620s but remained weak. Export volumes recovered but failed to surpass their 1614 peak during his rule.[30] Already in 1630, it had become evident that the old unfinished-cloth trade would not recover.[31]

Other forms of activity continued to grow, however. War in Europe led to a "wave" of privateering in the colonies.[32] Puritan gentry, like the Earl of Warwick, launched massive plundering campaigns in the Americas.[33] They also used renewed tensions with Spain as an opportunity to establish the Providence Island and Massachusetts Bay Companies, in addition to adding more members to the Bermuda Company.[34] City merchants, however, pushed foreign policy in the opposite direction, seeking more amicable relations with Spain. War hurt their trading activities on the Continent.[35]

By 1630, the East India and Levant Companies became the most profitable joint-stock enterprises. Half of England's

imports came from these two countries, and one cannot under-
state the fact that *imports* were their principal source of profit.[36]
But as the Dutch massacre of English East India agents at
Amboyna showed, these trades entailed greater rivalry with the
Dutch. Commercial success enabled the Levantine merchants
to become the most influential economic faction, especially in
London's Aldermanic Court, during the reign of Charles I.[37]

In no other respect did these merchants become more
powerful, however, than the particular means by which they
came to influence the Crown: customs farming. Government in
the 1620s grew at an anemic pace, as a result of the economic
havoc the European trade collapse wrought on England's
narrowly concentrated export sector. When Charles I assumed
the throne, he inherited a large debt burden—£750,000—a
weak economy, and conflict with Spain.[38] That same year,
Parliament broke tradition and limited Charles' right to collect
import and export duties (tonnage and poundage) to no more
than one year. It felt justified in claiming greater authority
given both the deterioration of royal credit and general
economic conditions. Charles, however, asserted royal preroga-
tive and ignored Parliament. In 1629, he dissolved the body for
eleven years.

For his main source of funding, Charles turned to the
wealthy city merchants who could function as customs farmers.
These individuals made advances to the Crown in exchange for
the right to collect duties on imports. They also used their fiscal
influence to achieve peace with Spain in 1629, much to the
dismay of the Puritan gentry.

In addition to the latter, a new economic group arose to
challenge the interests of the City merchants. This group of
"new merchants" broadly consisted of small producers, retail-
ers, and shipowners who could undercut the merchants
through illegal interloping.[39] England's weak bureaucracy
made enforcement of regulations difficult.[40] As a result, such
groups, often operating from ports outside of London, were
able to skirt the Merchant Companies' export privileges.

Over time, the new merchants grew wealthy enough to buy seats in the Commons. By the 1630s, their ranks expanded, and they came to dominate the lower house.[41] Many of the new entrants were those whose commerce grew outside of guild regulation. One of these groups included individuals involved in tobacco planting and retailing. Another important segment were vendors of so-called new draperies produced in Lancashire, the only cloth segment that did well in the 1630s. New draperies manufacturers sought to emulate the Dutch in producing lighter cloth for mass markets, which was difficult under the strict guild controls on the cloth trade.[42] They developed shared interests with the Birmingham arms manufacturers, who also thrived outside of guild oversight.[43]

Finally, England saw the rise of a carrying trade that would pave the way for the Navigation Acts. Growing colonial settlement and crop production naturally led to an increase in transatlantic shipping. Renewed hostilities in Europe also allowed England to encroach on the Dutch carrying trade, particularly in bullion transport for Spain.[44]

## The Road to Civil War

Crown finances continued to deteriorate under Charles' tenure. Already in 1630, the king faced annual financing needs of £300,000 per year (roughly 5 percent of GDP), which he sought to pay without the help of Parliament.[45] Of this amount, ordinary revenues, less ordinary expenses, contributed a reasonable deficit of £50,000 per year. But to repay the Crown's debt, Charles needed to find another £150,000. Finally, the rise of privateering in English waters required still further expenditures for naval armament.[46]

Had the economy returned to the robust performance of his father's early reign, Charles may have had a far more manageable situation with revenue growth restoring fiscal health over time. But it did not, and the Crown expanded its practice of borrowing on advances from customs farmers; the latter extended their lending to multiyear terms and even allowed the king to incur overdrafts.[47]

Persistent weakness in royal finances and, more generally, England's economy revealed a rotting political regime. It remained mired in unwieldy rent-seeking arrangements that hobbled its tradable goods sector. The status quo, however, continued to benefit influential City merchants. They profited from clientelist relations with the Crown, and their willingness to extend credit to the king prolonged economic decay.

Without Parliament, though, Charles was unable to rectify his finances, and his attempts to acquire new sources of revenue grew more egregious in the 1630s. He abused his powers to grant monopolies by issuing patents on numerous trades: soap, salt, coal, tobacco, and starch.[48] Additionally, Charles levied new "ship money" taxes using naval rearmament as a pretext. Such taxes had traditionally only applied to maritime towns, but he extended them to other areas.

The Crown also attempted to raise revenues through fines on land reclamation projects. Higher demand for food and heating coal produced a boom in speculative land improvement among the gentry. The king viewed this as an opportunity to extract revenues from people who encroached on royal forests.[49] His advisors also infuriated the gentry further by establishing an enclosure commission to prosecute landowners for "depopulating" the countryside.[50]

War in Scotland provided an opportunity for change. In 1639, the London Corporation rejected Charles' appeals for a £200,000 loan to organizing forces and demanded that he first call Parliament. Desperate, Charles finally convened the Short Parliament, which he dismissed after three weeks in April of the following year. The king then took several drastic measures. First, he threatened to debase the coinage with brass money, and next, he forcibly borrowed pepper from the East India Company, selling it immediately on the market.

His most disastrous decision, however, was seizing a shipment of Spanish bullion. English ships were carrying it on behalf of Spain and temporarily housed it at the Mint. The act sparked a chaotic bout of monetary flight and caused England's economy to suffer a "sudden stop" —a term economists use to describe modern crises in emerging markets.[51] The resultant calamity forced Charles to reconvene Parliament, which would remain active for eight years.

Parliament during the next two years announced an aggressive series of measures that led to civil war. It reasserted limits to non-parliamentary taxation, declared that it would regularly convene every three years, and gave itself control over military appointments. It also rendered customs-farming agreements odious, dissolved Charles' myriad patents, and convicted the king's ministers of conspiring against its authority.

At the same time, the parliamentary opposition coalesced with a newly empowered opposition in the City. A diverse pro-Parliament coalition took control of the Common Council and wrested power from the oligarchic Aldermanic Court. The group included both new merchants and radicals seeking to reform inequities within the guild system.

### The Interregnum

By the time civil war erupted in the 1640s, the new merchant groups had accumulated sufficient wealth to more aggressively challenge London's old guard. A large part of these fortunes came from colonial trade. Tobacco sales in England, for example, had soared from two hundred thousand pounds sold in the 1620s to three million by 1640.[52]

Emboldened by their success, the new class took advantage of the civil war to form interloping syndicates attacking the Levant and East India Companies.[53] They looked to apply the colonial model to the eastern trades by vertically integrating domestic retailing and shipping with foreign trade. These interlopers also sought to establish outposts in West Africa that would supply bullion for trade in Asia. Under pressure, the East India Company opened its membership to the new interests and adopted capital investment plans that it had previously resisted. Nevertheless, the Company's conflicts with interlopers would persist and shape Whig and Tory party divisions later in the century.[54]

Parliament's willful neglect of interloping was one example of the liberalization of commerce in England. As mentioned, it also took away numerous monopoly privileges granted by the Stuart administrations. After England became a Commonwealth, Oliver Cromwell (Lord Protector from 1653 to 1658) allowed demobilized soldiers to enter protected economic activities.[55]

Despite the considerable transformation of England's economy by mid-century, one problem still lingered: foreign trade. Export volumes in 1648 were 33 percent lower than their 1614 level. Furthermore, privateers, likely on the Dutch payroll, preyed on England's lack of defenses.

At first, Cromwell sought a union with the Republic. After the Dutch balked, Parliament instituted the first Navigation Act in 1651, which restricted the import of goods to English vessels. Thirty years earlier, Parliament had scuttled a similar proposal. But since then, enough interests had emerged that benefited more from trade aggression than peace. This not only included English shipowners who were the direct beneficiaries of the Acts but also stakeholders in the East India Company, whose bitter rival was the VOC.

After the passage of the Act, English cruisers began seizing Dutch ships not only near the Isles, but also in neutral waters.[56] When a Dutch delegation visited England, English officials made strong demands for reparations and concessions to commerce in the Indies that the Dutch refused.[57] What ensued was the first of three trade wars fought between England and the United Provinces. England lost the war, which lasted from 1652 to 1654, but captured one thousand seven hundred Dutch ships.[58] Additionally, the British navy—forced to combat privateering and conduct raids of its own—built more new vessels between 1651 and

1660 than in the four decades of James's and Charles's reigns.[59]

The war, however, added to the country's already high indebtedness. Already, Cromwell had waged an expensive campaign suppressing the Irish rebellion that saw him conduct a brutal massacre of 1500 to 2000 troops, priests, and civilians at Wexford in 1649. He had also invaded Scotland, which England added as a possession in 1654.[60]

To raise funds, Cromwell proceeded to raid Spanish possessions in the Americas, which led him to annex Jamaica.[61] But this policy naturally failed to improve government finances. After Cromwell died in 1658, England's debt reached £2.5 million, bringing the country to the brink of bankruptcy.[62] Nevertheless, Cromwell's foreign policy marked the beginnings of the rank militarism that characterized England's "old colonial system."

## The Birth of the Old Colonial System

After Cromwell's death, economic conditions became dire, with England suffering another painful bout of capital flight in 1659.[63] Reconciliation between moderate members of the gentry led to the restoration of the Stuart monarchy under Charles II. He agreed to the end the royal discretionary courts, which his father had used to target political enemies. More importantly, the Crown's ability to collect extra-parliamentary revenue was greatly curtailed. At the same time, the scope of Parliament's activities expanded considerably; it now oversaw affairs in military, religion, and foreign trade under a new civil service.[64]

The Restoration carried little risk of returning to the policies of the ancien régime, not least because the character of industry had changed considerably during the interregnum. Significant government purchases had helped stimulate manufacturing in the towns outside of London.[65] For example, the Birmingham arms makers who supplied guns to the parliamentary armies became a challenger to the London gunmakers company.[66] Provincial industries were producing a host of new items, especially textile products: threads, stuffs, silks, satins, velvets, and fustians.[67] The most notable development was that England was at this point making finished cloth while exports of unfinished cloth had mostly disappeared.[68]

These industries, however, had not improved the dismal condition of English trade. Charles II had an incentive to fix the problem as he was receiving less in customs revenue than his father had twenty years earlier.[69] Parliament moved quickly to address the situation, and between 1660 and 1663, the Committee of Trade oversaw a series of acts that would remain influential until the nineteenth century.

Improvements to the Navigation Act were the most important new policy. A major weakness of the 1651 version was the difficulty in identifying the nationality of ships. Under the new 1661 act, all foreign-built vessels had to be registered.[70] Additionally, it further stipulated that the colonies could only export certain goods exclusively to England: sugar, tobacco, cotton, wool, ginger, and dyes. The new legislation also raised the required proportion of Englishmen on a crew to three-fourths from one-half. Parliament amended it two years later to require all traffic from the colonies to be routed through England on English ships.

Telling was the fact that George Downing, who led a belligerent "Navy Party" faction, spearheaded the Committee of Trade's policies. Downing sought to enhance England's naval power, which would back its long-distance commerce.[71] Under the old structure of regulated merchant companies, individual merchants had to provide for their own defenses. But the East India Company's past failures against Dutch competition demonstrated the necessity of heavy fortifications at foreign outposts.[72]

Management of the Royal African Company was representative of the new approach. The company had formed in 1660 and sought to capture a share of the gold and slave trade from the Dutch. The first expedition was accompanied by three naval ships, which immediately ran afoul of the existing Dutch operation.[73] The Company was still able to establish a permanent foothold though its skirmishes with the Dutch would persist.

Combined with battles elsewhere, British clashes with the Dutch in Africa set the stage for the Second Anglo-Dutch War —a war that brought military and commerce into further intimacy. After the East India Company acquired Bombay from the Portuguese, the Company came into further conflict with the Dutch, who had a presence in nearby Surat. Dutch smuggling in the Americas was another source of tensions; the awkward position of New Amsterdam on the Atlantic Seaboard made enforcement of the Navigation Acts difficult.

Anti-Dutch interests coalesced to lead the drumbeat for war, and a shift in political winds was evident as jingoism united previous rivals.[74] The Second Anglo-Dutch War broke out in 1665 and lasted two years. Though the Dutch won the war, the British gained control of New Amsterdam, which the Dutch failed to defend due to their neglect of the West India Company. Furthermore, England maintained control of its slave-trading interest in Cape Coast Castle in modern-day Ghana.[75] By linking the colonies and gaining a stake in the slave trade, it closed the remaining loopholes in the Navigation Acts.

**The Road to Global Conflict**

The Second Anglo-Dutch War offered a preview of the colonial wars that would come to ensnare Europe, North America, and South Asia for more than a century. It ended quickly since the Dutch, already drawing significant profits from European trade, had minimal interest—aside from slave transport—in the New World. The same was not true for England, where militarism attracted a larger investor bloc than peace.

England suffered from an economic crisis immediately

after the end of the war. A plague, the Great Fire of London, and war all added to an already sizable stock of debt.[76] Additionally, the start of a long depression in the Republic led to more general economic weakness in Europe.

Compounding the problem were the exorbitant interest rates on Charles II's loans—as high as 10 percent. Furthermore, it was *prospective* rather than *realized* tax revenue that backed those debts.[77] Financial desperation, combined with a desire to see his nephew William accede to the stadtholdership in the United Provinces, caused the king to sign a secret treaty in 1670 with Louis XIV, pledging to aid France against the Dutch Republic in exchange for subsidies.

But the Crown's financial accounts were so dire that Charles forced a "stop of the exchequer," defaulting on advances made to him by goldsmith bankers. This led to bank runs and money market instability as English merchants failed to meet their obligations on foreign bills of exchange.[78] The episode showed that although England's economy had diversified since the beginning of the century, it had not developed enough to overcome its vulnerability to capital flight.

The crisis led to a shift in sentiment toward the Crown. Goldsmiths argued before Parliament that the stop had caused distress to "widows and orphans."[79] Corruption in the king's fiscal dealings also became apparent, eventually leading to the impeachment of the secretary of state. Although the king started a third Anglo-Dutch War in 1672, it became unpopular with the broader public, and Charles II submitted to Parliament's requests for peace in 1674.[80] Of course, the accession of Charles' nephew William III to the Dutch stadtholdership, following France's invasion of the Republic in 1672, also helped.

Party divisions grew starker in the late 1670s and 1680s. The king's proximity to France, in addition to his attempts to expand the rights of Catholics, contributed to rising anti-Catholic sentiment. Country Whigs, whose colonial interests and Puritanism made them hostile to France, helped stoke such feelings. Dutch propaganda also played a role since the Republic's printers had the world's most prolific publishers.

During these years, the Whig faction of the East India Company, led by Thomas Papillon, split from the Royalists, led by Josiah Child. Papillon wanted to expand the East India trade's membership and was forced to flee to the Dutch Republic after becoming an enemy of the king's brother.[81] Similarly, the rivalry between arms makers in Birmingham and London intensified, especially since the latter had been the principal suppliers of arms to the East India and Royal African Companies.[82] Birmingham's Member of Parliament was suspected of conspiring to kill the king and had his armory seized in 1683.[83]

Unsurprisingly, James II—a Catholic—met considerable opposition when he succeeded his brother to the throne in 1685. After James attempted to expand the political rights of Catholics, the Whig gentry invited William III of Orange, husband of James' daughter Mary, to invade England. A relatively peaceful transition of power saw James deposed and succeeded by William and Mary in the Glorious Revolution of 1688.

The Glorious Revolution marked the end of a lengthy period of institutional transformation that led to parliamentary rule. Under the Bill of Rights, only Parliament could dispense and suspend laws, and it alone had the power to levy taxes. The Bill also provided for free elections, freedom to petition, and just treatment by courts. Additionally, the Crown could only maintain a standing army with parliamentary consent.

William's ascent to the English throne quickly led to a global conflict that saw England and the Dutch Republic ally against Spain: the Nine Years' War. War provided considerable stimulus to shipbuilding, mining, and, of course, arms manufacturing. The Whig alliance with William proved rewarding as the English Ordnance Office commissioned Birmingham to make new Dutch-style guns.[84] Subsidized by permanent warfare, the gun industry would have an immense role in stimulating industrial development through its spillover effects in the eighteenth century.[85]

The influx of French Huguenots also provided a stimulus to manufacturing. Their entry, together with the war, caused patent applications to boom in the 1690s.[86] An observer noted the acceleration of technological development in 1695: "New projections every day set on foot to render the making of our woolen manufactures easy. . . The same for our product—mines and pits are drained by engines and aqueducts instead of hands."[87]

Conditions had also become ripe for an expansion of domestic credit. Together with Dutch capital flows, sustained bullion inflows from trade provided financial stability that had proven elusive to a country long beleaguered by capital flight. Deposit banking had already emerged during the Restoration with the goldsmiths' offerings; by the 1670s, goldsmiths were issuing early versions of checks and banknotes.[88] Even after the stop of the exchequer, demand for banknotes persisted.[89]

Together with the fiscal limitations enacted by the Bill of Rights, the Bank of England's charter in 1694 introduced the financial infrastructure required to grow domestic credit. In order to raise £1.2 million for the Nine Years' War against France, Parliament offered subscribers the right to incorporate as a bank. The Bank would possess the rights to issue banknotes, deal in bills, and transact in bullion. In no small part due to greater trust in the government's fiscal apparatus, the Bank obtained one thousand three hundred subscribers in ten days. A combination of 60 percent equity capital and the remainder in bank bills funded the purchase of the government's loan.[90] Only a few decades later, interest rates on the government's debt would drop from 8 to 3 percent, converging with Dutch yields.[91]

What ultimately allowed England to catch up to and eclipse the Republic was the demand shock unleashed by war. The War of the Spanish Succession, especially, forced the United Provinces to reverse their austere fiscal policy and raise expenditures to "unprecedented levels."[92] This policy change coin-cided with a sharp increase in prices and an almost 50 percent decline in the stock of metals at the Bank of Amsterdam.[93] The Republic conducted its largest military buildup in history and committed twice as many ground forces as England to the joint Anglo-Dutch army on the European continent.[94]

Already by the close of the seventeenth century, an abrupt change in the Anglo-Dutch trade balance had been visible, in favor of England.[95] Demand from the continental army—and more generally the opening of the Dutch monetary spigot—accelerated this trend, boosting England's export of cloth and grain.[96] Estimated export volumes registered a 75-percent increase from the beginning of the Nine Years' War in 1688 to the end of the War of the Spanish Succession in 1714.[97]

War with the French Empire also helped England surpass its Dutch ally in shipping. Even though the size of their merchant fleets were roughly equal, the Anglo-Dutch naval agreement of 1689 stipulated that the two countries provide ships at a ratio of five-to-three.[98] Furthermore, increased export volumes supported the English carrying trade through the restrictions imposed by the Navigation Acts.

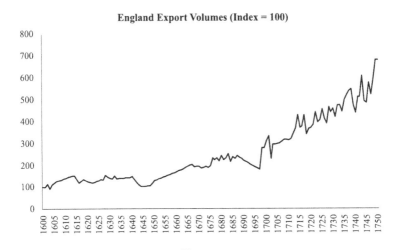

*Figure 7.2*

**Figure 7.2** depicts English export volumes, which remained anemic for much of the 17th century. War between the United Provinces and France, however, ended fiscal austerity in the Republic and unlocked Dutch demand for English exports. Source: Ryland Thomas and Nicholas Dimsdale, "A Millennium of Macroeconomic Data," Bank of England, 2017, https://www.bankofengland.co.uk/statistics/research-datasets.

## The Old Colonial System

The Nine Years' War marked the beginning of a period in which England engaged in near perpetual conflict. Over this period, size of the English army more than tripled.[99] This was no accident: the corrupt military-monopoly complex—which later drew the ire of Adam Smith—generated immense profits through government contracting.

An extended period of Whig dominance also began in this period, in which the country party used its grip on the state machinery to subsidize manufacturing outside of London. Birmingham gunmakers, Priya Satia writes, formed "the backbone of wider industrial development."[100] The Ordnance Office spread the spoils of the arms trade by establishing a division of labor in the gun-making process. More importantly, gun manufacturing served as a template for the emergent factory system of the late eighteenth century.

As discussed in Chapter 3, the gun industry also produced spillover innovations vital to the industrial revolution. England's naval buildup had a similar effect through the demand it created for nautical instruments. Together with gun manufacturing and clock-making, navigational devices pushed forth considerable advancement in precision-part construction. It is no coincidence that several of the men associated with England's industrial development—John Kay, Benjamin Huntsman, Thomas Newcomen, and James Watt—started as precision-instrument makers.[101] The spread of development to the outer towns explains why many of these manufacturers, like the Quaker gunmaker Samuel Galton, also happened to belong to nonconformist religions; such individuals would later agitate for radical reforms in the early nineteenth century.

Colonial wars not only stimulated arms demand but also secured end markets for English manufactures. Famous for their role in the American Revolution, protectionist legislation such as the Hat and Iron Acts subsidized mainland production at the expense of colonists. No subsidy, however, was greater than that provided by the millions enslaved in Africa. After winning the War of the Spanish Succession, England acquired *the asiento*—the right to transport them on behalf of Spain.

By 1750, English militarism established a global network of trade that surpassed that of the Dutch. No fact exemplified this more than the East India Company's dominance over the VOC.[102] And perhaps no institution was more representative of the old colonial system than the Company. In addition to contracting arms purchases, it provided for the Bengali calicoes exchanged in Africa for slaves. Between 1699 and 1774, the Company accounted for 13 to 15 percent of England's imports, and at mid-century it financed 10 percent of England's deficit.[103]

But having remained in power for too long, the East India Company, too, succumbed to decay, bringing the old colonial regime down with it. By the late nineteenth century, England had, over 150 years, transitioned from peripheral status to hegemony. Its old system of protections was ill-suited for an economy that had attained clear technological primacy. The decline of this system birthed a new configuration of the world, one that was not dissimilar to present times.

# 8

## WHERE THE SUN NEVER SET

L ike the Dutch Republic in the seventeenth century, the British Empire was alone at the helm of the global economy from the second half of the eighteenth century until the early twentieth century. Even when excluding Britain's vast territorial possessions, market organization by the beginning of this era had already spread over a population far greater than that of the Republic. It would only expand further by 1900.

By the time the Industrial Revolution arrived, England had found itself at the frontier of technological innovation. It had outgrown the policies of colonization and protections that had fueled its ascendance. Instead, Britain's new innovators—and, shortly after them, a fledgling financial sector—saw greater profits in peace and free trade.

The British had become monopsonists in a global market, using their know-how to organize production for maximal profit in other countries, especially the newly independent states in the Americas. With outsized purchasing power, they became the vendor-financers for the rest of the world. American cotton, Chilean copper, German grain before 1850, and then Argentinian beef, South African gold, and Malaysian rubber after 1850, all put these areas at the mercy of Britain's economy.[1] For the entirety of the nineteenth century, the substantial rents British investors derived from their extensive foreign investments were not only unmatched but also unavailable to nearly any other nation.

Although economic cooperation with Britain often produced one-sided results, some countries did benefit immensely. The most notable was Germany, which took advantage of agricultural outsourcing from Britain and used the export receipts to pursue industrialization. By 1870, it would begin to mount a challenge to its trading partner's hegemony.

The timing of such competition, first from the Germans and then from the Americans, was determined by developments within Britain. Bookended by the demise of the colonial joint-stock monopoly and the emergence of the modern corporation, British hegemony saw the economic phenomena distinguishing Dutch primacy reappear. Rising inequality coincided with financialization and growing demand deficiency. And stagnation became evident after the engorgement of the financial sector culminated in the Panic of 1866.

Per-capita income in Britain quadrupled over course of the nineteenth century and was the highest in the world. But wages followed a different trajectory, staying unchanged from the end of the Napoleonic Wars to the start of the Crimean conflict. In a century that saw an expansion in the number of citizens with voting rights, the share of the wealth owned by the top 1 percent in Britain grew from 50 to 70 percent.[2] Between 1810 and 1875, the average personal estate of members of the peerage increased fivefold, while financiers saw their wealth rise twentyfold.[3]

Rising asset values were the principal mechanism through which inequality appeared. Share prices in the United Kingdom increased nearly tenfold between 1820 and 1870. Though property prices for the entire century are difficult to source, housing prices rose 22 percent between 1845 and their peak in 1873.

Available price data also show that deflationary forces became increasingly pronounced.[4] GDP deflator estimates decelerate from 1813 until the twentieth century, with only mild inflation of 1.5 percent per annum between 1850 and 1870. Indices of wholesale producer and consumer prices show similar behavior. And the strongest signal, market interest rates on government debt, exhibit a trend decline.

Financialization accompanied disinflation. The twenty years between Peel's market reforms (1846) and the Panic of 1866 saw especially feverish growth in monetary aggregates. Following financial liberalization in the 1840s, the stock of commercial bills of exchange—the principal money market instrument—nearly tripled by 1870.[5] Similarly, total deposit liabilities (excluding the Bank of England's) increased from £20 million in 1824 to £50 million in 1844 and accelerated to £200 million over the next twenty years.[6]

By tying Bank of England notes to bullion reserves, the government stayed on the gold standard for a century. Say's Law justified such thinking: a gold standard ensured the most efficient economic order. Supply, after all, created its own demand and maximum price stability would ensure the best conditions for production. Of course, classical school ideas served as a pretext for a monetary regime that preserved the value of financial rents. After the end of the Napoleonic wars, the restoration of convertibility conferred significant gains on claimants of Britain's sizable stock of government debt.

Instead of keeping the economy in balance, however, maintenance of the gold peg exacerbated violent boom-bust patterns in the business cycle. As mentioned in Chapter 4, concerns about the adequacy of gold reserves acted as a belated hard brake on animal spirits. But England was never truly at risk of a destabilizing "external drain." Earnings from shipping, insurance, and foreign rents consistently offset the trade deficit.[7] More generally, bullion movements corresponded to the risk appetite of British investors. Investors sent gold abroad during times of exuberance and kept it at home when foreign investment was unattractive; exchange rates moved in favor of Britain in every crisis.[8] Even the massive gold discoveries in California would eventually find their way back to the world's monetary source.

Fiscal stringency went together with a rigid monetary regime. In the words of the essayist Perry Anderson, "the doctrine of 'Treasury Control' made the Exchequer the real nerve-center of the state, the dominant department of government enforcing its discipline on all others."[9] Behind this doctrine was the so-called "Treasury Mind"—technocrats subscribing to the view that budget balance and minimal expenditure were consistent with optimal policy.[10] Between 1820 and 1870, fiscal outlays in the country that could afford them most hardly grew in nominal terms and declined relative to output.[11] Expenditures in the rest of Europe, on the other hand, trebled.[12]

Unsurprisingly, seismic political changes accompanied Britain's economic transformation. The newly wealthy could organize lobbying campaigns, which were at times prone to fervent agitation. In the second half of the nineteenth century, their wealth surpassed that of the landed aristocracy.

Like the States Party earlier and the centers of each American party later, a new coalition—the Liberal Party—assembled to oversee Britain's long uncontested reign over the world. A combination of the old Whig aristocracy, Tory free traders, and radicals, the Liberals supported free trade, minimal state expenditure, revolution abroad (where convenient), and the extension of political and religious rights at home.[13] But this alliance grew more tenuous as the British economy succumbed to stagnation after 1870.

Scrutiny toward empire and inequality polarized the political establishment in the final quarter of the 19th century.

Disputes over Irish home rule split the Liberal Party. The resulting alliance between Liberal Unionists and Conservatives more broadly sought to preserve the considerable income from Britain's foreign possessions and military activities abroad.[14] Likewise, trade unionism and labor militancy soured relations between liberals and radicals. Meanwhile, the Conservatives weaponized a growingly anachronistic House of Lords to obstruct progressive reforms. Only after industry and finance fully displaced agriculture were the Liberals able to defang the Lords and briefly re-establish control. Yet by this point, the decline of both their party and the British Empire was all but assured.

*Figure 8.1*

**Figure 8.1** shows the rise in share prices during the Liberal Era in Britain. Following the end of the Napoleonic Wars, Britain's embrace of market liberalization coincided with increasing inequality and hoarding in financial assets. **Source:** Bank of England, Share Price Index (Weighted by Market Capitalisation) in the United Kingdom [MSPIUKM], retrieved from FRED, Federal Reserve Bank of St. Louis.

## Colonial Rot

England in the 1760s found itself at a crossroads between a rotting "old colonial system" and a nascent industrial revolution. It was in this decade that the spinning jenny and the water frame appeared. Within twenty years, these two innovations were combined to form the steam-powered spinning mule—enabling the factory production of textiles.[15] Manufacturing towns had already emerged with merchants, under the putting-out system, loaning instruments to cottage artisans. A boom in canal construction was also underway to ease bulk transport, especially in coal and iron, between growing towns.[16]

At the same time, the old colonial system experienced one final speculative run. In 1769, a corrupt and financially mismanaged East India Company saw its share price peak.[17] Three years later, leveraged speculation led to a crash in shares, causing the Anglo-Dutch money market to freeze.[18] Before the dust had settled, 525 banks had failed. It was the worst crisis since the South Sea bubble.[19]

By the end of the eighteenth century, both the Dutch East India Company and the Bank of Amsterdam, which had concealed overdrafts to the former, suffered insolvency. England, too, had accumulated a mountain of war debt from a century of colonial wars with France. Subsequent stabilization efforts famously incited rebellion in the American colonies.

"Old Corruption" drew increased scrutiny. Radicals harangued the "pensions," "sinecures," and "reversions" employed by the establishment, especially George III (r. 1760–1820), to influence Parliament.[20] Many individuals involved in defense, administration, and government contracting—like the East India official Robert Clive—were accumulating ill-gotten fortunes. Such malfeasance came at the expense of the general population, which shouldered war debts through heavy excise taxes.[21] By the eighteenth century, England's taxes on ordinary citizens had become more burdensome than those of the Republic.

Signs of a new economic order began to appear as early as 1774 when Richard Arkwright, who invented the water frame, successfully petitioned Parliament to make it lawful to wear goods made entirely of cotton and to reduce taxes on goods mixed with the fiber. In 1784, newer manufacturing interests united to successfully lobby a repeal of the cotton tax and formed the General Chamber of Manufacturers of Great Britain.[22] Two years later, the Chamber sought to expand to foreign markets and lobbied for the Eden Treaty, which liberalized trade relations with France.[23]

The treaty marked the beginning of a new developmental path for England. Technological primacy and opposition to further taxation created incentives to eschew warfare and open the world to English commerce. But "Little Englandism," which favored informal over formal empire, would have to wait.

## William Pitt's New Deal

Revolution in France ended the Anglo-French Eden Treaty of 1786 and led to war in 1793. What followed figures as one of the greatest monetary experiments in human history. Rising expenditures caused England's net borrowing surplus of 1 percent of GDP in 1794 to become a deficit of –13 percent by 1797. Concerns about banknote issuance, in turn, led gold reserves at the Bank of England to fall from £7 million in 1794 to £1 million, which forced Prime Minister William Pitt (the Younger, in office 1783–1801, and again 1804–6) to suspend convertibility.

From the beginning of the conflict to its end in 1815, England's indebtedness increased by 50 percent of GDP while prices doubled. The gentry, in particular, benefited as grain and coal prices increased. But the demand shock accompanying war helped other sectors too.

The military was the largest consumer of a range of goods, including iron and textiles, and produced several innovations that would be repurposed by industry.[24] Demand for bulk materials likely contributed to the canal boom that drove the business cycle upswing between 1803 and 1808. This cycle also saw new investments in a variety of domains, including brewing, insurance, mining, heating, and lighting. Share listings doubled by the end of the cycle.[25] New securities, together with trading in a growing volume of government bonds, contributed to the financial sector's resurgence.[26]

Rising economic fortunes along with wartime jingoism ushered in a "High Tory" era that saw Tory factions maintain almost uninterrupted control of Parliament until 1830. Whigs, on the other hand, remained divided between aristocratic elements and progressives seeking institutional reforms. Nevertheless, higher costs of living offered an opportunity to fix a social order that had come under attack by radical movements. Pitt introduced taxes on luxuries, inheritance taxes, and, finally, an income tax in 1799. Under the Speenhamland system, officials in the countryside supplemented wages and linked relief to the price of bread. Rather than an act of paternalistic magnanimity, however, Speenhamland's aim was to stave off insurrection. It also had the adverse effect of tying rural laborers to their parish.[27]

Another effect was that Speenhamland became a subsidy to farmers who adjusted wages in anticipation of parish support for their workers. This phenomenon was just one example of a "bloated war establishment" that had only grown larger over time.[28] Between 1797 and 1815, the number of central government officers grew by 66 percent.[29] Army, navy, church, and law appointments were in the several hundred thousand while their expenses grew to a massive £20 million per year.[30] Additionally, almost three hundred out of the 658 members of the peerage held newly created seats.[31]

As hinted, securities issuance during the Napoleonic Wars gave rise to a new investment bloc that the polemicist William Cobbett derided as the "paper aristocracy." Cobbett, who echoed Paine's criticisms from the political right, feared that such "loan jobbers" were upending the traditional order by taking over the estates of the gentry.[32]

David Ricardo was representative of such men. Ricardo had amassed a substantial fortune trading government bonds during the war with Napoleon and parlayed it into land and a seat in Parliament as a Whig. After the end of the war in 1815, Ricardo and holders of government debt helped push calls for budgetary austerity and resumption of convertibility.

After the war ended, the government implemented draconian policies of fiscal consolidation and price stability. A deficit of –7 percent of GDP sharply reversed into a surplus by the end of the decade.[33] From a peak of £26 million in 1815, Bank of England notes in circulation dropped below £17 million in 1823 and did not recover their former peak until 1876.[34] Producer prices embarked on an extended period of decline, only bottoming in 1822, 33 percent lower than their mark seven years earlier.[35] Money demand increased as the 5-percent rates on government securities became more compelling than falling profit opportunities elsewhere.[36] Bullion reserves, which had bottomed in 1815, increased sixfold to achieve a new high in 1821.[37] The severity of the government's policy on the general population is evident in employment estimates. Unemployment doubled from 5 percent in 1815 to 10 percent four years later—the year of the violent massacre at Peterloo where economic difficulty led to a protest for Parliamentary reform.[38]

The agricultural sector, too, saw its fortunes turn as prices fell. In one last demonstration of lobbying might, landowners persuaded Parliament to pass the 1815 Corn Laws that restricted imports of foreign grain. But proponents of free trade had only grown stronger since the Industrial Revolution and, together with a new bloc of international financiers, would overtake protectionist interests in influence.

## The Rise of Multinational Interests

Once deflation led to a sufficient accumulation of gold reserves at the Bank of England, Parliament, with Ricardo's endorsement, reinstated the gold standard under Peel's Act of 1819. The economy continued to stagnate until 1821 when investment began flowing into several domains: mining, gas, steam, insurance, trading, and rail. Wartime demand had helped spark the growth of these industries.[39] Like financialization in the United States after Paul Volcker (chair of the Federal Reserve 1979–87), peripheral banks also began to expand their lending practices. These banks, which issued their own small-denomination banknotes, increased their volume of discounted bills—short-term loans to merchants.

Concurrently, a "bewildering array of new financial assets" emerged in the 1820s, particularly in the category of foreign investments.[40] Independence in Latin America had created a new market for exporters and resulted in new share listings for foreign commodity ventures. Sovereign listings were especially notable: Chile, Colombia, and Peru—not to mention Sir Gregor MacGregor's fictional country of Poyais—all debuted bonds with approximately 6 percent yields.[41]

Bank of England directors, whose principal concern was paying dividends to shareholders, began participating in the foreign "carry trade." As mentioned earlier, they loaned their bullion holdings to Nathan Rothschild, who arbitraged the difference in money market rates between France and Britain. Between 1818 and 1822, Rothschild had also arranged two large loans totaling £8.5 million to Germany to finance infrastructure and industrial projects.[42]

But the export of bullion for investment abroad pressured domestic gold holdings.[43] An "internal drain" on gold also followed in 1825, when overstretched lending led to a wave of country bank failures. Alarmed, Bank of England directors raised their discount rate to the maximum 5 percent, which cemented the end of the early financial boom.

*Figure 8.2*

**Figure 8.2** shows that London listings of foreign government bonds soared during the early stages of 19th-century globalization. **Source**: Marc Flandreau and Juan H Flores, "Bonds and Brands: Foundations of Sovereign Debt Markets, 1820–1830," *The Journal of Economic History* (2009): 646-84.

As share prices tumbled, Parliament launched an investigation into the practices that had fueled speculation. The South Sea share bubble of 1720 was still a recent memory and the Bubble Act of 1720 prohibited the incorporation of joint-stock companies—whose ownership could be transferred with shares—without Parliament's approval. Members of the aristocracy used the crisis as an opportunity to voice their hostility toward financial markets.[44]

Circumstances, however, had changed considerably in the one hundred years since the South Sea bubble. The political establishment could not deny the role of new ventures in bringing England out of the postwar depression. More came to believe that the corporate structure possessed an unrivaled capacity to organize significant sums of capital for investment. Indeed, in addition to the expansion of British foreign investment, the most important development of the early 1820s boom was the emergence of joint-stock companies resembling the modern limited liability corporation.

Liberal Tories broke with their more conservative allies to voice their support for the new corporations. The President of the Board of Trade, William Huskisson, argued, "If there was any one circumstance, to which more than any other, this country owed its wealth and commercial advantages, it was the existence of joint-stock companies."[45] Editorials in the *Morning Chronicle* also appeared, appealing to the "sacred and golden principle of political economy," governmental non-interference.[46] On the grounds that it created unnecessary fear of severe penalties, Parliament repealed the Bubble Act in June 1825 with the understanding that shareholders still faced unlimited liability.

In that decade, the liberal wing also managed to push through several measures promoting freer trade. Among these was the Reciprocity Duties Act of 1823, which permitted individual trade agreements with other countries, and looser restrictions on the export of machinery in 1828.[47] Parliament also made the Corn Laws subject to a sliding scale and granted most-favored nation status to Prussia.[48]

Following the 1825 crisis, the economy languished. Meanwhile, the Speenhamland system in the countryside had reduced agricultural workers—unable to leave their parishes— to a state of pauperization, prompting riots.[49] By this point, industrial growth had only led to further concentration of the population in industrial cities.

Middle-class businessmen threatened an economic boycott if Parliament did not reform England's archaic electoral system. Fear of insurrection prompted by renewed instability in France finally allowed a Whig government, together with a minority of Tory liberals, to pass John Russell's 1832 bill that extended the franchise to members of the middle class (property owners).[50] Among the first significant pieces of legislation pushed by the newly empowered industrial interests was the Poor Law Amendment of 1834, which ended the Speenhamland system and made labor more subject to market forces. The Whigs also managed to abolish slavery, satisfying a longstanding demand of their Quaker constituency. These reforms, however, absorbed much of the Whig government's political goodwill in the 1830s.[51]

Aside from a brief business-cycle upturn, coinciding with speculative lending to the United States, economic weakness persisted in the 1830s. Although the new Poor Law created a flexible labor market, combined with stagnation, it caused unemployment to increase to 12 percent by 1841—the highest level in the nineteenth century. Industrialists took advantage of such conditions to organize a new round of agitation, this time targeting the Corn Laws. They echoed arguments that Ricardo had made earlier, that import restrictions made food costs, and therefore wages, more expensive than elsewhere in the world.

Manufacturers like Richard Cobden also viewed anti-Corn Law agitation as a means to increase industry's voice in Parliament.[52] This environment, one in which Parliament began fearing the effects of middle-class boycotts on unemployment, caused the liberal coalition to coalesce. Led by Robert Peel, who himself came from a manufacturing family, the liberal Tories joined with the Whigs and radicals to pursue more aggressive policy changes.

### The Birth of the Liberal Party

Peel's most important reform was his decision to substitute import duties with an income tax. In 1830, the Whigs unsuccessfully argued that raising consumption through lower duties would increase revenues. A growing fiscal deficit, however, allowed Peel to implement the proposal in 1842. Parliament reduced duties on exports in addition to tariffs on some 750 items.[53]

Four years later, in 1846, famine in Ireland provided an opportunity to eliminate the Corn Laws. Despite opposition from two-thirds of his party, Peel gathered enough votes to pass a repeal. The bill, however, permanently split the Tory Party and led to Peel's resignation.

In addition to passing fiscal reform and trade liberalization, the Peel administration streamlined the process for incorporation. Earlier, Parliament, after repealing the Bubble Act, had made gradual attempts to simplify the registration of joint-stock companies. In 1834, it expedited the process for official approval by transferring the power to Crown administrators. Then, in 1837, it declared that shareholder liability ceased after shares changed hands.[54]

With the Joint-Stock Companies Act of 1844, Peel made the formation of private corporations even easier. The act allowed individuals to incorporate through the simple act of registration, though they still had to disclose finances to the public. For the first time in five hundred years, incorporation did not require the explicit approval of the state.[55] Full limited liability remained another decade away, and the bill excluded the banking and railway industries. But its effects were evident in the sheer number of entities filing for corporate status.

What ended economic malaise, however, was not policy but railway mania. Railways had been among the few profitable investments in the 1830s. By the early 1840s, they acquired "a reputation for security and profit," as Bishop Carleton Hunt has described it.[56] Between 1843 and 1849, railway miles increased two-and-a-half times; the surge in real investment caused unemployment to fall below 3 percent. A corresponding frenzy for railway shares fueled a stock market boom that legitimized share ownership in the eyes of the broader public.

The spread of railroads to other countries was another economic development that helped strengthen the liberal coalition. British pig iron joined machine-spun yarn as an intermediate industrial input for countries like Prussia that were still industrializing.[57] More importantly, capital-intensive railroad construction increased foreign dependence on London finance. Free trade and free movement of money favored British investors more than ever before.

As the Dutch and American cases show, the term *free* trade belies the role foreign policy aggression played in creating a global trading regime suitable to Britain. The liberal coalition, through the efforts of its nationalist faction led by Lord Palmerston, relied on military force to secure open trade and finance. During the depression of the late 1830s, Palmerston—prefiguring Reagan-era officials in the 1980s—advocated using the Royal Navy to keep foreign markets open for dumping British wares.[58]

"House-breaking" also became a preferred policy weapon, and the foreign ministry deployed "experts" to offer legal advice to post-revolutionary regimes in Latin America and Europe.[59] Through his various roles, Palmerston armed insurgents against absolutist governments, like those in the Italian states, that did not bend to economic requests. And under his direction, the foreign ministry originated a policy of gunboat diplomacy that other nations would later copy. During the Sulphur Crisis of 1840, for example, Palmerston ordered a naval blockade of Sicily after the Kingdom gave a sulfur monopoly to France. He also actively used the navy to intimidate nations occupied in the slave trade—not out of benevolence, but rather to force these nations to better integrate their economies with Britain's. Indeed, few individuals contributed as much to the destruction of slavery.

For the rest of the century and the early part of the next, the liberal coalition would grapple with the balancing act of spending enough to maintain an informal empire—in addition to its formal one—while keeping public expenditures at a minimum. The Tory opposition, however, lacked a budget philosophy. Rebranded as Conservatives, they used the unpopularity of Peel's income tax to retake Parliament in 1852.[60] But delivering an acceptable budget—one that kept tariffs low while maintaining military expenditures—proved impossible. The Conservative budget's failure led to a final break with the liberal Tories, who joined the Whigs to form the Liberal Party (official in 1859).

The triumvirate leading the Liberal Party—Palmerston, John Russell, and William Ewart Gladstone—defined its policy. Gladstone, who became chancellor of the Exchequer after the Conservative government collapsed in 1852, set the economic agenda and eventually became the face of the party. While helming the Exchequer, he extended Peel's budget and made tariff elimination all but permanent.

### The Era of "Laissez-Faire"

Faith in unfettered markets guided Liberal Party legislation through the 1850s and 1860s. The Joint-Stock Companies Act of 1856 finally introduced limited liability to most forms of enterprise. Despite revelations of fraud after the end of the railroad bubble, the bill rolled back provisions that Gladstone's 1844 bill had made for disclosure and transparency. Only a few years later, Parliament extended limited liability to banks too, ending what to *The Times* seemed an "unintelligible distinction" between trade in money and all others.[61]

On trade, the liberal Parliament signaled a new era by ending the remaining vestiges of the Navigation Acts in 1854. Six years later, the Cobden-Chevalier Treaty eliminated tariffs on most major items of trade between Britain and France. The treaty helped the French railroad industry obtain iron, which domestic producers could not adequately supply.[62] More notably, France proceeded to strike similar treaties with other nations, causing free trade to become more general across Europe.

Meanwhile, financialization proceeded apace, in no small part due to parliamentary deregulation of joint-stock banking. Total bank deposits had grown from £55 million in 1846 to £120 million in 1856. The stock of bills of exchange, which had not increased in the prior decade, doubled over the same period.[63]

Foreign bills grew even faster, to fourfold their volume in 1846, indicating further internationalization of British finance. Even more foreign banking houses—Anglo-Austrian, Anglo-Italian, Anglo-Egyptian—appeared in the 1850s.[64] After the Panic of 1857, Parliament's inquiry took note of "a remarkable development of banks and of credit."[65]

By the 1860s, money had become its own business, just as it had in the Dutch Republic and would in the United States. Limited liability legislation led to new financial engineering practices that transformed existing rent streams. Similar to private equity in today's world, a new mania arose to convert private enterprises to joint-stock companies and remit their profits to shareholders as dividends.[66] Owners of legacy firms were often keen to sell their enterprises at lofty valuations in the share market.

A new kind of company—the "finance company"—appeared with a purpose as vague as its name.[67] Companies of this sort peddled investment expertise and the benefits of diversified asset ownership. They offered exposure to "operations as an experienced and intelligent capitalist might effect on his own account," combining "the Bank, the discounter, the railway. . . and that specious form of limited liability which induces the hope of profits on a very large sum with the risk of a very small one."[68]

A second type of company—the "discount company"—also grew popular. These companies sought to capitalize on limited liability by raising large amounts of capital to compete with banks in discounting short-term bills.[69] Less scrupulous than banks, these entities evolved to become money market funds, taking short-term financing and holding bills for investment.

As the *Economist* complained in February of 1866, the

boundary between the finance company and the discount company was blurring.[70] False perceptions of permanently cheap money, shaped by new gold discoveries abroad, sparked a yield grab—blind acquisition of assets bearing interest or dividends. Non-traditional financial institutions began to take on investments too risky for their staider counterparts.

The *Economist* also highlighted another cause for concern. While troubles on the asset side of financial balance sheets had been a regular occurrence, British financial institutions, for the first time, exhibited systemic funding risks. First, more financial companies were seeking cheaper financing in the form of short-term, callable deposits.[71] Second, asset hypothecation (pledging an asset as collateral to secure a loan) was taking place on specious terms, with private securities serving as collateral for lending. In one instance, a railway company issued securities to a construction company, which used them, in turn, to raise funding from a finance company.[72]

The Panic of 1866 was triggered by the failure of Overend, Gurney & Co. The well-regarded bank had extended its operations from bill brokering to investing. Trouble came when a court ruling against one of its investments prompted a run on the bank. The Bank of England refused a request for aid, leading to a large-scale financial crisis. Money demand soared, and the resultant shock caused the Bank of England to lose almost 50 percent of its reserves in a single day.[73]

## Britain's Secular Stagnation

The crisis exposed the flaws of the classical theory that backed mid-Victorian economic doctrine. Asset prices, however, continued to rise, and peaked in the early 1870s. That point marked not only the beginning of a long depression but also the start of Britain's relative decline.

Asset price behavior since the end of the Napoleonic Wars had been consistent with hoarding, declining real investment, and general overcapacity. While share prices rose inexorably until 1873, the yield on British consols (bonds with no maturity date) had fallen from its peak of 6 percent in 1798 to 3 percent. This decline only accelerated with the onset of stagnation, and yields fell further to 2 percent by 1897.

Equally revealing is the evolution of the balance of payments. As trade became more open, the trade balance deteriorated from a surplus of £4 million in 1816 to a deficit of almost *negative* £100 million by 1875. But a glance at other components reveals that the character of enterprise had changed. Over the same period, the balance of business services (including shipping) grew from £18 million to £98 million. And income from foreign investment exploded from a mere £2 million in 1816 to £50 million.[74] Growth in the latter two categories did not just offset the trade balance but drove its deterioration. Industries linked to these components, such as finance and steam-powered shipping, had been among the major investor blocs pushing for freer trade.

Trade liberalization indeed led to the gradual erosion of traditional export-sensitive sectors. For agriculture, which had to compete with cheaper grain from Eastern Europe and the United States, free trade spelled "universal catastrophe."[75] Textiles, too, began to decline after 1860 with the iron industry soon following in 1870.[76]

The growth of the financial and services sectors coincided with a redistribution of income from the provincial north and northwest to London. London's fortunes, however, were anything but well distributed. The Panic of 1866 exposed bitter inequality within it. Its relief system broke down, given the sheer number of impoverished citizens, and a cholera outbreak —a recurring feature of daily life—further compounded the misery.[77]

A general crisis in public health was perhaps the greatest indictment of Victorian-era economic policy. Opiate use became widespread, particularly among women, and forced Parliament to intervene, passing the Pharmacy Act in 1868. The formation of notable temperance groups in the 1860s was no coincidence as diseases of despair rose among men. More star-tling facts from the era show that malnutrition caused the average heights of English soldiers to drop by 2 centimeters between 1830 and 1860 and overall life expectancy to stall.[78]

## The Return of Nationalism

Economic distress following the Panic of 1866 prompted agita-tion for an expansion of the electoral franchise. Protectionist Conservative minister Benjamin Disraeli saw an opportunity to reintegrate his party with the working masses.[79] A brief-lived Conservative government passed the Reform Act of 1867. Although an immediate result of the act was the Conservatives' defeat in the 1868 elections, Disraeli returned to power in 1874. His ensuing six-year tenure was, by far, the longest of any Tory (non-liberal) government since 1830 and marked the end of the liberal coalition's domination of Parliament.

Disraeli won back office by appealing to imperialist senti-ment. He accused the Liberals, who had attempted to cut the colonial defense budget, of weakening Britain and espousing "cosmopolitan principles imported from the Continent."[80] Ushering in a new era of mass politics, he offered an alternative platform based on upholding tradition, maintaining the empire, and improving the conditions of the masses.[81]

Of course, his campaign did not lack support from select investor blocs. In addition to traditional backing from domestic agriculture, the new Conservative Party message attracted indi-viduals who had investments linked to colonial possessions.[82] These interests were also frustrated by the Liberals' aversion to policies based on imperial preference.

But no development contributed more to popular conser-vatism's appeal than the rise of Germany. Free trade, initially through British demand for its agricultural exports, allowed the German Customs Union (an economic coalition of German states, created in 1833) to pursue rapid industrialization. A rail-road boom, spurred by efforts to connect its disparate states, had considerable spillover effects on other sectors. Between 1825 and 1870, pig iron production, for example, grew from 40,000 tons to 1.4 million tons.[83] And in the 1840s, the German engineering company Krupp began producing firearms, followed by mass-produced steel after implementing the Bessemer process borrowed from England.[84]

German military victories in the 1860s drew attention to the emergence of a new rival on the continent. In 1866, Prussia defeated Austria in battle, and then, four years later, won a war against France. In addition to conducting more aggressive foreign policy, it also began centralizing authority after Bismarck pushed through retroactive legislation of military expenditures in 1867. These events, along with the formation of the German Empire in 1871, caused apprehension in Britain due in no small part to the size of its larger neighbor.

The effects of stagnation and overcapacity in Britain reached Germany and the rest of Europe in 1873. Following the crisis of that year, trade cooperation collapsed while protectionism on the continent began to increase with new tariffs in France and Germany. Disraeli did not reinstitute protections, but the chorus for new import duties grew louder in the Conservative camp into the twentieth century.

From 1868 to 1910, the economic interests of Conservative MPs underwent a noticeable change in composition. Throughout this period, the share of Tory MPs linked to manufacturing rose from 4 to 20 percent.[85] New groups, such as the National Fair Trade League and later the Tariff Reform League, found a home among Conservatives.[86] Leading party members even supported bimetallism (pegging the currency to both gold and silver), seeking to adjust the value of British exports.[87] Campaigns like those of the imperialist Joseph Chamberlain sought to woo working-class voters in the depressed North by railing against hard-money rentiers who were forcing England, as Chamberlain put it, "to sink into the position of Holland, which is rich but an inconsiderable factor in the world."[88]

Although Conservative governments passed bills such as

the Merchandise Marks Acts of 1887—introducing the label "Made in Germany" to encourage citizens to avoid German products—they stopped short of abandoning free trade. While manufacturing's representation among Conservative MPs increased, that of finance, too, rose from 10 percent in 1868 to 21 percent by 1910. In addition to investors in imperial possessions, this group likely included rentier proponents of gunboat diplomacy who had shifted over to the Conservative side. In 1902, for example, the Balfour government sent warships to Venezuela after it reneged on payments to British creditors. The Conservatives were reluctant to upset former Palmerston liberals who stood to lose from any deviation from orthodox economic policy.[89]

*Figure 8.3*

**Figure 8.3** illustrates the rise and fall of European trade cooperation. Trade openness peaked in 1873, marking the end of British-led globalization. As stagnation became more severe, Britain's trade partners began to embrace protectionist policies. **Source**: Michel Fouquin and Jules Hugot, "Trade Globalisation in the Last Two Centuries," *VoxEU*, September 17, 2016, https://voxeu.org/article/trade-globalisation-last-two-centuries.

### The Road to Calamity

The combination of an inflexible pound, which denominated much of the world's liabilities, and weak global demand created impossible circumstances for peripheral debtors. In 1882, exhaustion with Anglo-French mandated austerity prompted riots in Egypt. Urged by creditors (as well as by Liberal hawks, who sought to steal the Conservatives' patriotic thunder), the Gladstone government sent troops to secure British interests.[90] The invasion not only marked the beginning of Britain's long occupation of Egypt but was also representative of a more pronounced phase of imperialism that entangled the European powers.

Had economic conditions been more robust, military intervention to protect British foreign investments may have been less tempting than otherwise. Evidence suggests that the government was reluctant to give carte blanche to speculation.[91] But renewed perceptions of a zero-sum global economy reinforced insecurity about relative standing and concerns for "strategic" geographic interests.

The hard monetary shackles of British imperial finance helped foment the Second Boer War, which presaged the First World War. Export depression and indebtedness created resentment in South Africa among local Boers (Dutch-speaking settlers of the eastern Cape frontier), who revolted and won independence in 1881 during the first war.[92] But their new state, lacking an adequate productive base, remained dependent on the London-intermediated financial system. The discovery of gold in the Transvaal region offered a path for more sustainable independence. But English mining interests—and Cecil Rhodes, specifically—also coveted this resource. Together with the government's geostrategic concerns about its hold on the Cape of Good Hope, conditions became ripe for renewed conflict.

The role Germany played in this war is worth noting. When Britain tried to constrain the Boer Republics' ability to access finance, the Germans stepped in.[93] Germany also sold arms and provided volunteers during the war. Such actions only inflamed the rivalry between the two European nations.

The war also had another consequence: it revealed the sheer extent of resources available through taxation.[94] British economic stagnation in the late nineteenth and early twentieth centuries made it difficult for politicians to ignore the problem of unemployment.[95] Labor precarity gave way to more vocal trade unionism, as evidenced by the London dock strike of 1889 and the miners' strikes of 1910 and 1911.

At the same time, a new type of firm appeared: the manufacturing multinational.[96] Firms like Lever, Courtaulds, and Cadbury—like Ford and the Standard Oil spinoffs in America—could pay high wages and maintain a paternalistic relationship with their employees.[97] Such firms maintained strong ties to the Liberal Party, given its staunch support for free trade. The lower share of labor as a cost for these firms allowed them to back a Liberal Party increasingly dominated by reformist professionals.[98]

In 1906, led by H. H. Asquith, David Lloyd George, and Winston Churchill, these new Liberals won a resounding victory over the Conservatives, who had been in power for more than ten years. The election, which was also a referendum on tariffs, gave the Liberals a strong mandate to expand existing social welfare schemes. The most powerful of these was progressive taxation, which allowed the Liberals to placate labor while pursuing a naval arms race against Germany.

Military Keynesianism thus arrived well before the publication of the *General Theory*. Liberal Party reforms were too late and too insufficient to stop the grim events that soon followed. Only the magnitude of the First World War could break the century-long pound standard and Britain's rotting rentier empire.

When Adam Smith wrote *The Wealth of Nations* in 1776, he

attacked the monopolists and manufacturers—"the masters of mankind"—who pulled the strings of England's corrupt colonial system.[99] He could have hardly envisioned that a new set of interests would repurpose his ideas. But as Smith himself said, "all for ourselves and nothing for other people" is the vile maxim of every age.[100]

# 9

# A NEW BIRTH OF FREEDOM

Historians have often portrayed the newly independent United States of America as a closed and self-sufficient economy.[1] Although it had achieved formal separation from the British Empire, economic autonomy came more slowly. During the nineteenth century, it struggled to break free from the "quasi-colonial" influence of its mother country.[2]

Like all other nations, the United States was at the mercy of British investors. Volatile bullion flows from London drove cycles of boom and bust. Such patterns culminated in notable episodes of panic in 1797, 1819, 1837, 1857, 1873, and 1893; not until 1900 would the United States wean itself from foreign finance.

America's sensitivity to the London money market stemmed from the character of its economy. The US lagged behind Western Europe in development. Belgium, France, and Germany were all ahead in industrialization. Until 1870, almost 70 percent of US exports consisted of raw materials and commodities.[3]

Relative underdevelopment made economic relations with Britain the most important influence on party politics. George Washington may have warned against factional politics in his farewell address, but its rise was inevitable. During the French phase of the Revolutionary Wars, the American elite fractured into a "peace" party and a "war" party.

The Federalists, who were led by Hamilton and tied to merchants connected to London, sought reconciliation. On the other side, Jefferson remained sympathetic to France and favored territorial expansion.[4] The latter issue was fraught with risks, not only because it exposed Americans to conflict with Native American tribes and Canada—a fear behind the contentious Proclamation of 1763, which forebade settlement west of the Appalachian Mountains—but also because of its fiscal costs.

The end of the Revolutionary Wars in 1815 gave way to a new set of coalitions. Economic liberalization in Britain favored the assembly of a new party in the US—the Democrats—who favored free trade with the former motherland. The Democrats' agenda, which included supporting a minimal budget, suited the policy zeitgeist seizing the Western world.

In the context of America's relationship with Britain, one can identify parallels between American politics before the Civil War and politics in England before its own internecine struggle. The rival Whigs shared with their British namesake a dislike for the "king" Andrew Jackson—the patriarch of the Democratic Party. Among the Democrats' strongest backers were, like the London merchants connected to Amsterdam, New York City merchants who were agents of British banking houses.[5]

The Whigs, however, were a placeholder for a more formidable opposition: the Republicans. Disenchantment with free trade combined with technological progress to form the glue that bound this opposition. Spillovers from abroad—canals and textiles, followed by railroads, iron, and scientific agriculture—produced new investment blocs that sought a different route to development than the one offered by Britain. They arrived at the alternative of an expanded state that would more actively protect and subsidize industrial enterprise.

In their competition against each other, rival investment blocs co-opted opposing economic and non-economic interests: abolitionist against slaveholder, free soiler against cotton planter, immigrant against nativist, and those who belonged to the various progressive causes in the second half of the century. Such alliances between investors and popular movements allowed technological progress to erode old institutions and give birth to new ones. By 1900, the borders between the independent states that once formed a tenuous union had more fully dissolved. The unprecedented polyarchal experiment that had begun in 1776 was determined to last.

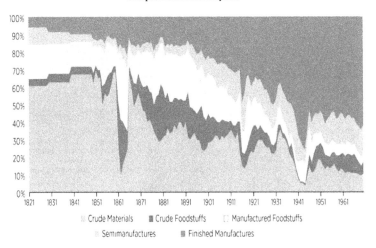

**Composition of U.S. Exports**

*Figure 9.1*

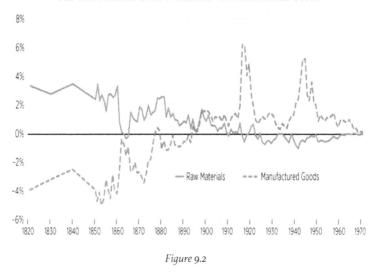

*Figure 9.2*

**Figures 9.1 and 9.2** show how for more than a century after independence, the U.S. was a commodity exporter and an economic periphery of England. The failure of British-led globalization fueled the rise of the Republican Party, which embraced more autarkic development. **Source**: Images from Brian Reinbold, and Yi Wen, "How Industrialization Shaped America's Trade Balance," Federal Reserve Bank of St. Louis, February 6, 2020. https://www.stlouisfed.org/publications/regional-economist/fourth-quarter-2019/industrialization-trade-balance.

## Early Financial Challenges

The parts constituting England's old colonial system were inseparable from the whole, and its decay spread to all of its organs. Though geographically distant, the fallout from East India Company corruption in South Asia found its way to the American colonies. In attempting to rescue the Company by granting it a monopoly on tea, the English government infuriated American merchants and shippers who were middlemen in the tea trade. Thomas Paine keenly observed, "it is somewhat remarkable that the produce of that ruined country [India], transported to America, should there kindle up a war to punish their destroyer."[6]

Mercantilist rot inflamed tensions in other ways too. Debts that accumulated from colonial wars that had benefited gunmakers and West Indies planters led to stricter enforcement of duties and smuggling. Additionally, turmoil in the Anglo-Dutch money market—in part resulting from speculation in East India shares—forced English bankers to call back loans issued to Virginia planters.[7]

When war between the colonies and England commenced in 1775, the colonies lacked any infrastructure for obtaining finance for the Continental Army. The Bubble Act of 1720 had forbidden the prior formation of joint-stock companies without parliamentary approval. Between 1775 and 1779, the Continental Congress attempted to issue its own currency, but capital flight and a lack of reserves caused the value of the Continental dollar to quickly erode.[8] The untenable monetary situation led Alexander Hamilton to devise a plan in 1779 to swap $200 million in severely depreciated claims for equity and debt in a new continental bank, which would be backed by loans from European allies.[9]

Although Hamilton's plan failed to materialize, the financier Robert Morris—Hamilton's friend and, later, political ally—obtained a charter for the Bank of North America. Morris used the bank to fund the Continental government soon after the British surrender at Yorktown.[10] The bank was backed significantly by foreign capital, with France contributing $250,000 in specie. By the end of the century, European investors held 13 percent of its stock.[11]

The newly independent states were thus dependent on foreign largesse. By the time of the Treaty of Paris, America owed $4.4 million to France and $1.8 million to the Dutch Republic, with another $10 million loan issue planned for the latter.[12] In sum, foreign indebtedness in 1783 represented 15 percent of total debt, which grew to 29 percent by 1789.[13] A revealing fact about America's relative development is that the years 1775 to 1795 was the only period with debts denominated in foreign currency.[14]

Although European allies had been a source of funds, the reality of Britain's economic dominance was hard to ignore. This consideration caused America to recognize pre-war debts owed to British creditors—a rude shock to indebted planters. As the French and the Dutch had their own revolutions to contend with, recourse to London finance became more important. Hamilton, in particular, had found Dutch and French credit to be insufficient.[15]

It was Northeastern merchants predominantly engaged in shipping and retail trades who were in favor of resuming economic ties with England. These interests, represented by the Federalists, had pre-existing financial ties to the former mother country; their operations had depended significantly on trade bills discounted by British banks.[16] Opposed to these interests, of course, were planters who resented the discriminatory credit practices of northern financiers like Morris.[17]

Under the government formed by the Articles of Confederation (1781–89), lack of economic coordination among the states led to monetary disarray. In addition to formulating their own trade laws, state loan offices issued their own bills. Furthermore, war debts remained unresolved, and the Continental Congress' liabilities traded as low as twenty cents of face value (an attractive gamble for speculators with Federalist ties).[18]

The Constitutional Convention of 1787 opened a path to resolving these institutional shortcomings, especially by endowing the federal government with new fiscal authority. Following Hamilton's *Report on Public Credit*, Congress passed the Funding Act of 1790, which allowed the government to assume state debts. The *Report on a National Bank* proposed the creation of a national bank in which the federal government would hold its deposits and own a 20 percent equity stake, while new national powers to raise revenues through excise taxes and tariffs would provide a means to retire debt.

## The Revolutionary Wars Resumed

An economic turn became palpable in the 1790s. Foreign investment returned as England's "canal mania" spilled over to the United States with British investors funding canal construction on the Connecticut River.[19] The first turnpikes also appeared and were built by companies in concert with state legislatures. It was also in this decade that Samuel Slater brought Arkwright's textile machinery to the United States.

No development, however, was more consequential than the rise of cotton production. The American South provided the ideal conditions to meet British textile manufacturers' insatiable demand for the crop. Simultaneously, Eli Whitney's invention of the cotton gin in 1793 cleared a major bottleneck in the production process. In just one decade, US cotton production soared from 1.5 million pounds to 36.5 million pounds. And exports to Britain grew almost 100-fold between 1791 and 1800.[20]

A new war between Britain and France, however, threatened to drag the United States back to conflict (the War of the First Coalition, 1792–97). Relations with Britain remained tense since it maintained its military posts in the Northwest Territory (today's American Midwest), refused to allow trade with the West Indies, and was seizing American ships. It also remained aggrieved over unpaid debts from planters. Worried about the effects renewed conflict would have on the nascent economic recovery, the Federalists pushed forth a treaty of neutrality—the Jay Treaty—in 1794.[21] Unsurprisingly, the treaty heightened divisions between the northern merchants and the planters, who favored commercial sanctions against Britain.

As the upturn continued, the American financial sector expanded greatly. The number of banks in operation grew from three in 1791 to twenty-nine in 1800 to ninety by 1811. Significant investment came from abroad, with foreign investors, mostly British, holding a 40 percent stake in the Bank of the United States by 1803.[22]

British ownership of US securities, in general, was extensive by the turn of the century. London held almost a quarter of US debt and 20 percent of corporate securities.[23] And several contemporary observers noted the new loans it made to planters, commenting that the British had once again come to dominate Virginia's trade.[24]

Economic change also contributed to the rise of new investor blocs. "Out-group" merchants like John Jacob Astor and Stephen Girard, who operated outside Federalist circles, became associated with the Democratic-Republican Party.[25] With the expansion of banking, Wall Street in New York emerged as a rival to Chestnut Street in Philadelphia. Aaron Burr, for example, obtained a charter for Manhattan Bank in 1799 (under the pretense of starting a water utility). And most importantly, the cotton boom produced a rapid rise in new slavery-based fortunes in the South.[26]

By the election of 1800, the Federalists had become mired in a "quasi-war" with France, which felt the Jay Treaty had violated its earlier commercial agreement with the US. The Adams government expanded the military in response and levied an unpopular tax to raise the requisite funds. Additionally, paranoia about domestic unrest and the threat of Jacobinism led the Federalists—imitating Pitt's Tories—to pass the heavy-handed Alien and Sedition Acts.

These events launched a new era in American politics by helping Jefferson's Democratic-Republicans wrest control of the government. His new coalition not only consisted of fellow Southern planters but also New York merchants lured by patronage. Jefferson saw an opportunity to win allies in the Northeast by breaking the Federalist hold on banking. In a letter to his Treasury Secretary Albert Gallatin, Jefferson wrote, "I am decidedly in favor of making all the banks Republican by sharing deposits among them in proportion to the dispositions they show."[27] Indeed, the alliance of New York merchants and Southern planters helped pro-slavery administrations maintain a grip on the White House until the Civil War.[28]

Jefferson's tenure at the White House illuminated one axis that separated the major investor blocs of the nineteenth century: fiscal policy. While Hamilton believed that perpetual debt would benefit the United States, Jefferson, and Gallatin sought to eliminate it. This stance marked the beginning of a series of Democratic administrations pursuing the classical school doctrine of minimal government.

Of course, as British gunboat diplomacy later demonstrated, liberal ideas were mere justification for pre-existing preferences, and their application was selective. Few examples are better than the Louisiana Purchase, which Jefferson accomplished with loans arranged by the British bank Barings. Although they favored budgetary austerity, the Democratic coalition would continue to make an exception for expenditures on the territorial expansion of slavery.

What Jefferson refused to prioritize was also revealing. He reversed course on the Federalist naval expansion, which was intended to protect Northern shipping interests. His refusal to allocate spending to the navy continued to anger the opposition as the Royal Navy began seizing American ships when its war with France re-escalated.[29] Naval policy would only change after the Civil War when Republicans would exhume centuries-old ideas tying mercantile strength to maritime supremacy.

The seizure of mercantile vessels persisted, however. Jefferson's reluctance to engage in a costly war led him to resort to economic sanctions instead, through the Embargo Act of 1807.[30] The act, which restricted trade with foreign nations, provided a fillip to domestic industry, notably textiles and iron.[31] Between 1807 and 1811 alone, the number of cotton mills grew from fifteen to eighty-seven.[32]

Nevertheless, British naval aggression continued, and hawks eyeing territorial expansion—such as Henry Clay and John Calhoun—successfully lobbied for a declaration of war in 1812. After three years of conflict, a truce in 1815 (and Napoleon's defeat at Waterloo) concluded the Revolutionary Wars. The demarcation of the Canadian boundary settled the territorial disputes between America and Britain that had begun with the Proclamation of 1763. Americans were now free to pursue expansion without British interference.

### Re-colonization under Britain's Empire of Free Trade

Peace marked the beginning of America's integration, like that of other countries, into a new system of free trade centered in London. A deluge of British investment poured into the United States, financing the capital investments behind the expansion of cotton slavery in the South and more general settlement in the West. As beneficiaries of the new economic regimes, the ascendant Jackson Democrats and their Southern base would embrace the principles of laissez-faire: minimal central government, free trade, and free banking.

Foreign investment returned quickly after the end of the war. Individual states became the beneficiaries of the British mania for foreign securities that raged from the late 1810s through the 1820s. "New York 6 percents" debuted as the first state issue in London, leading a boom in New York-specific investment that included the Bank of New York and the Erie Canal Project.[33] Pennsylvania and Maryland followed suit in 1824 to obtain financing for their own canal projects.[34]

That same year, Louisiana issued bonds to fund its new system of planter banks, which other states were quick to copy.[35] These banks sought to subsidize financing costs for planters, who required long-term borrowing and were perennially indebted.[36] Their importance demonstrates that the Southern states, in particular, came to depend on Britain not only as a destination for cotton exports—which roughly doubled in the 1820s—but also as a source for investment.[37]

Linking Britain and the South was a new group of New York City merchants, who served as intermediaries in the cotton trade. These merchants solidified the Democratic investor coalition that Jefferson had fostered. Employing their connections to British finance, they purchased cotton from, and extended credit to, planters.[38] They also financed the bulk import of manufactured goods from across the Atlantic. In this respect, they were not unlike the seventeenth-century Merchant Adventurers of England, who were middlemen connected to the credit source of Amsterdam.

A more general expansion of banking also took place alongside the growth of planter banks and Anglo-American finance. By 1829, the number of banks had risen to 329 from ninety in 1812.[39] These new banks joined the cotton interest to form the investor coalition backing Jackson's Democrats.

The newer banks sought to end the charter for the Second Bank of the United States. Excessive banknote issuance and the loss of reserves during the War of 1812 had caused the Madison administration to change its policy and support a new charter for the national bank. But by the late 1820s, private banks had grown resentful of the Bank's restrictions on credit expansion. With the comfort of sustained bullion inflows from Britain, Jackson opposed a new charter and pursued a policy of unregulated free banking.

Jackson also liberalized trade relations with Britain. In 1830, his administration struck a deal with the British to open US ports to their vessels in exchange for the reciprocal opening of West Indian and Canadian ports. Three years later, the Compromise of 1833 promulgated a gradual reduction in tariffs, which fell in most of the years before the Civil War.[40]

In the absence of an income tax, tariffs were the principal source of revenue for servicing debt. Budgetary austerity was thus necessary to keep tariffs low. Jackson not only vetoed many spending measures but, via land sales, fully paid down US debt in 1835—the only time in history when the country was free of debt.

Of course, government land sales also served to satisfy the speculative frenzy for land in the 1830s. Curtailment of the Bank of the United States' regulatory authority gave way to unrestrained credit expansion, which helped stoke the land bubble. Further underlying the mania was a surge in "hot money" inflows from London; these flows caused the US stock of specie to triple between 1833 and 1837.[41]

Eventually, the mania became overstretched, with turmoil in the Anglo-American money market causing panic in 1837 and 1839. The US subsequently experienced one of its worst depressions over the next ten years. Illinois, Indiana, and Pennsylvania defaulted temporarily; Michigan, Arkansas, and Louisiana partially repudiated their debts; the Florida territory and Mississippi fully defaulted.[42] Likewise, Texas had to be relieved from its obligations in an 1850 compromise that enabled California's accession to the union. The fallout from the crisis invited men like Friedrich List to voice their criticism of laissez-faire and offer an alternative economic agenda whose adherents would multiply in the years leading to the Civil War.

## A New Economy Emerges

As slavery expanded in the South, the rest of the American economy was undergoing a slow convergence with the industrialized world. A popular narrative once attributed the Civil War to the rise of manufacturing in the North and, consequently, conflict over the issue tariffs. But Northern manufacturers, specifically those in the textile industry, sold their output to the South and were reluctant to upset commercial relations. Instead, it was westward expansion and the associated growth of industrial agriculture that tipped the balance in favor of the antislavery camp.

Although the Constitutional Convention had established greater union between the independent states, America's internal market—like England's before the eighteenth century—remained disconnected. Development in the West, especially, required government for "internal improvements," which often came in the form of public-private partnerships at the state level. Among the greatest proponents of government-subsidized infrastructure was the Whig leader Henry Clay, who also happened to prosper from personal investments in land and manufacturing in Lexington, Kentucky. Proponents of infrastructure spending were indeed motivated by the sizable profit opportunities it could bring, and Clay's "Bluegrass System"—a tripartite policy of protectionism, central banking, and subsidized infrastructure—served as a development template for other western states.[43]

For farmers, infrastructure provided market access. Such access became more important over time as advances in industrial agriculture raised farm productivity. Inventions such as McCormick's reaper and Deere's plow mechanized farming and helped boost settlement in the Midwest.

Opponents of the Democrats took advantage of the agricultural revolution to form a rival mass politics, which the Federalists had been unable to accomplish. To counter the New York State Democratic machine in the late 1820s, for example, future Republicans William Seward and Thurlow Weed helped form the Anti-Masonic Party, which organized farmers enriched by the Erie Canal.[44] More generally, Seward was a prominent backer of public support for scientific agriculture and "the leading exponent of progressive Whig economic policy."[45] Previewing the post-Civil War Republican agenda, he framed agriculture in terms of economic nationalism. Seward warned in 1851 that "even, therefore, if we should continue to neglect agricultural improvement, England, Ireland, France, Spain, Italy, Germany, and Russia would not."[46]

From 1840 to 1860, a new phenomenon was noticeable in the Midwest: the growth of cities. Over this period, Chicago's population rose from 4,500 to 112,000; Detroit and Cleveland grew more than fivefold.[47] A large part of this increase came from immigrants drawn to the new factories engaged in activities such as flour processing, sugar refining, meat packing, or the manufacture of agricultural equipment.[48] In the case of the Germans escaping the failed Revolution of 1848, some, bringing new technical skills in agriculture and manufacturing, established their own enterprises.

The political ramifications of one statistic, in particular, cannot be understated: the slave states' share of total population had shrunk from 50 percent in 1790 to 35 percent by 1860.[49] Such a result was inevitable as the industrial ecosystem drew greater numbers into its fold organically, while the slave system relied on brute geographic expansion. In general, slave states struggled to attract new settlers.[50]Even though territorial expansion had added new slave states, it had not been sufficient to stop slaveholding interests from becoming a permanent minority in Congress by the 1850s.

### The Rise of the Republican Party

Recognizing that their control of government was slipping, proslavery interests developed more aggressive plans for expansion in the decade before the Civil War. They sought to introduce slavery to the large territory acquired in the Mexican-American War, which led to the controversial Compromise of 1850 and an especially draconian Fugitive Slave Act. Planters, along with their merchant allies in New York City, even contemplated invading Cuba to balance slave and free states.[51] Some launched campaigns, albeit failed ones, to annex new territory in Mexico and Central America.[52]

Antislavery interests, however, responded with a more hardened stance. Increasingly, Northern businessmen felt that the disproportionate power of slaveholders "prevented necessary reforms in the banking, currency, credit, and transportation systems."[53] The Polk administration, in office from 1845 to 1849, continued to pursue laissez-faire policies that incensed those who were demanding a more activist national government. The Independent Treasury Act of 1846, mirroring Peel's Bank Act, created a stricter bullion standard, and the Walker Tariff reciprocated the Corn Law repeal with tariff reductions. Furthermore, President James Polk rebuffed key internal improvement initiatives such as the Rivers and Harbors Act.

Although the Federalist Party had long disappeared, the

New England shipping merchants who constituted its backbone had not. Hailing from prominent families—the Forbeses, the Russells, the Lows, the Tappans, and the Perkinses—they accumulated sizable fortunes trading silk, opium, and tea in China during the Jacksonian Era. Their business challenges in Hong Kong and Canton strengthened their support for a strong naval policy. In 1843, for example, John Murray Forbes urged Secretary of State Daniel Webster to have a naval fleet accompany trade negotiators to China. Writing in blunt terms, he declared that "no foreign nations ever yet gained any disputed point by peaceful negotiations" with China. Furthermore, he wrote that it had "conceived the idea that we have but few ships of war, owing to their never having seen more than two at a time."[54]

By the 1850s, the "aristocratic opposition" had another reason to oppose the extension of slavery. Forbes and his peers had parlayed their shipping wealth into railroad investments, which boomed as railway mania reached the US. Given the scale and logistics of railroad construction, the profitability depended on state aid. Sectional differences became especially pronounced as Congress debated the location of the transcontinental railroad—a decision consequential for existing investments.[55]

Not unlike the seventeenth-century Puritan aristocrats who had helped settle their ancestors in Massachusetts Bay, the New England aristocracy helped sponsor "free soil" settlers in the West and the more general cause of abolitionism.[56] Their cultural exchange with the outside world, Anglophilia (Britain had banned the slave trade in 1833), and the Federalist heritage had already predisposed them to abolitionism. But this position was also inextricable from the investment considerations that informed the New England merchants' opposition to Jacksonian laissez-faire.

They were joined in the 1850s by a growing antislavery bloc in New York state, where the Democratic machine had earlier elevated the Jacksonians to power. Here, commerce with the

Midwest, facilitated by the Erie Canal and new railroads, had grown enough to challenge the cotton trade.[57] More private interests in the state thus began to favor autarkic development over the free trade principles espoused by the Anglo-American merchants in New York City.

Tensions over the slavery question escalated once Congress passed the Kansas–Nebraska Act in 1854. Hoping to establish a transcontinental railroad with Chicago as its eastern terminus, Illinois Senator Stephen Douglas brokered a deal with Southern interests to repeal the Missouri Compromise, which prohibited slavery north of the 36°30′ parallel. This distressed free soilers who believed that the extension of slavery would eliminate opportunities for individual homesteads, which had grown more attractive after the Corn Law repeal.[58] More anti-slavery moderates began to believe that a few hundred thousand planters should not have disproportionate control of the government and therefore joined the New England merchants in funding Kansas Aid societies promoting free settlement in that state.[59]

Fighting in Kansas split both parties and led to the Whig Party's dissolution. The Republican Party rose in its place with a less compromising stance on slavery. Its platform vowed to implement a more activist government through tariffs, home-steads, and state support for agriculture.[60] Although the Republicans lost the 1856 presidential election, the Panic of 1857 boosted support for more radical change. Causing bankruptcy among western farmers, the Panic led many to blame the slave states for a "conspiracy" hindering economic progress.[61] Three years later, Abraham Lincoln's presidential victory pushed the Southern states to secede.

## To the Victor Go the Spoils

The secession of the Southern states naturally removed the principal obstacle to industrial policy in the United States. The Union states did not hesitate to pass preferred legislation, and shortly before the Civil War began, Congress enacted the Morrill Tariff in 1861. Delivering on its promises of state support for agriculture, the Republican Party established the Homestead Act and a Department of Agriculture the following year. And in 1863, Congress passed the National Banking Act, which created a system of national banks that could buy government debt and issue notes under a uniform currency.

Although the war had a detrimental effect on the American economy, forcing capital flight and the suspension of convertibility, it provided a significant stimulus to the industrial sector. War demand spurred the development of iron-ore mining in the Lake Superior region, whose sulfur-free ores were necessary in the new Bessemer process used to produce steel in Western Pennsylvania.[62] Military contracting also caused many iron and apparel manufacturers to run at capacity, and one firm, Morgan Iron Works, built forty-three steamers for the Navy.[63]

When the war ended in 1865, the industrial shock fueled a new investment rush. By 1870, annual railroad construction jumped to five thousand seven hundred miles from one thousand five hundred a decade earlier.[64] Over the same period, mining and manufacturing output expanded 33 percent in real terms, while agricultural output grew 50 percent.[65] The rapid development of the latter sector was also evident in US grain exports to Britain, which quickly surpassed those of Germany after the end of the war.[66]

To say nothing of the human cost of deaths, growth in these sectors were cross-subsidized by workers and the South. Real wages for day laborers fell 20 percent between 1860 and 1865.[67] And in the Southern states, agricultural output took nearly two decades to recover.[68] Nor did their consumption levels recover until the turn of the century.[69]

Industrial growth and the concurrent protectionist impulse would favor Republican Party rule until the election of Woodrow Wilson. Over this period, the average tariff on imports ranged from 40 to 50 percent. In many cases, like the

Woolens Act of 1867, Congress passed legislation designed by manufacturers themselves with little modification.[70] Indeed, favors and government contracts for private industry in exchange for political support characterized a more outwardly corrupt "spoils system" in the final quarter of the nineteenth century. Tariff revenues also provided the Republicans with a vital resource for acquiring favors.[71]

The Panic of 1873, which ended European trade cooperation, did not spare the US. It put a stop to the post-Civil War land speculation mania and forced the country, buffeted by bullion outflows, to commit itself to the gold standard. For more than twenty years, America, like the rest of the world, would experience volatile growth and painful deflation— conditions which fomented popular unrest.[72]

Amid such dire economic circumstances, a narrowly contested election of 1876 forced the Republicans to remove troops from the South. The end of Reconstruction heralded a new era of terror on African Americans and allowed Democrats to maintain control of the region for almost a century. Nevertheless, they only occupied the presidential office for two terms during the period between 1860 and 1912.

For the railroad industry, stagnation provided an opportunity to consolidate and wield its disproportionate market power. By the early 1880s, forty-one railroads had market capitalizations over $15 million, while Carnegie Steel's, in comparison, was only $5 million.[73] Such sheer size allowed railroad magnates, in the words of Henry George, to exert political influence "by controlling the press, manipulating legislatures, and filling the bench with their creatures."[74] Railroads were also able to force other enterprises, such as importers, to show their accounts and share profits.[75]

Frustrated with railroad power, Republican tariffs, and the spoils system, Democrats—supported by oldline merchants trading with Britain, Anglo-American financiers, and importers —carried Grover Cleveland to the White House first in 1884 and again in 1892.[76] But Cleveland was unable to overcome the tariff consensus. Republicans were able to make successful appeals to Anglophobia to undermine his administrations, which were staffed with members of the "Cobden Club"—named after Liberal British minister Richard Cobden.[77]

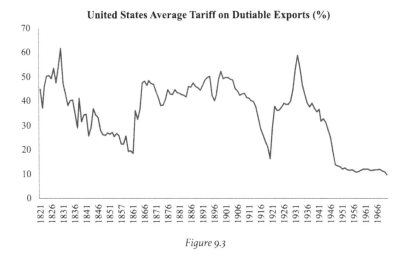

*Figure 9.3*

**Figure 9.3** maps the course of tariff duties in the United States. Following the demise of the Federalists and the rise of the Jacksonian Democrats, average tariffs on dutiable exports fell as America embraced freer trade alongside Europe. Tariff policy returned after the Civil War and peaked under Hoover in one last hurrah for the Republicans before the New Deal. **Source**: Bicentennial Edition: Historical Statistics of the United States, Colonial Times to 1970, United States Census Bureau (1975), https://www.census.gov/library/publications/1975/compendia/hist_stats_colonial-1970.html.

## The Expansion of Empire

An influential group of Cleveland's supporters were opponents of imperialism, in large part due to their opposition to state expenditures. These individuals had voiced their criticism of the annexation of foreign territories as early as 1870 when President Grant attempted to claim the Dominican Republic.[78] Although Grant believed that the island could be a destination for former slaves, he also had commercial interests in mind. He argued that it "will become a large consumer of the products of Northern farms and manufactories," which would allow the US to generate an export surplus to repay foreign debt.[79]

Like elsewhere in the world, the decline in trade cooperation only strengthened imperialist urges. In the 1880s, Republican politicians James Blaine of Maine and Henry Cabot Lodge of Massachusetts, supported by textile interests in that state, continued to advocate aggressive foreign policy initiatives.[80] Pushing naval rearmament, they raised the threat of the Royal Navy to America's coastal defenses and, of course, the need to secure foreign markets against British competition. The publication of Alfred Thayer Mahan's *The Influence of Sea Power upon History* in 1890 bolstered their case, though Mahan favored a close alliance with Britain.[81] That year, Republicans used tariff revenues to upgrade the navy and fund a pension act for Civil War veterans, which grew to account for 40 percent of expenditures.[82]

In 1890, Republicans also passed the McKinley Tariff, raising the average import duty to an all-time high of 49.5 percent. Democrats assailed the Republicans as the party of big business and lifted Grover Cleveland back to the White House in 1892.[83] But his second term was beleaguered by a new panic in 1893. The failure of Barings Bank, which had significant investment in Argentina, prompted a reversal of London's appetite for foreign investment. By 1893, the US government's gold reserves had fallen below the critical psychological threshold of $100 million, which caused bullion outflows to accelerate.[84] Two years later, the US Treasury had to seek a bailout of $66 million in gold from a syndicate of J. P. Morgan & Co. in New York and J. S. Morgan & Co. and N. M. Rothschild & Sons in London.[85]

The crisis, however, would mark the last serious external drain on American finances. After a twenty-year malaise, animal spirits—evidenced by an enlivened stock market and rising interest rates—returned to Britain. Industry consolidation helped its iron, coal, and steel industries recover.[86] A new revolution in road transport, with the appearance of bicycles, the motor engine, and the "horseless carriage," also helped spark a resurgence in investment.[87]

Mirroring a similar development in Britain (with the appearance of firms like Dunlop and Lever, mentioned earlier), a new type of firm, the manufacturing multinational, emerged in the US.[88] Such integrated industrials utilized continuous production processes and combined mass manufacturing with mass distribution.[89] And their organizational structure built on existing innovations in mass transport and communications.[90]

Such firms reflected, more generally, productivity advancements America had made in a range of industries, including timber, steel, crude oil, meat packing, and telephones.[91] Combined with the recovery in British demand, advances in these categories enabled the US to achieve, for the first time, a manufacturing surplus.[92] Total exports rose by 80 percent between 1895 and 1900 while the trade balance rose to a surplus of 3 percent of GDP.[93] With an improved external sector, the US stock of monetary gold nearly doubled between 1896 and 1900.[94] America had begun a new phase in which it would be the world's leading exporter.

Manufacturing growth coincided with a peak in the power of the tariff lobby during the decades adjoining 1900. With more investors having a stake in protections, the Democrats lost significant support from the business community, which rallied behind William McKinley in the 1896 presidential election.[95] At the same time, however, popular movements like the People's Party were now able to enter the Democratic Party, which retained support from select interests, such as silver companies.[96] The party was thus able to platform Williams Jennings Bryan's campaign for redistributive bimetallism, which sought to expand the money supply by creating money backed by silver.

Although the Republicans gained control of all three branches of government after winning the presidency, they still had to contend with popular discontent. Like their Tory counterparts across the Atlantic, Republicans found nationalism—in the form of the Spanish-American War—to be an effective rallying cry for unity in 1898.[97] The war helped the Republicans retain control of Congress in the midterms of that year, and added Guam, Puerto Rico, and the Philippines to US territory.

Claims that business interests led America into the war are dubious. Nevertheless, foreign policy aggression gained more adherents in the 1890s, with many in the business community echoing Grant's earlier sentiments that Latin America represented the best market for US manufacturers.[98] Even before the war, the United States had sent marines to Nicaragua in 1893 to protect the Maritime Canal Company's concession. It had also sent military personnel to Panama in 1895 to protect banana planters.

### The Grim Path to Hegemony

Persistent manufacturing surpluses in the early 1900s signaled America's developmental convergence with industrialized Europe. A steadier inflow of bullion, the result of a more robust external sector, created an economic environment favorable to the expansion of credit. In the first decade of the new century, bank lending began to spill over to the foreign sphere. US portfolio investment abroad jumped from $50 million in 1897 to almost $900 million in 1908.[99]

Increased foreign lending marked the beginning of a new international role for the dollar. With the rise of both multinational finance and multinational manufacturing, the Republican investor coalition faced a more formidable policy rival. In 1909, the Republicans stepped too far in passing the Payne-Aldrich Tariff Bill, which hiked duties once again. The bill only cemented perceptions that the Republicans served a corrupt tariff-monopoly complex. In the following year, Democrats, for the first time in nearly twenty years, won control of the House of Representatives. In 1912, a coalition of multinational, mining, and agricultural interests helped Woodrow Wilson reach the presidency—the first Democrat to do so since 1892.[100]

Like Lloyd George and Churchill's New Liberals in Britain, Wilson paired the policy priorities of multinationals with a progressive economic agenda. This stark similarity reflected the fact that America had reached a point of economic maturation where it, too, could produce firms whose operations spanned the globe. With the Revenue Act of 1913, Wilson lowered tariffs. But the Democrats, instead of advocating for a smaller government as they had in the nineteenth century, substituted the lost revenues with an income tax (and an estate tax a few years later). Military spending was the budgetary item they hoped to restrain. Between 1898 and 1909, naval expenditures had quadrupled.[101] For Wilson, a policy of less overt imperialism proved a convenient stance.

During Wilson's first term, Congress also passed the Federal Reserve Act of 1913. Although the United States was by this point less vulnerable to external drains, it still had to contend with the problem of internal bank runs, as the Panic of 1907 demonstrated. During that crisis, the banking system had to once again rely on J. P. Morgan for short-term liquidity. Rival banks—notably Kuhn, Loeb & Co.—could no longer tolerate Morgan as the de facto lender of last resort. Additionally, such banks saw growing profits in foreign lending and sought to modernize American banking to the standards of rival financial centers.[102] For farmer-aligned Democrats like Wilson, suspicious of the "money trust," the Act brought the financial system under greater government control.[103]

The new Federal Reserve System, like the Bank of England, aimed to maintain a functional money market during episodes of panic. It could do so through the ability to issue Federal Reserve Notes in exchange for private bank assets.[104] Forty percent of these notes, however, had to be backed by gold. Given the considerable progress it had made in international commerce, America was in a better position to manage this constraint than ever before.

With the onset of the First World War, foreign affairs naturally took precedence over domestic reforms. But no country benefited from the war more than the United States. By ending what amounted to a century-long monetary straitjacket in Britain, the First World War produced the most impactful global demand shock since the Napoleonic Wars. Between 1914 and 1917, British expenditures increased fourfold while the budget balance sharply widened to a deficit of –25 percent of GDP.[105] The Bank of England's holdings of government securities increased nearly fivefold during the war.

One of the principal wartime windfalls to the US was the rise in demand it triggered. From the beginning of 1914 to the end of 1918, total US exports tripled in value. And during the war, the trade balance exceeded 6 percent of GDP—a sizable figure for what was then an already large economy.[106] By 1920, rapid export growth, in combination with the extensive damage inflicted on Europe's productive capacity, allowed the US to make significant inroads against Britain's economic dominance.[107] If it was not the larger partner in their shared hegemony, America was by this point at least the British Empire's equal. Almost 150 years after its founding, the United States had achieved independence.

# 10

# AMERICAN HEGEMONY AND ITS DECLINE

J ames Madison was stunned by the sad fate of the Dutch
Republic in 1787, when the once-great nation was
brought low by civil war and a Prussian invasion. He
registered his alarm in *The Federalist* no. 20: "This
unhappy people seem to be now suffering from popular
convulsions, from dissensions among the States, and from the
actual invasion of foreign arms, the crisis of their destiny. All
nations have their eyes fixed on the awful spectacle."[1] Madison
hoped that the newly created United States could avoid a
similar fate. Indeed, the drafters of America's Constitution were
eager to draw lessons from Dutch political institutions.[2] And
yet, in the twentieth century, the United States could not avoid
a course similar to the one taken during Dutch primacy.

By 1920, the US had managed to reach the farthest edge of
technological development by expanding its polyarchy over a
population two-and-a-half times that of Britain.[3] It had fully
integrated the loose assemblage of states that originally
composed it, albeit at the immense price of the Civil War, and
accommodated still greater numbers through territorial
conquest and immigration. This newfound position at the fore-

front of the global economy would reshape American institutions over course of the next century.

The threat of Communism defined the first era of US primacy. Like the Counter-Reformation and Jacobinism in earlier eras, the specter of the "red menace" helped shape the American fiscal-military state. Protecting foreign interests against revolution became especially critical as commerce took on a more global form. The US thus took over Britain's role in the nineteenth century as the world's security force.

Technological supremacy also led to the demise of protectionism and a fervent embrace of free trade. Trade priorities shifted as services and investment in the foreign sector supplanted manufacturing exports. After the 1970s, the waning of the Cold War permitted rigid enforcement of price stability, enabling American financial institutions to assume a more dedicated role as the world's bankers.

The symptoms that had marked the relative decline of America's predecessors once again reappeared. Financialization and demand deficiency accompanied the emergence of a rentier state after the end of the New Deal. And, as before, concentrating wealth, fueled by an inexorable increase in asset prices, underpinned these processes.

The end of the Cold War in the late 1980s ushered in a new era of cooperation among nations. Such cooperation facilitated the unprecedented economic growth of regions that had long been developmental laggards. China, as I discussed in Chapter 5, was the most notable example. But as the decade since the financial crisis of 2008 has demonstrated, cooperation once again rests on a tenuous foundation.

## The Rise of the Multinational Bloc

The demand shock of the First World War accelerated the technical progress of American industry. This phenomenon contributed to the further development of multinational enterprises in the 1920s. Their ranks included names such as Ford, General Electric, Coca-Cola, Colgate, Eastman Kodak, National Cash Register, RCA, Harvester International, and, most importantly, Standard Oil of New Jersey.

Notably, in contrast to older industries, such companies derived far greater costs from fixed capital than from labor.[4] As a result, they were more amenable to labor concessions than the textile, shoes, steel, and packaged meat companies that comprised the latter group. From Ford's eight-hour workday to Eastman Kodak's profit-sharing initiatives to Standard Oil's funding for "Industrial Relations Counselors," these corporations embraced progressive labor policies well in advance of the reforms that followed the New Deal. They even carried over their relatively generous wage policies to European operations.[5]

As already mentioned, the new multinationals sought greater certainty for their business operations abroad. Foreign tariffs represented the most cumbersome impediment to these entities. In many cases, tariffs imposed a greater burden than labor costs. Many of these multinationals thus became invested in preventing reciprocal tariff wars and, more generally, preserving open markets abroad. New industry and old industry, for example, clashed on the issue of the League of Nations, which old-industry interests characterized as "simply a rally ground for free traders and all who are opposed to the doctrine of 'adequate protection' for industries and labor of the United States."[6]

The industry that incurred the most significant foreign political risk, "Big Oil," would emerge to be the most politically influential into the next millennium.[7] Although the world's first oil well was drilled in 1859, oil's use had initially been limited to kerosene for lamps and lubricants. But as the twentieth century approached, the internal combustion engine revolutionized industry. Suddenly, oil demand became limitless.[8]

Before the First World War, the American government tended to lag behind Britain in its support for the foreign expansion of its oil interests. The war, however, created anxiety that the US would exhaust its domestic supply.[9] Between 1921 and 1922, for example, Standard Oil of New Jersey, Standard of Indiana, and Gulf all entered contracts to develop Venezuela's Maracaibo oil basin.[10] By the end of the decade, Venezuela would become the second-largest producer of crude oil despite having had virtually no production before 1917.[11] By the 1930s, American oil companies had investments in areas as far ranging as Iran, Bahrain, and Borneo.

As was already evident in the return of the Democrats in 1910, members of the financial sector, too, helped form the internationalist investor bloc. Firms such as Lehman Brothers, Goldman Sachs, and Bank of America had grown more prominent and sought to make inroads into J. P. Morgan's empire.[12] Unlike the latter, which had investments in legacy tariff-protected industries, these banks had closer ties to new multinational companies.[13]

Furthermore, American banks' foreign business had multiplied in the 1910s. The number of foreign branches and subsidiaries increased from twenty-six in 1913 to 156 by 1919. In the First World War's aftermath, more financial firms, like their counterparts in the real sector, had a vested interest in institutions promoting international cooperation and, consequently, recovery in war-damaged economies.[14]

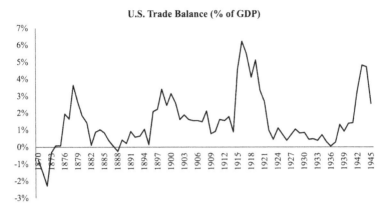

*Figure 10.1*

| Year | U.S. Gold (mt. tons) |
|------|----------------------|
| 1870 | 107 |
| 1875 | 86 |
| 1880 | 209 |
| 1885 | 371 |
| 1890 | 442 |
| 1895 | 169 |
| 1900 | 602 |
| 1905 | 1148 |
| 1910 | 1660 |
| 1915 | 2568 |
| 1920 | 3679 |
| 1925 | 5998 |
| 1930 | 6358 |
| 1935 | 8998 |
| 1940 | 19543 |
| 1945 | 17848 |

*Table 10.1*

**Figure 10.1** shows the acceleration of U.S. export growth during the First and Second World Wars. **Table 10.1** demonstrates how during the Great Depression (1930-1940), bullion flowed to the U.S. seeking a safe haven—a marked change from the crises of the 19th century when the U.S. suffered from external drains of its gold reserves. **Sources**: Timothy Green, *Central Bank Gold Reserves: An Historical Perspective Since 1845* (London: World Gold Council, 1999), retrieved from https://www.gold.org/goldhub/research/central-bank-gold-reserves-historical-perspective-1845; Measuring Worth; National Bureau of Economic Research, Total Imports for the United States retrieved from FRED, Federal Reserve Bank of St. Louis.

## The New Deal

The unpopularity of the war, which led to steep income tax hikes on the wealthy, allowed the tariff interest to retake control of the government. Holding both Congress and the presidency in the 1920s, the Republicans proceeded to substitute revenues from income taxes with higher tariffs under the Fordney-McCumber Act of 1922. Nevertheless, that decade saw another attempt at international cooperation as Europe returned to the gold standard. Even the Soviet Union, under its New Economic Program, reintroduced market institutions and opened itself to foreign investment.[15]

As the next decade demonstrated, the international order of the 1920s rested on precarious footing. To maintain its pre-war gold parity, Britain undertook draconian austerity measures that raised its primary surplus to 7 percent of GDP and its current account balance to 4 percent of output.[16] Capital flight from political instability forced similar efforts in France under the Poincaré administration. Germany, of course, faced the Sisyphean task of servicing its massive war indemnity. And outside of Europe, Japan's struggles were indicative of its decision to be the first to renege on its commitment to fixed exchange rates. Neither Britain nor the United States stood ready to fill the vacuum in global demand and instead "nailed their flag to the mast of Say's Law," as the historian Eric Hobsbawm put it.[17]

Indeed, the postwar recovery masked the severe demand deficiency that had resulted from Britain and America's stubborn maintenance of their respective rentier and export empires. The decayed international order was no longer sustainable, as evidenced after the Wall Street Crash of October 1929. In response to the escalating tariff war, the Republicans passed the Smoot-Hawley Tariff in 1830, which, in the wake of depression, brought on the long demise of the protectionist bloc.

Following Roosevelt's famous election in 1932, multinationals —fearing the socialist impulse that had gripped the rest of the world—strengthened their ties to progressivism. With the support of large oil companies, cyclical industries, and the Rocke-feller-controlled Chase Bank, Roosevelt—almost forty years after Bryan's first campaign—abandoned the gold standard in 1933.[18] He also oversaw the investigation of J. P. Morgan that year and the passage of the Glass-Steagall Act, which was, in part, intended to weaken the latter.[19] Among the most consequential bills passed the following year was the Reciprocal Trade Agreements Act of 1934. The act allowed the President to adjust tariffs and make bilateral trade agreements without Congressional approval; the negotiations under it served as a template for the global General Agreement on Tariffs and Trade (GATT) signed in Geneva the following decade.[20] Finally, in 1935, Congress passed the Social Security and Wagner acts, which strengthened labor and attracted opposition from labor-intensive industries like steel.[21]

## Hegemony Realized

The outbreak of the Second World War in 1939 unleashed a demand shock large enough to end the Great Depression. From that year to 1943, the fiscal deficit widened from –3 percent of GDP to –27 percent. Output increased nearly two-and-a-half times during the war, while exports rose almost fivefold, growing faster than they had during the First World War. By the war's end, the United States was producing half of the world's output.

Like the Dutch admiralty boards and the British Ordnance Office, new military research departments spurred several innovations. In 1940, fearing German technical progress, the government established the Office of Scientific Research and Development headed by Vannevar Bush.[22] The OSRD not only launched the Manhattan Project but also created a network of laboratories that would become the main conduit for funding scientific research.[23] Military research initiatives during the war, as Fred L. Block, and Matthew R. Keller have written, "built thousands of planes and tanks, developed the atomic bomb, the hydrogen bomb, civilian nuclear power, the computer, the transistor, the semiconductor, and made major advances in airplane, radar, and missile technology, and completed much of the preparatory work for the laser."[24] After the onset of the Cold War in the 1950s, these efforts evolved into the creation of institutions—most notably DARPA and NASA—dedicated to pushing the technological boundary.

Of course, military research and development occurred in close collaboration with private industry. For example, Frank Jewett, president of Bell Labs joined Bush, and Charles Stark Draper developed anti-aircraft sight technology with Sperry Gyroscope Company, which had already been commercializing his research.[25] Military R&D also contributed to the expansion of several prominent defense companies, including Teledyne, General Dynamics, and Raytheon.

As already evident in negotiations of the lend-lease arrangements with Britain during the war, America's outsized share of production allowed it to dictate the terms of the postwar order to its allies.[26] Through the GATT agreements, the Democrats were able to resume their project of reducing tariffs and opening world trade. And under the Bretton Woods system, Britain had little choice but to accept a monetary arrangement that ran through the dollar. Its relegated economic status was especially apparent in 1949 when, facing a shortage of dollars, its government devalued the pound by 30 percent. Even the *Economist* entertained "the Communist thesis that it is the deliberate and conscious aim of American policy to ruin Britain and everything that Britain stands for in the world."[27]

Indeed, the lure of communism in Western Europe, where Soviet influence remained strong, meant America could not ignore the welfare of its allies (and its largest export market). As a result, the United States extended considerable aid to Britain and the continent through the Marshall Plan and grants for European reconstruction. America's provision of money—and consequently influence—also expanded beyond Europe through the IMF, World Bank, and USAID (later on). In 1948 alone, foreign aid represented 17 percent of federal expenditures and would retain a 7-percent share in the next decade.[28]

War in Asia helped the Republicans return to the presidency in 1952. Tasked with balancing the budget, President Dwight Eisenhower opted to maintain expenditures and, as a result, disappointed many in his party who sought lower income taxes. Keynesian policy had retained its appeal. Even corporate advocates, such as the Committee for Economic Development, touted its mutual benefits for both firms and labor.[29] A substantial portion of government spending, however, went to armaments, which led Eisenhower to issue his famous warning about "the military-industrial complex."

Through the "New Look" strategy, Eisenhower had managed to keep defense expenditures stable after the end of the Korean War. But Democrats were able to take advantage of frustration with Eisenhower's fiscal policies to recapture the White House in 1960. The Kennedy and Johnson administrations adopted proposals from the Committee for Economic Development and Ford Foundations to implement Keynesian "supply-side" tax reductions. Kennedy cosigned an investment tax credit in 1962 and paved the way for the 1964 Revenue Act, which reduced income and corporate tax rates by 20 percent and 8 percent respectively.[30] The Democrats also revived military spending, which rose almost 70 percent between 1960 and 1970, as tensions in Asia re-escalated. Finally, the "Kennedy Round" of GATT talks also oversaw among the most aggressive reductions to tariffs—30 percent on average—in history.[31]

## The Decline of American Manufacturing

The 1960s GATT rounds, uncoincidentally, occurred during an unprecedented period of global economic growth. Cold War allies—most notably Japan, Germany, and later the Asian tigers —saw their economies rapidly industrialize. World GDP growth in real terms reached 6.7 percent in 1964 and hovered close to 6 percent until 1973—levels not attained since.[32]

What enabled such high levels of output growth were the maximally Keynesian policies, centered on armaments production, pursued by the United States.[33] In addition to military expenditures, public sector employment grew 50 percent during the 1960s—its highest increase in any decade after the Second World War.[34] With broadened distribution, expansionary policy caused money velocity to accelerate and capacity utilization to reach almost 90 percent after 1965.[35]

Armaments spending and, more generally, strong global aggregate demand, created optimal conditions for the export markets of certain Cold War allies. West Germany, which stood on the dividing line between capitalism and communism, and Japan, the bulwark against communism in Asia, were natural beneficiaries of such an environment. Equally telling is that all four "Asian Tigers"—South Korea, Taiwan, Hong Kong, and Singapore—were also vital to the Western bloc. Although conventional wisdom has credited the industrialization policies of these countries, all were beneficiaries of targeted demand. Furthermore, armaments had absorbed a significant part of the productive capacities of incumbent manufacturers like the US, the United Kingdom, and the Soviet Union.[36]

Industrialization in the economies of America's Cold War allies helped plant the seeds for the New Deal's collapse. Already by the 1950s, Japanese and German manufacturers began to capture the profit share of their American counterparts. The American share of advance-country manufacturing exports fell from 27 to 21 percent between 1950 and 1963, only to fall further, to 17 percent, by 1971.[37] Meanwhile, the import penetration of foreign manufacturers had doubled from 6.9 percent in the early 1960s to 16 percent by the early 1970s.[38]

While American policy contributed to the rise of foreign manufacturers, it also contributed to a loss of competitiveness at home. As mentioned earlier, domestic manufacturing benefited from military spending, which had quintupled between 1950 and 1970. Although such demand mitigated the impact of competitive pressures in the short term, beneficiaries of military largesse had little incentive to improve their ability to operate without subsidies.[39] Defense contracts helped companies such as General Dynamics and Studebaker, which founded the Committee for Economic Development, survive their business struggles.[40]

Unions' peculiar role in the New Deal coalition also helped undermine the competitiveness of domestic manufacturing. Recall that internationalist multinationals had supported progressive labor policies against the interests of the pro-tariff, labor-intensive manufacturers that backed the Republican Party. This meant that wage pressures in sectors such as materials and apparel, which faced the onslaught of imports, were less of a concern for the investor bloc backing the New Deal agenda.

Prominent unions were also able to leverage their critical role in anti-communism. Since the days of the Gompers-led AFL in the early part of the century, they had helped counteract the activity of more radical labor movements. During the 1960s, the AFL-CIO's support for Cold War policies became important as domestic opposition to US foreign intervention grew stronger. Not only did the AFL-CIO actively support the invasion of Vietnam, but its affiliate, the American Institute for Free Labor Development, channeled funds from government agencies to US-friendly political groups in Latin America.[41] As a result, unions were not only able to obtain intervention in disputes from Democrat administrations but also the support of Republicans like Nixon, who famously declared, in 1971, "I am now a Keynesian."[42]

As a result, real wages in manufacturing grew 15 percent in the 1960s despite increased foreign competition. The extent of the sector's global uncompetitiveness would become evident in the next decade when the real exchange rate priced in manufacturing unit labor costs would collapse by almost 50 percent. On the other hand, Germany and Japan benefited from lower real wages after the Second World War and what effectively amounted to (US-backed) one-party rule, which limited wage pressures.[43]

Profitability differentials between domestic and foreign industries were substantial. Average net profit rates in both Japan and Germany between 1950 and 1970 were almost double that of the United States. In manufacturing, the stark contrast between Japan and the United States during this period is especially noteworthy: 40 percent versus 24 percent.[44] Consequently, the relative size of the material sector, which mainly consisted of manufacturing firms, suffered a sizable contraction. Its share of the S&P 500 shrunk from 26 percent in 1957—the biggest—to 10 percent by 1973, behind the energy and consumer discretionary sectors.[45]

### "Stagflation"

The United States, however, had reached a developmental position in which it could exploit factor availability on a global scale. Firms thus responded to new profit opportunities in manufacturing abroad by increasing their foreign investments. As such, the ratio of foreign to domestic manufacturing investment by US corporations tripled from the late 1950s to the early 1970s.[46] Likewise, the overseas assets of major American Banks jumped from $3.5 billion to $53 billion in the 1960s.[47]

Demand for foreign investment in conjunction with high aggregate demand, fueled by armaments spending and a business cycle upturn, tested the dollar-gold peg of $35. Already by 1960, dollar liabilities equaled America's stock of gold.[48] In October of that year, the London gold market briefly priced gold at $40 per ounce on the prospect of Kennedy winning the presidential election. Given Kennedy's criticism of the Eisenhower administration's budgetary austerity, speculators began to cast doubts on the US government's ability to commit to the official price. In March of the following year, Germany relented to speculative pressures and revalued the deutsche mark by 5 percent. As a result, the Kennedy administration had to impose capital controls through the interest equalization tax. But evasion mechanisms—available to multinational enterprises—rendered such controls ineffective.[49]

Through the 1960s, efforts to defend the gold fixing caused America's stock of the metal to decline from $19 billion at the beginning of the decade to less than $13 billion in 1967. The escalating conflict in Vietnam only made price stability more difficult to attain. The international system of fixed exchange rates finally unraveled that year when Britain, where domestic profits had also diminished in relative terms, was forced to devalue the pound by 14 percent in November 1967. By March of the next year, the US stock of gold fell further, to $10 billion, and the US ceased intervening in the London market. Gold convertibility finally ended in August 1971 after the parallel rate rose above $42.

Despite the failure to maintain convertibility, no crisis occurred in the real economy. Unemployment had fallen from 7 percent in 1961 to 3.4 percent in 1969. Meanwhile, the S&P 500 rose by 50 percent (25 percent in real terms). Particular segments of the stock market had done even better with large multinational stocks (the "Nifty 50") peaking in 1972 with twice the valuation of the broader index.[50] The Sixties had also seen a revival of Wall Street with the emergence of mutual funds and conglomerates. The latter would acquire diversified businesses, often struggling manufacturers, mostly with inflated shares but also occasionally with heavy borrowing.[51] Amid the era's financial exuberance, (non-financial) private credit as a share of GDP had increased by 20 percent between 1960 and 1973.[52] The rabid speculative appetite of "the go-go years" had drawn comparisons to 1929, contributing to the hesitancy of economic officials to slow the economy down in the name of price stability.[53]

Nevertheless, by the early 1970s, the struggling manufacturing sector became a dead weight on the economy. Between 1965 and 1973, profitability in the manufacturing sector declined more than 40 percent compared to 13 percent for the non-manufacturing sector, which was more able to pass on cost increases.[54] Overcapacity began to emerge in global manufacturing that decade, especially as the East Asian Tigers increased their share of US imports to 6.7 percent in 1973 from just 1.6 percent a decade earlier.[55] As demand "leaked abroad" at the expense of domestic industry, the efficacy of monetary stimulus declined; even though the money supply grew faster from the beginning of 1971 to the end of 1973, unemployment fell only 1.2 percent.

Meanwhile, inflation accelerated from 5 percent to 9 percent over the same period. Inflationary pressures were exacerbated by the appreciation of other currencies against the dollar—a phenomenon driven by speculative demand for foreign securities. The Japanese yen appreciated 20 percent as the Nikkei stock index increased by 150 percent between 1971 and 1973. From the beginning of 1977 to the end of 1978, the yen again appreciated 33 percent, while the mark appreciated 20 percent. The rise in these currencies created a false perception that the United States was suffering from capital flight.

Instead, what caused the sharp appreciation of foreign currencies was the highly profitable activity, principally by American banks, of borrowing dollars domestically and speculating in financial assets abroad via subsidiaries.[56] Not coincidentally, the 1970s also saw the beginnings of the hedge fund industry and professional trading in futures contracts.[57] The magnitude of currency moves in these years reflected the shallowness of foreign capital markets, which were not yet fully developed in comparison with those of the United States. Furthermore, speculative flows of capital dwarfed trade balances in size.[58] "Stagflation" indeed possessed only a superficial resemblance to the crises of financial flight in less-developed economies. Speculators were already aware at the time that "a strong and growing US economy meant a weak US dollar," as Michael Moffit observed.[59] Hence, fears about the US trade deficit have failed to manifest even as it has widened since the 1970s.

Additionally, aggregate demand conditions were responsible for that decade's oil "shock," which exacerbated inflationary pressures.[60] Oil price increases were preceded by a rise in industrial commodities sensitive to the business cycle.[61] Concurrent demand from commodity-intensive industrializing countries revealed a short-term supply constraint in oil. But such a commodity-specific bottleneck hardly amounted to evidence for the existence of a more general aggregate supply constraint, as many used the crisis to claim. A similar phenomenon later occurred during the foreign investment boom of the 2000s when oil prices increased by a comparable magnitude. Then, too, foreign currencies rapidly appreciated against the dollar, only to fall sharply when risk aversion led a retreat to US dollar assets.

Ultimately, imbalances in manufacturing had grown too large to both sustain employment in that sector and contain inflation. By this point, the US economy had matured beyond export-led development, which was more appropriate for those countries whose growth depended on outcompeting legacy American firms. Unsurprisingly, the share of the population employed in manufacturing fell 20 percent between 1970 and 1980 while the share in services increased by 14 percent.

## The End of the New Deal and Liberalism's Rebirth

The New Deal coalition's objectives had, in the end, become too numerous. Inflationary pressures rendered impossible the simultaneous pursuit of Cold War military aims, the economic development of allies in that war, and the protection of economic sectors under threat from such development. When inflation finally reached 10 percent in the second half of the 1970s, circumstances had changed enough to cause price stability to supersede employment as a priority.

Perhaps the most important change was the Soviet Union's stagnation and the Warsaw Pact countries' growing dependence on the external world. Recurring grain harvest failures caused the Soviet Union to import grain and agricultural machinery from the West while diminishing returns to investment contributed to increased imports of foreign technology.[62] At the same time, its Comecon partners, like Poland, turned to an import-led development strategy.[63] To fund its imports, the Soviet Union began relying on oil exports, which benefited from the price boom of the 1970s. Greater oil sales to the West, however, also created resentment among allies who depended on subsidized prices.[64] The fraying of the Warsaw Pact, coupled with internal dissent among the diverse cultural constituents of the Soviet Union, heralded the beginning of the latter's decline.

These events, in addition to Nixon's détente with China, not only spelled the end of the Cold War but also, consequently, an end to the fiscal-military regime of the New Deal. In "one last hurrah" for the New Deal coalition, free trade interests—upset with Nixon's import surcharges and general protectionist impulses—supported Jimmy Carter's presidential campaign in 1976.[65] Beleaguered by inflation, however, Carter began implementing fiscal austerity in 1979 and appointed noted inflation hawk Paul Volcker as chair of the Federal Reserve.

By 1980, Republicans were able to assemble a new coalition of investors—one that would allow them to control the executive branch for twelve years. The demise of domestic manufacturing enabled Ronald Reagan to pivot to a tentative embrace of free trade.[66] Together with a moderation in his foreign policy stance on China, this allowed Reagan to win support from multinational enterprises.[67]

Another set of investors also helped strengthen the Republican coalition: financiers. New financial interests, such as those who offered products like CDs and mutual funds, had only grown since the 1960s. Nixon had already courted such firms, who were hampered by the Democrats' "heavy-handed bureaucratic regulatory schemes."[68] Likewise, the nascent mergers and acquisitions industry also belonged to the camp of financiers opposing regulation. Its first incarnation, the conglomerate bubble, had ended when "the establishment" united against the takeover of old-economy icon Chemical Bank.[69] Union-friendly officials stood in the way of the new business of acquiring legacy firms, severely cutting their costs, and maximally extracting their profits.

Equally important was the growth of securities and investment divisions at major banks. Just as securities issuance during the Napoleonic Wars had given rise to the "stock jobbers" and "paper aristocracy" that had drawn William Cobbett's scorn, the policies of the late New Deal contributed to the growth of their twentieth-century incarnation. Such departments profited from trading and speculation in domestic debt, foreign debt, corporate securities, and commodities. They stood to benefit from policies pursuing price stability that would boost the value of their holdings and the orderly function of their business.

Finally, Reagan benefited from a general corporate backlash against New Deal regulations. Since the publication of Rachel Carlson's *Silent Spring,* a vocal segment of the Democratic Party called for increased environmental oversight. This new activist movement, along with Carter's attempts to tax windfall profits on oil, hastened international oil's shift to the Republican side.[70]

Under Reagan, laissez-faire—dormant since the decline of Victorian Britain—reappeared. His administration created a formula for successive administrations at home and abroad: cut income taxes, reduce social spending, defang unions, eliminate regulations, and pursue rigid price stability. Under the Economic Recovery and Tax Act of 1981, effective tax rates for businesses fell from 32 to 16 percent, while the corporate income tax share of federal revenues fell to 6 from 15 percent in the prior decade.[71] At the individual level, tax rates were cut by 23 percent, but increases to social security taxes *raised* rates on those who earned less than $30,000.[72]

Reagan's crusade against "big government" spared the military. Military expenditures rose 39 percent in real terms between 1980 and 1985.[73] Summoning Palmerston's tactics 150 years earlier, the Reagan Doctrine armed rebels against Soviet-friendly regimes such as Afghanistan, Nicaragua, and Angola under the banner of democracy. The strategy, which avoided direct confrontation, sought to undermine the weakening Soviet Union, whose dissolution shortly afterward removed a significant obstacle to American investment abroad.

In a reversal of the budget policy of the Eisenhower administration, the Reagan Treasury attempted to offset tax cuts and military expenditures with reduced social spending. Discretionary grant programs, implemented by the Johnson administration, were cut by 45 percent while overall social outlays fell 10 percent.[74] Whereas unemployment insurance covered 80 percent of those without jobs in the early 1970s recession, it only covered 25 percent in 1984.[75] Regulatory agencies also became a convenient target for spending cuts. The EPA's budget, for example, was reduced by 35 percent.[76]

Nowhere was the power to withhold regulation more evident than in White House efforts to weaken unions. The backlog of cases against employer violations of the National Labor Relations Act grew from four hundred to one thousand seven hundred cases between 1980 and 1984.[77] At the same time, the proportion of dismissed suits against employers for unfair labor practices grew from 16 to 48 percent.[78] The most successful action against unions, however, was arguably a symbolic one when, in 1981, Reagan banned thirteen thousand striking air traffic controllers from government employment.

## A New Liberal Era

The actions carrying the most weight came from the Federal Reserve. With tacit acceptance from the White House, the central bank maintained an interest rate as high as 20 percent, which had increased from 11 percent since Volcker became Chairman. Rate hikes had their intended effect: unemployment rose to a post-Depression high of 11 percent by the end of 1982, while inflation collapsed from 10 to 5 percent. The blunt instrument of interest rates had proven so effective that Volcker's measures rapidly unwound speculation in foreign currencies and US officials had to intervene, under the 1985 Plaza Accord, to stop dollar appreciation.

Under the still new experiment of a monetary standard unfettered by gold, many perceived successful disinflation as an achievement. No consensus existed on what inflation rate was appropriate, except that the Federal Reserve could utilize interest rates to ensure price stability. But a curious development cast doubt on the anti-Keynesians. High unemployment, above 7 percent, persisted until 1987 even though growth had recovered. In the shadow of the stagflationary 1970s, economists rationalized this phenomenon as the result of interest rates that were too high or a high natural rate of unemployment. Under the first solution, the Federal Reserve needed only to induce further money supply growth by lowering interest rates. Under the second, the government needed to do more—or rather "less"—to improve the private sector's confidence (and willingness to supply jobs).

While price stability exacted a significant toll on employment, it was a boon to holders of dollar-denominated financial assets. Interest rates on government obligations began a long march downward while stock market valuations began a long trajectory in the opposite direction. These trends would parallel their real economy counterparts in falling inflation, rising profits, increasing demand deficiency, and growing wealth disparity.

By stabilizing long-term interest rates, disinflation was conducive to the expansion of financial activity. New securities, most notably so-called "junk bonds" with high yields, proliferated. The conglomerate boom of the 1960s returned in friendlier political circumstances under the new vessel of "private equity." With the help of greater investor appetite for debt, such entities aimed at increasingly larger targets (as famously recounted in *Barbarians at the Gate)*. In general, lending expanded as creditors felt more certain about inflation and as more individuals substituted debt for lost purchasing power. Total private credit as a share of GDP, which had increased by less than 20 percent of GDP since 1960, began to accelerate in 1981 and would almost double over the next twenty years.[79]

At the end of the 1980s, the first meaningful bout of banking instability since the Depression took place: the Savings and Loan Crisis. Resembling the country bank failures that followed resumed convertibility in 1820s England, the crisis saw bankruptcies in thousands of regional lenders. With reduced Keynesian demand buffers, its effects were felt more keenly.

Reagan-era economic struggles, however, did not rekindle faith in Keynesianism. But twelve years out of power had provided the Democrats sufficient time to assemble a competitive investor coalition. Like the British Cobdenite Liberals who opposed Palmerston's aggression in the nineteenth century, and the Dutch States Party supporters of peace with Spain in the seventeenth century, influential segments of multinational business grew critical of Reagan's foreign policy, which had antagonized friendly sections of Europe and Latin America. Groups such as the "Inter-American Dialogue," some of which looked to Eastern Europe for future business, felt that the Reagan Doctrine undermined détente and also wanted to protect Latin American and the Caribbean from involvement in tensions between the superpowers.[80]

But no group proved more indispensable to the Democratic revival than new interests within the financial sector. Members of the insurance industry, the emergent hedge fund sector, and the immensely profitable proprietary investment arms of investment banks—most notably soon-to-be Treasury Secretary Robert Rubin—grew disenchanted with Reagan's fiscal deficits.[81] In their view, deficits were behind the high interest rates crippling foreign economies and creating volatility in long-term bond markets, and were therefore bad for business.[82]

At the same time, divisions between the free trade and protectionist wings of the Republican Party surfaced like those within the Tory Party during the Corn Law debates. Conservative businessman Ross Perot ran on a third-party platform opposing the North American Free Trade Agreement and calling for stricter immigration policies.[83] Perot obtained the largest vote for a third-party candidate since 1912. Though he lost the election, his coalition would re-emerge with force twenty-four years later, solidifying its parallels with Disraeli's Tories after the 1860s.

Though Democrats won the 1992 election, the line dividing the economic policies of the two parties became thinner. Officials under the Clinton administration pursued "Rubinomics" —a policy of fiscal consolidation and strong sensitivity to the negative effects of government policy on market confidence. Influenced by the prevailing economic zeitgeist, the Clinton Treasury subscribed to the classical-school idea that the public and private sectors competed for savings. Reduced government indebtedness would drive interest rates lower and, in turn, reduce borrowing costs for the more efficient private sector. Informed by the contemporary crises in less-developed countries, they also believed that higher government debt could provoke "bond vigilantes" into demanding punitively higher interest rates.

In reality, Clinton-era fiscal policy was intended to appease one vigilante in particular: Federal Reserve Chairman Alan Greenspan. Serving as chair from 1987 to 2006, Greenspan was a "lifelong libertarian Republican" who believed in the "Reagan Revolution against government interference in the economy."[84] His tenure at the Federal Reserve imposed a fetter on fiscal policy: any attempt to increase welfare spending could prompt Greenspan to raise interest rates in disapproval. Clinton officials thus pursued policies that would coax Greenspan into lowering rates, especially as inflation trended down.

Of course, the economic beliefs of Greenspan and the Clinton Treasury strongly overlapped. Their free-market dogma conveniently appealed to a private sector that wielded increasing political influence. Between 1974 and 1990, the average cost of a winning Congressional campaign had grown from $60,000 to $400,000. It had subsequently tripled to $1.2 million by 2006.[85] Political contributions from the financial sector, in particular, quadrupled between 1990 and 2006, while those from the securities and investment industry increased six-fold.[86]

Unsurprisingly, the 1990s and early 2000s saw considerable bipartisan deregulation of the financial sector. The Riegle-Neal Act of 1994 enabled further consolidation of the banking sector by repealing restrictions on interstate banking.[87] Following financial panic in 1998, the Graham-Leach-Bliley Act created a new category of financial holding companies that could participate in a broad range of activities, thus giving rise to so-called megabanks.[88] Finally, in 1999, the Clinton Treasury, together with Greenspan, produced the "Over-the-Counter Derivatives Markets and Commodity Exchange Act," which exempted many new securities from federal regulation.[89] Authorities, in essence, enabled financial entities to regulate themselves.

Whereas the financial sector's share of domestic corporate profits had been no more than 16 percent in 1985, it had reached 41 percent by the 2000s.[90] The combination of deregulation and market expansion had made a vast array of rent streams available to financial institutions. Like investors in the Victorian-era "Finance Company" or the earlier Dutch partnerships, stakeholders in megabanks placed excessive faith in the power of diversification to reduce risk. By adding leverage to their myriad of investments—as much as thirty-three times underlying capital—they were able to generate outsized profits, at least while animal spirits were in their favor.[91]

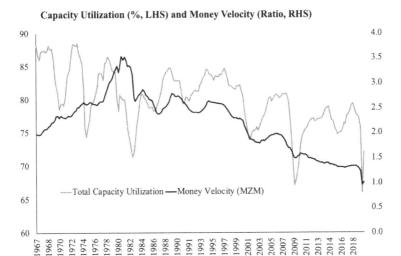

Capacity Utilization (%, LHS) and Money Velocity (Ratio, RHS)

*Figure 10.2*

**Figure 10.2** shows that capacity utilization and money velocity have incurred a protracted decline since the end of the New Deal and the beginning of post-1980 market liberalization. **Source**: Federal Reserve Bank of St. Louis, Velocity of MZM Money Stock [MZMV], retrieved from FRED, Federal Reserve Bank of St. Louis; Board of Governors of the Federal Reserve System (US), Capacity Utilization: Total Index [TCU], retrieved from FRED, Federal Reserve Bank of St. Louis.

## Building a Rentier Empire

Alongside financial liberalization, the free trade agreements of the 1990s marked a new epoch of global cooperation, unseen since the repeal of the Corn Laws. Already in motion since the GATT talks of the 1960s, trade openness accelerated after the collapse of the Soviet Union.[92] Following in the footsteps of the

Republic and Britain, the United States—through the Washington Consensus trio of the Treasury, IMF, and World Bank—convinced more countries to open their borders to American investment.

Appealing to revived classical-school trade theories, the Consensus argued that unregulated trade and financial flows would accelerate growth in the less-developed world. As evidenced by recurring foreign-exchange crises, however, such policies exposed countries to the vagaries of American speculators. Money could flow out as quickly as it flowed in, creating a destabilizing cycle of boom and bust. Often, market liberalization offered a means of self-enrichment to corrupt authorities. The latter could cheaply acquire privatized state assets or siphon away scarce dollars obtained through government debt issuance.

All the while, officials at the US Treasury, starting in the 1990s, embraced "a strong dollar." In their supply-determined view of the world, dollar strength reflected foreign confidence in the American economy.[93] This policy was a sharp reversal from the Reagan administration, which had caved to protectionist pressures to weaken the dollar. But dollar strength became less of a concern as American firms were free to seek the lowest costs anywhere in the world. The share of imports-to-GDP grew from 5 percent in 1970 to 10 percent by 1990, and a further 18 percent by 2008. Additionally, a substantial proportion of imports were intra-firm—almost half by 2014.[94]

Like France during the Dutch Golden Age and Germany during the Victorian period, China was able to take advantage of the re-location of foreign production, initially from its industrialized Asian neighbors, to fuel its development. In stark contrast to the Soviet model, it grew through cooperation with the West via selective adoption of market institutions. Centralized authority allowed the Chinese government to offer a large pool of inexpensive labor in the service of foreign textile, apparel, and toy manufacturers in the 1980s and 1990s, and then into higher value-added electronics assembly.[95] By 2002, foreign-owned firms accounted for more than 85 percent of China's "high-tech" exports.[96] But dollar earnings from its labor services funded domestic investment and, eventually, a home-grown technology industry.

Between 1990 and 2008, US imports from China increased twentyfold. Over this period, the US current account deficit widened from a surplus of 0.7 percent of GDP to a deficit of −5 percent. At the same time, China, through its current account surpluses, managed to accumulate almost $500 billion dollars in treasuries. Many economists, most notably new Federal Reserve Chairman Ben Bernanke, began to draw a causal link between the two phenomena in the early 2000s. Applying the "loanable funds" paradigm to the international economy, they argued that savings in China and other Asian economies were funding America's trade deficit with the outside world. They also pointed to the parallel decline in long-term interest rates, which had fallen from 16 percent (ten-year) to 4 percent since the 1980s. Thus, in their view, the United States had become vulnerable to a withdrawal of foreign savings.

But such arguments succumbed to the fallacious assumption that the United States was like any other economy. Instead, the trade deficit was the inevitable outcome of a unique developmental trajectory that saw America transition from domestic production to increased foreign investment—the same path pursued by the Dutch and British at the apex of their hegemony. As global exchange became more open, US firms had become less constrained by domestically available factors of production.

Thus, like its predecessors, America was able to employ its technical advantages to build a global investment empire. In contrast to other countries with external deficits, America's international accounts exhibited certain paradoxical features. Accumulated current account deficits caused the US net international investment position—foreign assets minus foreign liabilities—to decline from a balanced position in 1990 to −27 percent of GDP by 2008, and then to −60 percent by

2019.[97] And yet, net foreign income over these respective periods grew from 0.5 to 0.8 to 1.1 percent of GDP. Despite issuing more liabilities to foreigners over time, the United States continued to earn more from them than it paid out.

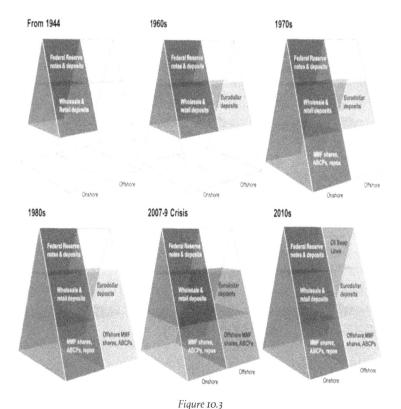

*Figure 10.3*

**Figure 10.3** illustrates financialization in the modern United States and the internationalization of the dollar (in the "offshore" segment). Both processes signaled developmental maturity for the American economy. The terms MMF and ABCP refer to money market funds and asset-backed commercial paper. Additionally, C6 swap lines refer to swap agreements among the six major central banks ensuring foreign access to U.S. dollars. **Source of image**: Steffen Murau, Joe Rini, and Armin Haas, "The Evolution of the Offshore US-Dollar System: Past, Present and Four Possible Futures," *Journal of Institutional Economics* 16, no. 6 (2020): 767–83.

While American ownership of foreign assets had doubled from 20 percent of GDP in 1976 to 40 percent in 1990, it tripled between 1990 and 2008. A persistent decline in interest rates indeed contributed to outsized US earnings on foreign investment. But contrary to the "savings glut" idea, interest rates did not decline because foreign savings increased. Instead, foreign savings increased because American investment poured outward. What caused interest rates to fall was the same reason the US was able to earn persistent and outsized returns on its foreign holdings: the market power of American firms. As profit margins reached record levels and wealth concentrated in narrower hands, so too did hoarding in financial assets.[98] A commensurate decline in money velocity and capacity utilization, already underway since the end of the New Deal, was also evident.

That US ownership of foreign assets exploded alongside more general financialization is no coincidence. By the 2000s, money had become its own business. And as in Britain in 1866 and the Dutch Republic in the mid-seventeenth century, this phase of development culminated in crisis.

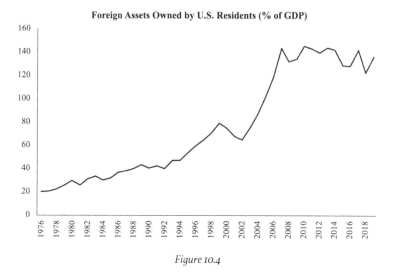

*Figure 10.4*

**Figure 10.4** shows how American technological primacy coincided with increased investment abroad and the acquisition of claims on the foreign sector. **Sources:** U.S. Bureau of Economic Analysis, U.S. Assets [IIPUSASSA], retrieved from FRED, Federal Reserve Bank of St. Louis.

---

## The End of Trade Cooperation

As some have observed, the crisis of 2008 did not lead to any fundamental change in economic policy. The architects of the Washington Consensus returned under a new Democratic administration—a development that should not have seemed so surprising at the time given the financial sector's early campaign donations to the new president.[99] Though many at the time compared the crisis to the Great Depression, this analogy, as should now be evident, was a poor one. Yet authorities had hailed the lessons they had learned from the 1930s, especially after monetary easing provided sufficient time for the technology sector to lead a new investment cycle.

Nevertheless, precarity in the broader population had become difficult to ignore. While post-1980 business cycles oversaw periods of low unemployment, employment alone indicated little about standards of living. Greenspan himself admitted that greater insecurity accompanied the robust employment market of the 1990s.[100] Alongside stagnant wage growth, Americans faced rising costs of living associated with debt and healthcare expenses.[101] The latter amounted to a modern-day "poll tax," increasing annually without any improvement in efficacy.[102]

Life expectancy for large segments of the population had regressed. Those worst affected were the so-called Rust Belt states, which uncoincidentally had possessed seven of the ten most unionized states in 1974.[103] Mortality rates in these areas had bucked declines elsewhere in the developed world as cases of "diseases of despair" increased after the 1990s.[104] As was the case in the Republic and Britain, America's undisputed hegemony did not coincide with improved living standards for all citizens.

Like the Orangists after 1670 and the Tories after 1870, Republicans successfully channeled the grievances of the Rust Belt states in 2016. Echoing Disraeli's attack on cosmopolitanism, Donald Trump, who had earlier attempted a run with Perot's Reform Party, blamed "globalists" for decimating American manufacturing and empowering China. And as Joseph Chamberlain had done more than a century earlier, Trump exhumed the instrument of tariffs.

But hardly any protectionist investor bloc remained in 2016. Instead, a coalition of investors naturally opposed to Democratic policies stood behind Trump.[105] Among these were Wall Street, private equity, and high-frequency trading interests who sought to undermine post-crisis financial regulation, as well as Democratic proposals to close the carried-interest loophole and proposals to tax trading. Support also came from energy interests who had opposed the environmental protections of the 2016 Paris Peace Agreement. Prominent members of the private sector indeed filled the early cabinet and oversaw a massive reduction in corporate taxes.

Notable among Trump's backers were elements in the technology sector who profited from government security contracts.[106] Unsurprisingly, his administration saw technology companies and the government become more proximate. Palantir Technologies, for example, provided software that helped Immigration and Customs Enforcement (ICE) conduct raids on immigrants. With its $10 billion JEDI project, the Department of Defense sought technological upgrades for "increasing the lethality of [the] department."[107] Likewise, new private-sector groups such as the Defense Innovation Board sought to find military applications for Silicon Valley technology.[108] Its founder, the former CEO of Google, warned that the industry could not outcompete China without government support.[109] Such opinions likely informed global bans the Trump White House placed on sales of semiconductor chips to Chinese firms. These restrictions sought to impede the Chinese tech sector's ability to compete against US rivals in new custom artificial intelligence chips.[110]

Increasing animosity between the US and China is being caused, in no small part, by failing global exchange. After peaking in 2008, global trade volumes relative to GDP have stagnated.[111] The slowdown in trade has weighed on China's economy, which is now, to a considerable extent, driven by an insatiable demand for property.[112] China's property boom stems from a rise in inequality parallel to that of the United States. The deliberate restriction of vehicles for savings drives hoarding in real estate. As anti-China rhetoric provides a convenient distraction from inequities in the United States, it does so equally in a country where bureaucrats have accumulated sizable fortunes.[113]

Amid languishing growth, the state in China looks to reassert itself, not unlike France during the Fronde and Germany during the Kulturkampf.[114] Anti-corruption initiatives offer a pretext for the re-centralization of authority.

Economic disparities between the coast—favored by market reformers—and inner regions, also offer an excuse for interventionism.[115]

The failure of cooperation risks the renewed ascendance of the cult of the nation, not only in the world's foremost powers but in every corner of the globe. With the global market disappointing the hopes of the many for progress, the appeal of centralizing forces within will only grow stronger. What lies ahead is not unfamiliar.

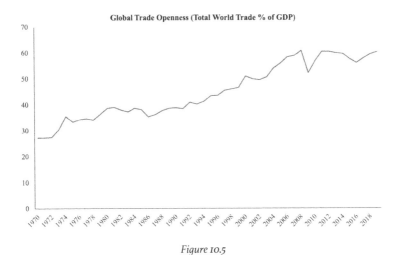

*Figure 10.5*

**Figure 10.5** indicates that trade openness, as represented by total world exports to GDP, peaked in 2008. **Source**: World Bank. https://data.worldbank.org/indicator/NE.TRD.GNFS.ZS

# 11

# CONCLUSION

T he historical pattern continues before our eyes. As trade cooperation diminishes, calls for a more assertive state abound. As this book has shown, however, the state has always had an active role in economic organization. So-called eras of laissez-faire or free markets were no exception. What matters is how investor blocs choose to direct state intervention. Since the Reagan Revolution, the government of the United States has prioritized securing market institutions at home and abroad. Free trade, as in its Dutch and British incarnations, did not arise on its own. It required the state to both establish and maintain the foundation on which it rested.

Priorities now seem to be shifting back toward state support for investment through increased application of new technology toward military ends. Particularly in semiconductor fabrication, which may be the bleeding edge of innovation in more than one sense, military use provides a convenient subsidy for the sheer scale of projected costs.[1] Reminiscent of the long-distance trades in the late seventeenth century and steel in the second half of the nineteenth century, the technology sector's rapid growth over the past decade may be the final catalyst for the end of the Pax Americana. A sector that has historically depended on government subsidies will require them even more so in a world of demand deficiency. Yet as market organization fails, states may once again supply such aid in the form of militarism.

Meanwhile, England's other former colony, India—arguably the most unwieldy polyarchy in human history—embarks on a path of autarkic development not dissimilar to the path Britain and the United States followed. Its current government, like the Whigs and Republicans earlier, succeeded the failed neoliberal regime that had held power since the Emergency of the 1970s. Through the "Make in India" and "Self-Reliant India" campaigns, authorities have sought to bring manufacturing within the country and capture the economies of scale offered by its 1.3 billion citizens.

In India, too, the influence of investor blocs is apparent.[2] A recent *Financial Times* article proclaimed that the influence of India's "Rockefeller"—the energy billionaire Gautam Adani—reflected a concentration of corporate power.[3] The analogy, however, runs deeper than its authors likely intended. With falling costs and the government providing considerable support through power purchase agreements, renewable energy looks to replace imported fossil fuels and clear a lingering developmental bottleneck.[4] As the leading nations remain tied to old sources of energy, renewables in India may have the same role that coal had for England and oil for the United States. And fledgling exports of renewable power to neighbors in South Asia may only offer a glimpse of how the sector may alter the relative standing of the Indian economy.[5]

A similar phenomenon is evident in India's internet sector.[6] Reliance Industries, reminiscent of the railway robber barons, continues to monopolize the country's telecommunications infrastructure and is locked in a bitter dispute with the U.S-owned firms who dominate e-commerce. Recent bans on Chinese smartphone applications also represent an effort to foster home-grown substitutes.

This last example provides an ominous glimpse of the future. India's recent border disputes with China, with whom it has historically had less than amicable relations, overlap uncomfortably with increasing animosity between China and the United States. How this trio fits past patterns is not difficult to see.

## The Road to Catastrophe

The world cannot afford the possibility that these nations, or any other for that matter, will initiate a new epoch of conflict. But it is the very existence of states that has given rise to the cycle of the past five hundred years. Putting an end to it therefore seems all but impossible.

To prevent catastrophe, the states of the world will have to create peace preemptively. They must not only more strongly affirm comity as a global public good—a collective responsibility of all nations, not just one—but acknowledge the structural vulnerability that undermines it: the maldistribution of political and economic power, both within and between states.

Like similar periods in the past, the most recent era of cooperation has been a false one. It has rested on the tenuous footing of might rather than the stronger foundation of benevolence and goodwill. As was the case during the Thirty Years War and after the Napoleonic Era, force cleared the way for globalization. Look no further than the Middle East where "blowback" —the sordid legacy of such tactics—beckons perennial military engagement. One can hardly call the deliberate application of state power to secure markets on behalf of a narrow set of interests "free trade."

Adam Smith would have recoiled at the tactics governments have used to impose market institutions in modern times as equally as he would have railed at the naval aggression employed by Liberals like Palmerston. His observations in *The Wealth of Nations* about the commercial relationship between the Dutch Republic and its peripheries are revealing:

The merchants, artificers, and manufacturers of those mercantile states which, like Holland and Hamburg, consist chiefly of this unproductive class, are in the same manner maintained and employed altogether at the expense of the proprietors and cultivators of land. The only difference is, that those proprietors and cultivators are, the greater part of them, placed at a most inconvenient distance from the merchants, artificers, and manufacturers whom they supply with the materials of their work and the fund of their subsistences—the inhabitants of other countries and the subjects of other governments.[7]

The peculiarities of economic arrangements are less relevant than the political structures behind them. So long as they reflect the desires of some privileged interest, institutions will be subject to decay. Politics may forever remain "the shadow cast on society by big business," as John Dewey put it.[8] A world in which all have equal voice likely represents a hopeful utopia. As Smith said, "Not only the prejudices of the public, but what is much more unconquerable, the private interests of many individuals, irresistibly oppose it."[9] Avoiding a renewed phase of conflict is in the interest of all. Yet now, a growing number, as at similar junctures in the past, associate cooperation with immiseration rather than improvement.

Like the Republic after the 1650s and Britain after the late 1860s, the US has succumbed to stagnation since 2008. Year after year, authorities have revised down specious projections of so-called potential GDP while the economy's actual performance has fallen short of even these estimates.[10] For the American worker, whose real wage has hardly changed over the last forty years, stagnation has been a fact of life for a much longer period.

Many in the United States blame trade and unfair economic practices by China to support its manufacturing sector for the present stagnation, but the true source of present stagnation is monetary in nature. The past forty years of globalization have been an encore of what occurred during Dutch and British hegemony: financial wealth concentrating in the hands of a few. What reflects an "imbalance" is not the US trade deficit, but the extraordinary invisible earnings American investors draw from profits and interest on investments abroad. And, of course, one cannot ignore the claims the latter hold on fellow citizens in the form of mortgages, student loans, and medical debt.

Financial hoarding has by no means been exclusive to American investors. Their counterparts in Japan, Germany, the United Kingdom, and Switzerland have also accumulated a sizable portion of global financial assets. The same is true for China and the less-developed countries, where select interests have taken to hoarding in global property.

Indeed, those who benefited from the supposed free trade of the past forty years were not monolithic states pursuing a national interest—a fictitious entity—but the governing few of each country who cooperated to impose markets on the whole of society from the top down. It should not be so surprising, then, that markets instituted in such a manner offer the few a means to extract rents from the many. The result is that the global economy is now succumbing to demand deficiency, which will persist so long as existing—and pervasive—channels for rent-seeking remain intact. Under present conditions, individuals will struggle to pay their debts, find adequate employment, and experience material progress, thus foreshortening demand. More worryingly, whole populations in the less-developed countries will be unable to improve their circumstances.

The IMF and World Bank have overlooked this last consideration. Countries do not grow in a vacuum, yet these multilateral organizations place great faith in unilateral policy. They insufficiently appreciate that, in a global market society, the less-developed nations are patients on life support and depend on external demand for survival. But as global demand weakens, the patient's risk of hypoxia rises. In conditions of weak external demand, such countries will find it nearly impossible to acquire sufficient foreign exchange to service debts and improve their relative technological standing.

Argentina's most recent experience is instructive. The election of a market-friendly government, combined with improved American risk appetite for emerging markets, led to a deluge of speculative finance into the country. Once animal spirits retreated, however, the woeful prospects of Argentina's export sector became apparent. Pressures on the exchange rate became intolerable, and it received the largest IMF loan in history. But the loan preconditions placed too much faith on the potential of structural reforms—fiscal consolidation and labor legislation—to act as a magic elixir on Argentina's ability to sustainably generate foreign exchange. Pressures on the exchange rate persisted, and the ratio of foreign debt liabilities to export receipts reached 250 percent by 2020—one of the worst among all countries.

The new government has restructured its foreign liabilities and plans to use the resultant fiscal space to stimulate domestic demand. But Argentina's ability to pursue such policy is highly constrained by its relative economic standing. Fiscal policy will only hasten monetary flight to dollars and exacerbate inflationary pressures as the country remains a prisoner of anemic external demand.

An aging population, through lower import demand, at least partly mitigates its economic troubles. More disturbing are similar predicaments in countries with more sizable, younger, and growing populations. Such demographic trends place a considerable strain on foreign exchange reserves in countries such as Nigeria, Pakistan, Iraq, and Egypt. Yet like Argentina, they suffer from scarce dollars, high interest rates, and low export-to-output ratios. Absent reliable paths to development, political stability in these nations will remain tenuous, especially as demand deficiency continues to limit their economic autonomy. Potential instability, in turn, risks creating dangerous new pretexts for rivalry among the "great powers."

The economic trends in these countries diverge sharply from trends in the more developed nations with aging populations. As is widely known, Japan offers the most salient example, with its population projected to shrink as much as 15 percent by 2040.[11] China's and Germany's populations are also likely to contract over the same period, while those of the United States and the United Kingdom will have more modest growth relative to the past.

These five countries, however, hold an inordinate share—72 percent—of global wealth.[12] And so long as present political arrangements remain in place, they will continue to do so. But the prospect of peace will also slip further away as hoarding in these rentier economies deters progress in the rest of the world.

## Establishing Sustainable Cooperation

The solutions for creating true and lasting cooperation are too complex to fit the confines of this or any other book. Nor can "expert judgment," forever prone to folly, substitute for the necessary devolution of authority. Technocratic panaceas cannot fix an institutional dilemma—the need to limit the influence of privileged interests—that has beleaguered human society since the recorded past. Nevertheless, I will attempt to outline the minimum economic adjustments necessary to establish some degree of trust in international exchange and prevent conflict.

The fundamental principle that all nations must embrace is the flexible adjustment of economic claims. Such adjustment entails alleviating individuals from "unfreedoms" imposed by markets.[13] These not only include burdensome debts but the deprivation of necessities that markets struggle to provide, such as adequate housing, healthcare, education, and environmental conditions. Society must have the ability to collectively reassign claims to these items. By ruling out such collective initiatives, markets only give individuals the freedom to "explore the box in which [they] are confined," to borrow a phrase from Charles Lindblom.[14]

When drafting his plan for what became the IMF, Keynes identified the fact that the rigid monetary foundations underlying markets produce adverse effects. Markets have an inherent deflationary bias as money becomes too reliable an outlet for hoarding. As Keynes put it, "The social strain of adjustment downwards," which characterizes deflation, "is much greater than that of an adjustment upwards" since "the process of adjustment is compulsory for the debtor and voluntary for the creditor."[15] Keynes was not unaware of how the rise and fall of rigid monetary arrangements has impacted societal progress. He alluded to "the vast development of trade and prosperity throughout the Mediterranean countries and beyond which followed the dispersal of the temple hoards of Persia by Alexander the Great."[16]

To sustain demand, the advanced countries—the United States, China, Germany, and Japan at least—will have to undertake coordinated efforts to combat hoarding in non-produced financial assets.[17] A means of doing so, as a former chief economist of the IMF has suggested, is to raise inflation targets, perhaps to a window of 3 to 6 percent.[18] As the persistence of disinflation demonstrates, however, present policies cannot accomplish this. Without targeting distribution, they will remain ineffective, and society will continue to underwrite monetary claims far too cheaply.

Global fiscal-monetary policy should then seek the objective of raising minimum incomes. Such an approach goes beyond the oft-touted universal basic income, which often masquerades as an attempt to abolish welfare programs. In advanced countries, income support should be tied to the inflation target and tuned appropriately. Several implementations already abound, ranging from a "negative income tax" to a "social dividend" from central bank asset holdings.[19]

Inflation-targeted redistributive policy in the financial centers would, in turn, restore conditions amenable to the progress of peripheral nations. But further reforms to the international economic architecture are needed to prevent exploitation arising from relative developmental disparities. First, a system of global minimum wage rules must set a floor on minimum wages across countries.[20] Not only would this improve the adequacy of living standards—it would also buttress demand. And, of course, global labor rules would prevent some economies from taking advantage of demand management in others (which decimated American manufacturing after the 1950s). Second, although higher inflation targets in the center economies should improve reserve adequacy on the peripheral ones, the IMF should have the ability to create special drawing rights (SDRs)—effectively its own money—and exchange them for reserve currencies. It should also have the means to adjust the supply of SDRs as necessary to support purchasing power in the developing nations. Third, countries must coordinate efforts to tax destabilizing financial outflows (and inflows). Such flows impose severe constraints on economic autonomy by making foreign-exchange scarce and enabling predatory finance. Fourth, they must devise new rules to penalize countries offering havens for tax avoidance or illicit wealth.

Finally, stronger multilateral cooperation on immigration flows is imperative. As mentioned, existing demographic imbalances are unsustainable, and countries must collectively recognize geographic mobility as a right. Such action will become more pertinent with time as environmental change renders parts of the world uninhabitable.

To reiterate, the policies outlined above will not substitute for the necessary expansion of political participation. They merely acknowledge the bitter lesson of similar eras in the past. As Karl Polanyi observed, "To allow the market mechanism to be the sole director of the fate of human beings and their natural environment, indeed, even of the amount and use of purchasing power, would result in the demolition of society."[21]

That modern times remain captive to the forces of the past

is a sobering indictment of our present conception of democracy. Markets and political franchise still leave consequential decisions well out of the hands of ordinary individuals. Sustainable cooperation, which is now a matter of humanity's survival, requires participation to extend to greater domains of life.

## From Polyarchy to Democracy

For almost half a century, market fundamentalists have employed a selective reading of Adam Smith to justify such a role for the market mechanism. As I noted in the introduction, Smith was by no means oblivious to the hold investors have over government. Furthermore, those who peddle mere individual self-interest as the only or essential requirement for a prosperous society have omitted a critical precondition set by Smith: justice.[22] As he argued in *The Theory of Moral Sentiments*,

> Beneficence... is less essential to the existence of society than justice. Society may subsist, though not in the most comfortable state, without beneficence; but the prevalence of injustice must utterly destroy it.[23]

In his eyes, justice did not come from the state, which provided an "imperfect remedy," but from mutual trust among citizens.[24] Such trust, however, depends on the outcomes a society produces for individuals; it strengthens or frays accordingly.

The moral sentiment of justice served as a foundation for the ideas in *The Wealth of Nations*. Even in the latter work, Smith claims, "The establishment of perfect justice, of perfect liberty, and of perfect equality is the very simple secret which most effectually secures the highest degree of prosperity."[25] This quote, in fact, immediately precedes his observations that Dutch merchants prospered at the expense of the less-developed nations that supplied them. One can infer then that

Smith believed that equality, justice, and liberty are owed not just to one's fellow citizens. They are also owed to members of other societies, if cooperation is to rest on anything but the most tenuous footing.

Since the beginning of the Dutch Republic, polyarchy has seen great progress. Power, over the past five hundred years, has diffused across wider segments of society. More importantly, individual rights have been strengthened, albeit through a painful and irregular process. This trend will likely continue, but only if humans can survive another epoch of conflict—a vital qualification at our present juncture.

# NOTES

## 1. Introduction

1. Simon Kuznets seems to have originated this anecdote.
2. Stefan Avdjiev, Robert N. McCauley, and Hyun Song Shin, "Breaking Free of the Triple Coincidence in International Finance," *BIS Working Papers*, 524 (October 2015).
3. Karl Polanyi, *The Great Transformation: The Political and Economic Origins of Our Time* (1944; repr., Boston: Beacon Press, 2001), 216.
4. The current account, here, means the net trade balance plus the net balance of services and the net balance of income from investments abroad.
5. P. J. Cain and A. G. Hopkins, *British Imperialism: 1688–2015* (New York: Routledge, 2016), 176.
6. Violet Barbour, *Capitalism in Amsterdam in the 17th Century* (Ann Arbour: University of Michigan Press, 1963), 85.
7. Simon Schama, *The Embarrassment of Riches: An Interpretation of Dutch Culture in the Golden Age* (Berkeley: University of California Press, 1988), 259.
8. Schama, *Embarrassment of Riches*, 259.
9. See Chapter 5.
10. A long list of such individuals includes List, Kindleberger, Wallerstein, Arrighi, Braudel, and Seligman.; The Dutch were likely not the first to achieve primacy, but missing data makes the formation of the Dutch Republic in the late sixteenth century the most convenient starting point for this book.
11. Adam Smith, *An Inquiry into the Nature and Cause of the Wealth of Nations*, ed. Edwin Cannan, introd. Max Lerner (New York: Modern Library, 1937), lvii.
12. Katharina Pistor, *The Code of Capital: How the Law Creates Wealth and Inequality* (Princeton: Princeton University Press, 2019), 9.
13. Distribution considers how economic output accrues to various members of society. It becomes an important consideration in any economic framework that introduces socioeconomic heterogeneity.
14. Comparative advantage represents a country's ability to produce a good or service at a lower opportunity cost than other nations.
15. Monopsony is the condition in which a market has a single buyer, who, as a result, is able to wield disproportionate bargaining power.
16. Peter Lindert and Jeffrey Williamson, "Unequal Gains: American Growth and Inequality since 1700," *VoxEU*, June 16, 2016, https://voxeu.org/article/american-growth-and-inequality-1700; D. L. Phillips, *Well-Being in Amsterdam's Golden Age* (Amsterdam: Amsterdam University Press, 2008),

44; Thomas Piketty, *Capital in the Twenty-First Century*, trans. Arthur Goldhammer (Cambridge, MA: Harvard University Press, 2014); L. Soltow and J. L. van Zanden, *Income and Wealth Inequality in the Netherlands, 16th–20th Century* (Amsterdam: Het Spinhuis, 1998), 38–41; Jan Luiten Van Zanden, "Tracing the Beginning of the Kuznets Curve: Western Europe during the Early Modern Period," *Economic History Review*, 48, no. 4 (1995): 643–64.

17. The term was coined by the political scientist Robert Dahl.

18. Hyman Minsky, *Stabilizing an Unstable Economy* (New York: McGraw-Hill, 2008), 158.

19. C. E. Lindblom, *Politics and Markets: The World's Political Economic Systems* (New York: Basic Books, 1977).

20. Elizabeth Clare Edwards, "Amsterdam and William III: The Role of Influence, Interest and Patronage on Policy-Making in the Dutch Republic, 1672–1684" (PhD diss., University of London, 1998), 168–69.

21. Friederich List, *The National System of Political Economy*, trans. Sampson S. Lloyd (London: Longmans, Green, 1909), 33.

22. List, *The National System*, 34.

23. Lindblom, *Politics and Markets*, 18.

24. C. Harline, *Pamphlets, Printing, and Political Culture in the Early Dutch Republic* (Dodrecht: Nijhoff, 1987), 115.

25. Smith, *The Wealth of Nations*, bk. 4, ch. 2, 437.

26. A work extensively cited in this book is Thomas Ferguson, *Golden Rule: The Investment Theory of Party Competition and the Logic of Money-Driven Political Systems* (Chicago: University of Chicago Press, 1995).

27. James Curran and Jean Seaton, *Power without Responsibility: Press, Broadcasting and the Internet in Britain* (London: Routledge, 2010), 35.

28. Jonathan Israel, *Empires and Entrepots: The Dutch, the Spanish Monarchy and the Jews, 1585–1713* (London: Bloomsbury, 1990), 82.

29. Thomas Ferguson, "From Normalcy to New Deal: Industrial Structure, Party Competition, and American Public Policy in the Great Depression," *International Organization* (1984): 41–94.

30. Jan de Vries and Ad van der Woude, *The First Modern Economy: Success, Failure, and Perseverance of the Dutch Economy, 1500–1815* (Cambridge: Cambridge University Press, 2010), 352–56.

31. Polanyi, *Great Transformation, 257.*

32. Randolf G. S. Cooper, *The Anglo-Maratha Campaigns and the Contest for India: The Struggle for Control of the South Asian Military Economy* (Cambridge: Cambridge University Press, 2003), 31; Yoko Matsui, "Japanese-Dutch Relations in the Tokugawa Period," *Transactions of the Japan Academy* 72, special issue (2018): 139–54.

33. Barbour, *Capitalism in Amsterdam*, 88; Charles Wilson, *England's Apprenticeship 1605–1763* (London: Longmans, 1965), 168.

34. A. G. Hopkins, *American Empire: A Global History* (Princeton, NJ: Princeton University Press, 2019), 294.

35. The reason likely stems from path dependency and sequencing of development, with France maturing before England and Germany before the United States. See Chapter 5.

36. Jonathan Israel, *The Dutch Republic: Its Rise, Greatness, and Fall, 1477–1806* (New York: Oxford University Press, 1995), 971.
37. N. W. Posthumus, *Inquiry into the History of Prices in Holland* (Leiden: Brill, 1946), I:cxvi.
38. Oscar Gelderblom and Joost Jonker, "Public Finance and Economic Growth: The Case of Holland in the Seventeenth Century," *Journal of Economic History* 71, no. 1 (2011): 1–39.

## 2. Uncertainty, Distribution, and Politics

1. J. M. Keynes, "The General Theory of Employment," *Quarterly Journal of Economics* 51, no. 2 (1937): 209–23.
2. I will use the term "animal spirits" extensively to describe herd investor psychology that tends to waver between extreme of greed and panic; Charles Mackay, *Extraordinary Popular Delusions and the Madness of Crowds* (New York: Barnes & Noble Books, 2004), xviii.
3. Jan de Vries and Ad van der Woude, *The First Modern Economy: Success, Failure, and Perseverance of the Dutch Economy, 1500–1815* (Cambridge: Cambridge University Press, 2010), 301.
4. Elasticity is the degree to which an economic variable changes in response to another (typically price).
5. John Maynard Keynes, *The General Theory of Employment, Interest, and Money* (Cham: Palgrave Macmillan, 2018), ch. 17, 203.
6. Real investment means investment in physical assets as opposed to monetary or financial assets.
7. Michael McLeay, Amar Radia, and Ryland Thomas, "Money Creation in the Modern Economy," *Bank of England Quarterly Bulletin* (2014), Q1, https://www.bankofengland.co.uk/quarterly-bulletin/2014/q1/money-creation-in-the-modern-economy
8. In *Reconstructing Macroeconomics*, Lance Taylor defines the principle of effective demand as the assertion that "changes in the level of output are the means by which savings and investment are brought into equality, with investment being determined independently of potential savings flows."; Lance Taylor, *Reconstructing Macroeconomics: Structuralist Proposals and Critiques of the Mainstream* (Cambridge, Mass.; London: Harvard University Press, 2004), 10.
9. Keynes, *The General Theory*, ch. 13, 160.
10. Keynes, *The General Theory*, ch. 13, 160.
11. Risk aversion, in economics parlance, is the tendency of investors to flee to assets with more certain returns.
12. Equilibrium, here, means some natural resting point for the economy under which supply and demand are in balance in all markets.
13. Keynes, *The General Theory*, ch. 23, 318.
14. Robert B. Barsky and Lutz Kilian, "Do We Really Know That Oil Caused the Great Stagflation? A Monetary Alternative," *NBER Macroeconomics Annual* 16 (2001): 137–83; Michael Moffitt, *The World's Money* (New York: Simon and Schuster, 1983), 143.

15. Keynes, *The General Theory*, ch. 23, 319.
16. Andrea Finkelstein, *Harmony and the Balance: An Intellectual History of Seventeenth-Century English Economic Thought* (Ann Arbor: University of Michigan Press, 2003), 210-211.
17. Finkelstein, *Harmony and the Balance,* 210-211.
18. Christine Gerrard, "Poems on Politics" in *The Oxford Handbook of British Poetry, 1660-1800,* ed. Jack Lynch (Oxford: Oxford University Press, 2016), 295.
19. Ha-Joon Chang, *Kicking Away the Ladder: Development Strategy in Historical Perspective* (London: Anthem Press, 2002), 32; Erik S. Reinert, "Diminishing Returns and Economic Sustainability; the Dilemma of Resource-Based Economies under a Free Trade Regime," The Other Canon, 1996, http://othercanon.org/wp-content/uploads/2020/02/Diminishing-Returns-and-Economic-Sustainability-The-Dilemma-of-Resource-based-Economies-under-a-Free-Trade-Regime.pdf.
20. E. J. Hobsbawm, *Industry and Empire: From 1750 to the Present Day* (London: Penguin, 1990), 104–5.
21. Hobsbawm, *Industry and Empire*, 104–5.
22. Hobsbawm, *Industry and Empire*, 104–5.
23. Finkelstein, *Harmony and Balance*, 207.
24. Malcolm Sawyer, "Kalecki on Imperfect Competition, Inflation and Money," *Cambridge Journal of Economics* 25, no. 2 (2001): 245–61.
25. Sawyer, "Kalecki on Imperfect Competition."
26. Under Kalecki's framework, savings not only equal investment, but investment in turn equals the sum of gross profits and capitalist consumption (though capitalist consumption tended to be negligible in his view). Gross profits here can also include non-wage compensation such as bonuses.
27. Sawyer, "Kalecki on Imperfect Competition."
28. Michal Kalecki, *Collected Works of Michal Kalecki*, vol. 7, *Studies in Applied Economics 1940–1967; Miscellanea*, ed. Jerzy Osiatyński, trans. Chester Adam Kisiel (Oxford: Clarendon Press, 1997), 85.
29. Kalecki, *Collected Works*, 7:87.
30. The Keynesian (and Kaleckian) view rejects the idea that individual supply functions across goods can be combined into an independent economy-wide supply function.
31. Kalecki, *Collected Works*, 7:285–86.
32. Kalecki, *Collected Works*, 7:286.
33. Kalecki, *Collected Works*, 7:286.
34. See Chapter 10.
35. Perry Anderson, *English Questions* (London: Verso, 1992), 140; Tom Burns, "Organization and Social Order," (unpublished manuscript), ch. 25, Retrieved from http://www.sociology.ed.ac.uk/tomburns/manuscript.html.
36. Joan Robinson, "Keynes and Ricardo," *Journal of Post Keynesian Economics* 1, no. 1 (1978): 12–18.
37. Robinson, "Keynes and Ricardo."

## 3. Politics as Investment

1. See Chapter 10.
2. John Brooks, *The Go-Go Years* (New York: Weybright and Talley, 1973).
3. Priya Satia, *Empire of Guns: The Violent Making of the Industrial Revolution* (Stanford: Stanford University Press, 2018), Chapter 3.
4. Arie Arnon, *Monetary Theory from Hume and Smith to Wicksell: Money, Credit, and the Economy* (Cambridge: Cambridge University Press, 2011), 104.
5. Hyman P. Minsky, "Prices in a Capital-Using Capitalist Economy I" (1976), Hyman P. Minsky Archive, Paper 37, http://digitalcommons.bard.edu/hm_archive/37.
6. Hyman P. Minsky, *John Maynard Keynes* (New York; London: McGraw-Hill, 2008), 164.
7. Minsky, "Prices i."
8. Hyman P. Minsky, "Prices in a Capital Using Capitalist Economy II" (1992), Hyman P. Minsky Archive, 36, https://digitalcommons.bard.edu/hm_archive/36.
9. Charles E. Lindblom, "Market and Democracy—Obliquely," *PS: Political Science and Politics* 28, no. 4 (1995): 684–88.
10. Harline, *Pamphlets*, 212–13.
11. Marjolein 't Hart, *The Dutch Wars of Independence: Warfare and Commerce in the Netherlands 1570–1680* (New York: Routledge, 2014), 132.
12. Priya Satia, *Empire of Guns: The Violent Making of the Industrial Revolution* (Stanford: Stanford University Press, 2018), introduction.
13. Satia, *Empire of Guns*, ch. 1.
14. Satia, *Empire of Guns*, ch. 4.
15. Satia, *Empire of Guns*, ch. 4.
16. Satia, *Empire of Guns*, ch. 4.
17. See Chapter 10.
18. See Chapter 8.
19. Cain and Hopkins, *British Imperialism*, 343.
20. Minsky, "Prices i."
21. Minsky, "Prices i." Emphasis added.
22. R. Brenner, *Merchants and Revolution: Commercial Change, Political Conflict, and London's Overseas Traders, 1550–1653* (New York: Verso, 2003), 394.
23. Christopher Hill, *The Century of Revolution, 1603–1714* (New York: Norton, 1982), 241.
24. Jonathan Israel, *The Dutch Republic: Its Rise, Greatness, and Fall, 1477–1806* (Oxford; New York: Oxford University Press, 1995), 785–91.
25. Ferguson, *Golden Rule*, 22-37.
26. Ferguson, *Golden Rule*, 38.
27. Lindblom, *Politics and Markets*, 207.
28. Lindblom, *Politics and Markets*, 213.

# 4. Global Investment

1.  Lindblom, "Market and Democracy."
2.  See Chapter 10.
3.  Karsten Kohler, "Gross Capital Flows and the Balance-of-Payments: A Balance Sheet Perspective," Post Keynesian Economics Society Working Paper Series, October 2020, http://www.postkeynesian.net/downloads/working-papers/PKWP2019.pdf.
4.  Claudio Borio and Piti Disyatat, "Global Imbalances and the Financial Crisis: Link or No Link?" *BIS Working Papers* 346 (May 2011); Maurice Obstfeld, "Does the Current Account Still Matter?" *American Economic Review*, 102 (2012): 1–23.
5.  Robert N. McCauley and Michela Scatigna, "Foreign Exchange Trading in Emerging Currencies: More Financial, More Offshore," *BIS Quarterly Review* (March 2011).
6.  Gustavo Adler, Camila Casas, Luis Cubeddu, Gita Gopinath, Nan Li, Sergii Meleshchuk, Carolina Osorio-Buitron, Damien Puy, and Yannick Timmer, "Dominant Currencies and External Adjustment," *IMF Staff Discussion Note* (2020).
7.  International Monetary Fund, "Namibia: Financial System Stability Assessment," Washington, DC: IMF Publication Services, 2018, https://www.imf.org/en/Publications/CR/Issues/2018/03/15/Namibia-Financial-System-Stability-Assessment-45723.
8.  Perry Mehrling, "Financialization and Its Discontents," *Finance and Society*, 3 (2017): 1–10.
9.  Jeremy Grantham and Ben Inker, *GMO Quarterly Letter* (2017).
10. Albert H. Imlah, "British Balance of Payments and Export of Capital, 1816–1913," *Economic History Review*, 5 (1952): 208–39; de Vries and van der Woude, *The First Modern Economy*, 87, 683.
11. See Chapter 10.
12. Maurizio Habib, "The Exorbitant Privilege from a Global Perspective," *VoxEU*, March 29, 2010, https://voxeu.org/article/how-exorbitant-dollar-s-exorbitant-privilege.
13. De Vries and van der Woude, *The First Modern Economy*, 87.
14. Barbour, *Capitalism in Amsterdam*, 45–46.
15. Barbour, *Capitalism in Amsterdam*, 124.
16. Barbour, *Capitalism in Amsterdam*, 124.
17. Barbour, *Capitalism in Amsterdam*, 124.
18. Henry William Spiegel, *The Growth of Economic Thought* (Durham: Duke University Press, 1991), 100–4.
19. Finkelstein, *Harmony and the Balance*, 51.
20. Barbour, *Capitalism in Amsterdam*, 74.
21. Spiegel, *The Growth of Economic Thought*, 103.
22. Barbour, *Capitalism in Amsterdam*, 51.
23. Barbour, *Capitalism in Amsterdam*, 125.
24. Barbour, *Capitalism in Amsterdam*, 132–35.
25. Charles P. Kindleberger, "The Economic Crisis of 1619 to 1623," *Journal of Economic History* 51, no. 1 (1991): 149–75.

26. Martha White Paas and John Roger Paas, *The Kipper und Wipper Inflation, 1619–23: An Economic History with Contemporary German Broadsheets* (New Haven: Yale University Press, 2012), 146.

27. Kindleberger, "The Economic Crisis of 1619."

28. John McCusker, *Essays in the Economic History of the Atlantic World* (London: Routledge, 2005), 71.

29. Johannes Gerard Van Dillen, *History of the Principal Public Banks* (London: Cass, 1964), 117.

30. Barbour, *Capitalism in Amsterdam*, 123.

31. Imlah, "British Balance of Payments."

32. Imlah, "British Balance of Payments."

33. Imlah, "British Balance of Payments."

34. Stefan Altorfer, *History of Financial Disasters 1763–1995*, vol. 1 (London: Pickering and Chatto, 2006), 188; Sidney Homer, Richard Eugene Sylla, *A History of Interest Rates* (Hoboken: Wiley, 2005), 183; Larry Neal, "The Financial Crisis of 1825 and the Restructuring of the British Financial System," *Review-Federal Reserve Bank of Saint Louis*, 80 (1998), 53–76.

35. Edward Victor Morgan, *The Theory and Practice of Central Banking, 1797–1913* (New York: Kelley, 1966), 110–11.

36. Morgan, *Theory and Practice of Central Banking*, 110–11.

37. The discount rate is the interest-rate charged by a central bank on short-term loans to financial institutions.

38. Rudiger Dornbusch and Jacob A. Frenkel, "The Gold Standard and the Bank of England Crisis in 1847" in *A Retrospective on the Classical Gold Standard, 1821-1931*, ed. Michael D. Bordo and Anna J. Schwartz (Chicago: University of Chicago Press, 1984), 234; Peter Fearon and Derek Howard Aldcroft, *British Economic Fluctuations, 1790-1939* (London: Macmillan, 1972), 40-43

39. Ryland Thomas and Nicholas Dimsdale, "A Millennium of Macroeconomic Data," Bank of England, 2017, https://www.bankofengland.co.uk/statistics/research-datasets.

40. Xu Chenzi, "Reshaping Global Trade: The Immediate and Long-Run Effects of Bank Failures." Proceedings of Paris December 2020 Finance Meeting EUROFIDAI – ESSEC, October 13, 2020. https://ssrn.com/abstract=3710455.

41. Xu, "Reshaping."

42. S. G. Checkland, "The Birmingham Economists, 1815–1850," *Economic History Review* 1, no. 1 (1948): 1–19.

43. Checkland, "Birmingham."

44. Attwood's family had manufacturing investments in Birmingham.; Checkland, "Birmingham."

45. Checkland, "Birmingham."

46. Checkland, "Birmingham."

47. Cain and Hopkins, *British Imperialism*, 176.

48. Cain and Hopkins, *British Imperialism*, 176.

49. See Chapter 8.

50. Ralph Fendel and David Maurer, "Does European History Repeat Itself? Lessons from the Latin Monetary Union for the European Monetary Union," *Journal of Economic Integration* 30, no. 1 (2015): 93–120.
51. Thomas and Dimsdale, "A Millennium of Macroeconomic Data."

# 5. The Iron Chains of History

1. List, *The National System*, 201.
2. List, *The National System*, 201.
3. List, *The National System*, 29.
4. See, in particular, Immanuel Maurice Wallerstein, *The Modern World-System I* (Berkeley: University of California Press, 2011).
5. Charles P. Kindleberger, *World Economic Primacy, 1500 to 1900* (New York: Oxford University Press, 1996), 6.
6. Jonathan Anderson, "How to Think about Emerging Markets" (Emerging Advisors Group, 2017).
7. Karel Davids, *The Rise and Decline of Dutch Technological Leadership: Technology, Economy and Culture in the Netherlands, 1350–1800* (Boston: Brill, 2008), 208; de Vries and van der Woude, *The First Modern Economy*, 17–18.
8. Davids, *Dutch Technological Leadership*, 209–10.
9. Davids, *Dutch Technological Leadership*, 211.
10. Davids, *Dutch Technological Leadership*, 214.
11. Hill, *The Century of Revolution*, 13–15.
12. Davids, *Dutch Technological Leadership*, 285–87.
13. Davids, *Dutch Technological Leadership*, 323.
14. Iain Clarkson, *The Industrial Revolution: A Compendium* (Basingstoke, Hampshire: Macmillan, 1990), 4; Davids, *Dutch Technological Leadership*, 297.
15. Robert Ashton, *The Crown and the Money Market, 1602–1640* (Oxford: Clarendon Press, 1960), 4–5.
16. Barbour, *Capitalism in Amsterdam*,122.
17. Cleona Lewis with Karl T. Schlotterbeck, *America's Stake in International Investments* (Washington, DC: Brookings Institution, 1938), 17–18.
18. Lewis, *America's Stake*, 17–18.
19. Lewis, *America's Stake*, 11.
20. J. S. Mill, *Principles of Political Economy: With Some of Their Applications to Social Philosophy* (New York: Appleton, 1895), 538.
21. J. E. Stiglitz, B. C. Greenwald, P. Aghion, and K. J. Arrow, *Creating a Learning Society: A New Approach to Growth, Development, and Social Progress* (Columbia University Press, 2014), 4.
22. Stiglitz, *Creating a Learning Society*, 15.
23. Stiglitz, *Creating a Learning Society*, 232.
24. Stiglitz, *Creating a Learning Society*, 86–88.
25. Y. Suzuki, *Japan-Netherlands Trade 1600–1800: The Dutch East India Company and Beyond* (Kyoto: Kyoto University Press, 2012), 14.
26. Suzuki, *Japan-Netherlands Trade 1600–1800*, 20.
27. Suzuki, *Japan-Netherlands Trade 1600–1800*, 111–12.

28. Bank of Japan Currency Museum, "The History of Japanese Currency," https://www.imes.boj.or.jp/cm/english/history/content/#EarlyModern.
29. See Chang and Stiglitz as examples.
30. Anderson, "How to Think about Emerging Markets."
31. Barry Emanuel Supple, *Commercial Crisis and Change in England, 1600–1642* (Cambridge: Cambridge University Press, 1959), 50.
32. F. W. Taussig, *The Tariff History of the United States* (New York: Knickerbocker Press, 1931), 57.
33. Taussig, *The Tariff History of the United States*, 58.
34. Brenner, *Merchants and Revolution*, 203.
35. Taussig, *The Tariff History of the United States*, 169.
36. Wilson, *England's Apprenticeship*, 195.
37. Clarkson, *Industrial Revolution*, 6.
38. Victoria and Albert Museum, "Flintlock Pistol," http://collections.vam.ac.uk/item/O97426/flintlock-pistol-monlong-pierre; Satia, *Empire of Guns*, ch. 1.
39. Anderson, "How to Think about Emerging Markets."
40. Anderson, "How to Think about Emerging Markets."
41. Anderson, "How to Think about Emerging Markets."
42. Van der Wee in M. Teich, R. Porter, and B. Gustafsson, *The Industrial Revolution in National Context: Europe and the USA* (Cambridge: Cambridge University Press, 1996), 65.
43. Davids, *Dutch Technological Leadership*, 132; De Vries and van der Woude, *The First Modern Economy*, 421.
44. B. A. Cook, *Belgium: A History* (New York: Peter Lang, 2002), 52.
45. Van der Wee in Teich, *The Industrial Revolution in National Context*, 66.
46. Cook, *Belgium*, 51.
47. Cook, *Belgium*, 52.
48. Erik Buyst and Ivo Maes, "Central Banking in 19th Century Belgium: Was the NBB a Lender of Last Resort?" *Financial History Review* 15, no. 2 (2008): 153–73; van der Wee in Teich, *The Industrial Revolution in National Context*, 71.
49. Oscar Gelderblom and Joost Jonker, "Exploring the Market for Government Bonds in the Dutch Republic (1600–1800)," November 2006, http://pseweb.eu/ydepot/semin/texte0607/GEL2006EXP.pdf.
50. See Chapter 7.
51. Thomas I. Palley, "Export-Led Growth: Evidence of Developing Country Crowding-Out," in *Globalization, Regionalism, and Economic Activity*, ed. Philip Arestis, Michelle Baddeley, and J. S. L. McCombie (Cheltenham: Edward Elgar, 2003), 175–97.
52. Davids, *Dutch Technological Leadership*, 274.
53. H. Heller, *Labour, Science and Technology in France, 1500–1620* (Cambridge: Cambridge University Press, 2002), 169, 199; William H. Scheifley, "The Father of French Agriculture," *Sewanee Review* 29, no. 4 (1921): 467–71.
54. Davids, *Dutch Technological Leadership*, 273.
55. De Vries and van der Woude, *The First Modern Economy*, 322, 374.
56. De Vries and van der Woude, *The First Modern Economy*, 322, 374.
57. De Vries and van der Woude, *The First Modern Economy*, 298, 308.

58. De Vries and van der Woude, *The First Modern Economy*, 296.
59. Robert Roswell Palmer and Joel Colton, *A History of the Modern World to 1815* (New York: Knopf, 1971), 142.
60. Barbour, *Capitalism in Amsterdam*, 30.
61. Barbour, *Capitalism in Amsterdam*, 30.
62. Tilly in Teich, *Industrial Revolution in National Context*, 98.
63. Charles P. Kindleberger, "Germany's Overtaking of England, 1806–1914," *Review of World Economics*, III (1975): 253–81.
64. Kindleberger, "Germany's Overtaking"; Kindleberger *Primacy*, 155.
65. T. Pierenkemper and R. H. Tilly, *The German Economy during the Nineteenth Century* (New York: Berghahn Books, 2004), 150.
66. Tilly in R. E. Sylla and G. Toniolo, *Patterns of European Industrialization: The Nineteenth Century* (London: Routledge, 1991), 175–93.
67. Tilly in Sylla, *Patterns of European Industrialization*, 175–93.
68. Kindleberger, *Primacy*, 155.
69. Y. Qian, *How Reform Worked in China: The Transition from Plan to Market* (Cambridge: MIT Press, 2017), 21.
70. Lee Branstetter and Nicholas Lardy, "China's Embrace of Globalization" in Loren Brandt and Thomas G. Rawski, *China's Great Economic Transformation* (Cambridge: Cambridge University Press, 2008), 633–82.
71. R. Brenner, *The Economics of Global Turbulence: The Advanced Capitalist Economies from Long Boom to Long Downturn, 1945–2005* (New York: Verso, 2006), 325.
72. See above; Benedikt Koehler, *History of Financial* Disasters, vol. 2 (London: Pickering & Chatto, 2006), 147. See also Chapter 10.
73. P. Hanson, *The Rise and Fall of the Soviet Economy: An Economic History of the USSR 1945–1991* (New York: Routledge, 2014), 45.
74. Hanson, *The Rise and Fall of the Soviet Economy*, 31, 49.
75. Hanson, *The Rise and Fall of the Soviet Economy*, 45.
76. See Chapter 7.
77. See Chapter 9.
78. Paul Krugman, "The Myth of Asia's Miracle," *Foreign Affairs* 73, no. 6 (1994): 62–78.

# 6. Pirate Empire

1. Harline, *Pamphlets*, 130.
2. Wallerstein, *Modern World-System* I, 185.
3. I. Wallerstein, *The Modern World-System II: Mercantilism and the Consolidation of the European World-Economy, 1600–1750* (Berkeley: University of California Press, 2011), 203.
4. 'T Hart, *The Dutch Wars of Independence*, 182.
5. Barbour, *Capitalism in Amsterdam*, 131.
6. Davids, *Dutch Technological Leadership*, 117.
7. Davids, *Dutch Technological Leadership*, 132.
8. De Vries and van der Woude, *The First Modern Economy*, 292–93.

9.  A. Thompson and C. R. Hickson, *Ideology and the Evolution of Vital Institutions: Guilds, the Gold Standard, and Modern International Cooperation* (New York: Springer, 2001), 103.
10. Barbour, *Capitalism in Amsterdam*, 118.
11. Barbour, *Capitalism in Amsterdam*, 119.
12. Barbour, *Capitalism in Amsterdam*, 103.
13. Barbour, *Capitalism in Amsterdam*, 102.
14. Roger Fouquet and Stephen Broadberry, "Seven Centuries of European Economic Growth and Decline," *Journal of Economic Perspectives* 29, no. 4 (2015): 227–44.
15. Phillips, *Well-Being in Amsterdam's Golden Age*, 44.
16. Barbour, *Capitalism in Amsterdam*, 141–42.
17. Barbour, *Capitalism in Amsterdam*, 74.
18. Barbour, *Capitalism in Amsterdam*, 76.
19. Barbour, *Capitalism in Amsterdam*, 92.
20. De Vries and van der Woude, *The First Modern Economy*, 636.
21. De Vries and van der Woude, *The First Modern Economy*, 636.
22. Barbour, *Capitalism in Amsterdam*, 94.
23. Barbour, *Capitalism in Amsterdam*, 30, 38n, 46.
24. M. Wilkins, *The History of Foreign Investment in the United States to 1914* (Cambridge, MA: Harvard University Press, 1989), 60.
25. Posthumus, *Inquiry into the History of Prices in Holland*, vol. 1, table 8.
26. 'T Hart, *The Dutch Wars of Independence*, 87.
27. 'T Hart, *The Dutch Wars of Independence*, 89.
28. 'T Hart, *The Dutch Wars of Independence*, 127.
29. 'T Hart, *The Dutch Wars of Independence*, 130.
30. 'T Hart, *The Dutch Wars of Independence*, 131.
31. Harline, *Pamphlets*, 6.
32. 'T Hart, *The Dutch Wars of Independence*, 131.
33. 'T Hart, *The Dutch Wars of Independence*, 132.
34. Davids, *Dutch Technological Leadership*, 98.
35. Davids, *Dutch Technological Leadership*, 282.
36. Davids, *Dutch Technological Leadership*, 282–97.
37. Barbour, *Capitalism in Amsterdam*, 116, 127; Wallerstein, *The Modern World-System II*, 206.
38. Barbour, *Capitalism in Amsterdam*, 132–34.
39. Israel, *The Dutch Republic*, 314.
40. Soundtoll Registers Online, http://dietrich.soundtoll.nl/public/index.php.
41. T. H. Aston, *Crisis in Europe 1560–1660* (New York: Basic Books, 1965), 10; L. Gomes, *Foreign Trade and the National Economy: Mercantilist and Classical Perspectives* (London: Palgrave Macmillan, 1987), 42; Israel, *The Dutch Republic*, 317.
42. Lodewijk Otto Petram, "The World's First Stock Exchange: How the Amsterdam Market for Dutch East India Company Shares Became a Modern Securities Market, 1602–1700" (PhD diss., Universiteit van Amsterdam, 2011), 81.
43. Israel, *The Dutch Republic*, 436–37.

44. Israel, *Empires*, 75.
45. Israel, *The Dutch Republic*, 333.
46. De Vries and van der Woude, *The First Modern Economy*, 28.
47. De Vries and van der Woude, *The First Modern Economy*, 30.
48. De Vries and van der Woude, *The First Modern Economy*, 30.
49. De Vries and van der Woude, *The First Modern Economy*, 29.
50. Israel, *The Dutch Republic*, 335.
51. De Vries and van der Woude, *The First Modern Economy*, 202–10.
52. De Vries and van der Woude, *The First Modern Economy*, 36.
53. J. I. Israel, *Dutch Primacy in World Trade, 1585–1740* (Oxford: Clarendon Press, 1989), 184.
54. De Vries and van der Woude, *The First Modern Economy*, 100.
55. Gelderblom and Jonker, "Public Finance."
56. P. J. Blok, O. A. Bierstadt, and R. Putnam, *History of the People of the Netherlands*, vol. 4, *Frederick Henry, John De Witt, William III* (New York: Putnam's Sons, 1907), 38.
57. Gelderblom and Jonker, "Public Finance."
58. De Vries and van der Woude, *The First Modern Economy*, 100.
59. Gelderblom and Jonker, "Public Finance."
60. Stephen Quinn and William Roberds, "An Economic Explanation of the Early Bank of Amsterdam, Debasement, Bills of Exchange and the Emergence of the First Central Bank" in Jeremy Atack and Larry Neal, *The Origins and Development of Financial Markets and Institutions: From the Seventeenth Century to the Present* (Cambridge: Cambridge University Press, 2009), 32.
61. Van Dillen, *Principal Public Banks*, 117.
62. Israel, *Empires*, 75.
63. 'T Hart, *The Dutch Wars of Independence*, 126–27; de Vries and van der Woude, *The First Modern Economy*, 99.
64. Blok, *History of the People of the Netherlands*, 4:71.
65. De Vries and van der Woude, *The First Modern Economy*, 465.
66. Harline, *Pamphlets*, 213.
67. Harline, *Pamphlets*, 216.
68. Harline, *Pamphlets*, 218.
69. De Vries and van der Woude, *The First Modern Economy*, 326.
70. De Vries and van der Woude, *The First Modern Economy*, 373.
71. De Vries and van der Woude, *The First Modern Economy*, 283.
72. De Vries and van der Woude, *The First Modern Economy*, 373.
73. Davids, *Dutch Technological Leadership*, 132.
74. Barbour, *Capitalism in Amsterdam*, 116; Israel, *The Dutch Republic*, 611.
75. De Vries and van der Woude, *The First Modern Economy*, 421.
76. Davids, *Dutch Technological Leadership*, 297.
77. Blok, *History of the People of the Netherlands*, 4:163.
78. Blok, *History of the People of the Netherlands*, 4:175.
79. P. Burke, *Venice and Amsterdam: A Study of Seventeenth-Century Élites* (London: Temple Smith, 1974), 45–46, 60, 81.
80. Gelderblom and Jonker, "Public Finance."
81. Gelderblom and Jonker, "Public Finance."

82. Van Dillen, *Principal Public Banks*, 118; Jan Luiten Van Zanden, "Prices and Wages and the Cost of Living in the Western Part of the Netherlands, 1450–1800," International Institute of Social History, accessed January 29, 2021, http://www.iisg.nl/hpw/brenv.php.

83. Barbour, *Capitalism in Amsterdam*, 74.

84. Barbour, *Capitalism in Amsterdam*, 80–81.

85. Barbour, *Capitalism in Amsterdam*, 81.

86. Barbour, *Capitalism in Amsterdam*, 81.

87. Harline, *Pamphlets*, 219.

88. De Vries and van der Woude, *The First Modern Economy*, 673.

89. Piet M. A. Eichholtz, "A Long Run House Price Index: The Herengracht Index, 1628–1973," *Real Estate Economics*, 25 (1997), 175–92.

90. De Vries and van der Woude, *The First Modern Economy*, 331.

91. De Vries and van der Woude, *The First Modern Economy*, 333.

92. 'T Hart, *The Dutch Wars of Independence*, 182.

93. O. Gelderblom, *The Political Economy of the Dutch Republic* (Farnham: Ashgate, 2009), 177–85.

94. De Vries and van der Woude, *The First Modern Economy*, 647.

95. De Vries and van der Woude, *The First Modern Economy*, 647.

96. Davids, *Dutch Technological Leadership*, 135–37; de Vries and van der Woude, *The First Modern Economy*, 321.

97. De Vries and van der Woude, *The First Modern Economy*, 217–18.

98. De Vries and van der Woude, *The First Modern Economy*, 286.

99. Davids, *Dutch Technological Leadership*, 127; de Vries and van der Woude, *The First Modern Economy*, 290.

100. De Vries and van der Woude, *The First Modern Economy*, 289.

101. Roos van Oosten, "The Dutch Great Stink: The End of the Cesspit Era in the Pre-Industrial Towns of Leiden and Haarlem," *European Journal of Archaeology* 19, no. 4 (2016): 704–27.

102. Thompson, *Ideology and the Evolution of Vital Institutions*, 103.

103. Barbour, *Capitalism in Amsterdam*, 71.

104. Van Zanden, "Prices and Wages."

105. Van Zanden, "Kuznets."

106. De Vries and van der Woude, *The First Modern Economy*, 609.

107. Israel, *Dutch Republic*, 335.

108. Barbour, *Capitalism in Amsterdam*, 83; Petram, "The World's First Stock Exchange," 80.

109. De Vries and van der Woude, *The First Modern Economy*, 267.

110. De Vries and van der Woude, *The First Modern Economy*, 322, 374.

111. Hobsbawm in Aston, *Crisis in Europe*, 10.

112. Israel, *The Dutch Republic*, 779.

113. De Vries and van der Woude, *The First Modern Economy*, 678.

114. Edwards, "Amsterdam and William III," 96.

115. Israel, *The Dutch Republic*, 784.

116. Israel, *The Dutch Republic*, 818.

# 7. The Country and the Court

1. Supple, *Commercial Crisis and Change in England*, 6.
2. Hill, *The Century of Revolution*, 31.
3. Brenner, *Merchants and Revolution*, 201.
4. Brenner, *Merchants and Revolution*, 320.
5. T. K. Rabb, *Enterprise and Empire: Merchant and Gentry Investment in the Expansion of England, 1575–1630* (Cambridge, MA: Harvard University Press, 1967), 28.
6. Brenner, *Merchants and Revolution*, 85.
7. Hill, *The Century of Revolution*, 33.
8. Hill, *The Century of Revolution*, 16.
9. Davids, *Dutch Technological Leadership*, 286–87.
10. Hill, *The Century of Revolution*, 18.
11. Brenner, *Merchants and Revolution*, 109.
12. Rabb, *Enterprise and Empire*, 66.
13. Hill, *The Century of Revolution*, 39.
14. Rabb, *Enterprise and Empire*, 31–32.
15. Rabb, *Enterprise and Empire*, 93.
16. Hill, *The Century of Revolution*, 39.
17. Hill, *The Century of Revolution*, 39.
18. Brenner, *Merchants and Revolution*, 248n.
19. Rabb, *Enterprise and Empire*, 77.
20. Brenner, *Merchants and Revolution*, 11, 25.
21. Thomas and Dimsdale, "A Millennium of Macroeconomic Data."
22. Ashton, *The Crown and the Money Market*, 157–59.
23. Gelderblom, *Political Economy*, 249.
24. Supple, *Commercial Crisis and Change in England*, 54–55.
25. Supple, *Commercial Crisis and Change in England*, 54–55.
26. Supple, *Commercial Crisis and Change in England*, 54–55.
27. Supple, *Commercial Crisis and Change in England*, 54–55.
28. Ashton, *The Crown and the Money Market*, 122–27.
29. Supple, *Commercial Crisis and Change in England*, 190.
30. Bank of England, Trade Volumes: Export Volumes in the United Kingdom [TVEXPUKQ], FRED, Federal Reserve Bank of St. Louis, accessed January 31, 2021, https://fred.stlouisfed.org/series/TVEXPUKQ.
31. Supple, *Commercial Crisis and Change in England*, 119.
32. Rabb, *Enterprise and Empire*, 85.
33. Brenner, *Merchants and Revolution*, 265.
34. Brenner, *Merchants and Revolution*, 269.
35. Brenner, *Merchants and Revolution*, 271.
36. Brenner, *Merchants and Revolution*, 25–29; Anne Mary Millard, "The Import Trade of London 1600–1640" (PhD diss., London School of Economics and Political Science, University of London, 1956).
37. Brenner, *Merchants and Revolution*, 89–90.
38. W. R. Scott, *The Constitution and Finance of English, Scottish and Irish Joint-Stock Companies to 1720*, vol. 1, *The General Development of the Joint-Stock System to 1720* (Cambridge: University Press, 1912), 187.

39. Brenner, *Merchants and Revolution*, 83–85.
40. Hill, *The Century of Revolution*, 29.
41. Brenner, *Merchants and Revolution*, 203.
42. Hill, *The Century of Revolution*, 29.
43. Hill, *The Century of Revolution*, 29.
44. Supple, *Commercial Crisis and Change in England*, 160–61.
45. S. Broadberry, B. M. S. Campbell, A. Klein, M. Overton, and B. van Leeuwen, *British Economic Growth, 1270–1870* (Cambridge: Cambridge University Press, 2015), appendix, p. 187; Scott, *The Constitution and Finance*, 206.
46. Scott, *The Constitution and Finance*, 206-207
47. Ashton, *The Crown and the Money Market*, 83.
48. Ephraim Lipson, *The Economic History of England*, vol. 3 (London: Black, 1943), 314.
49. Hill, *The Century of Revolution*, 20.
50. Hill, *The Century of Revolution*, 18.
51. Scott, *The Constitution and Finance*, 230.
52. Gary B. Nash, *The American People: Creating a Nation and a Society* (New York, NY: Longman, 1998), 32, 40–44, 47, as cited in Mike Davey, "The European Tobacco Trade from the 15th to the 17th Centuries," University of Minnesota Libraries, https://www.lib.umn.edu/bell/tradeproducts/tobacco.
53. Brenner, *Merchants and Revolution*, 169.
54. Daniel E. Bogart, "The East Indian Monopoly and the Transition from Limited Access in England, 1600–1813," *National Bureau of Economic Research Working Paper Series* No. 21536 (2015), https://www.nber.org/papers/w21536.
55. Wilson, *England's Apprenticeship*, 136.
56. Blok, *History of the People of the Netherlands*, 4:191.
57. Blok, *History of the People of the Netherlands*, 4:194.
58. Hill, *The Century of Revolution*, 155.
59. Hill, *The Century of Revolution*, 155.
60. Christopher Hill, *God's Englishman: Oliver Cromwell and the English Revolution*, (New York: Harper, 1972), 117-129.
61. Scott, *The Constitution and Finance*, 256–58.
62. Scott, *The Constitution and Finance*, 259.
63. Scott, *The Constitution and Finance*, 261–62.
64. Hill, *The Century of Revolution*, 223.
65. Hill, *The Century of Revolution*, 204.
66. Satia, *Empire of Guns*, ch. 1.
67. Joan Thirsk, *Economic Policy and Projects: The Development of a Consumer Society in Early Modern England* (Oxford: Clarendon, 1978).
68. Hill, *The Century of Revolution*, 205.
69. Scott, *Constitution and Finance*, 266.
70. Wilson, *England's Apprenticeship*, 163.
71. Wilson, *England's Apprenticeship*, 169; C. Wilson, *Profit and Power: A Study of England and the Dutch Wars* (The Hague: Nijhoff, 1978), 120.
72. Scott, *The Constitution and Finance*, 272–73.

73. Wilson, *Profit and Power*, 113.
74. Wilson, *Profit and Power*, 121.
75. Wilson, *Profit and Power*, 142.
76. Scott, *The Constitution and Finance*, 286.
77. Lipson, *The Economic History of England*, 3:233.
78. Lipson, *The Economic History of England*, 3:236.
79. Lipson, *The Economic History of England*, 3:237.
80. Blok, *History of the People of the Netherlands*, 4:415–18.
81. Nick Robins, *The Corporation That Changed the World: How the East India Company Shaped the Modern Multinational* (London: Pluto Press, 2006), 49.
82. Satia, *Empire of Guns*, ch. 1.
83. Satia, *Empire of Guns*, ch. 6.
84. Satia, *Empire of Guns*, ch. 1.
85. Satia, *Empire of Guns*, ch. 4.
86. Scott, *The Constitution and Finance*, 314.
87. Lipson, *The Economic History of England*, 3:54.
88. Lipson, *The Economic History of England*, 3:232
89. Lipson, *The Economic History of England*, 3:242
90. Lipson, *The Economic History of England*, 3:241
91. Homer, *A History of Interest Rates*, 175.
92. Israel, *The Dutch Republic*, 970; Gelderblom and Jonker, "Exploring the Market."
93. Van Dillen, *Principal Public Banks*, 120; de Vries and van der Woude, *The First Modern Economy*, 25; van Zanden, "Prices and Wages.".
94. Israel, *The Dutch Republic*, 970–71.
95. De Vries and van der Woude, *The First Modern Economy*, 485
96. D. Ormrod, O. David, C. Feinstein, P. O'Brien, B. Supple, P. Temin, and G. Toniolo, *The Rise of Commercial Empires: England and the Netherlands in the Age of Mercantilism, 1650–1770* (Cambridge: Cambridge University Press, 2003), 83–85; de Vries and van der Woude, *The First Modern Economy*, 485.
97. Thomas and Dimsdale, "A Millennium of Macroeconomic Data."
98. Israel, *The Dutch Republic*, 971; de Vries and van der Woude, *The First Modern Economy*, 685
99. Satia, *Empire of Guns*, notes to introduction.
100. Satia, *Empire of Guns*, ch. 4.
101. Christopher Hill, *Reformation to Industrial Revolution: The Making of Modern English Society* (New York: Pantheon Books, 1967), 205.
102. Robins, *The Corporation That Changed the World*, 55.
103. Bogart, "The East Indian Monopoly."

# 8. Where the Sun Never Set

1. Hobsbawm, *Industry and Empire*, 136.
2. Piketty, *Capital*, Figure 10.3.
3. Peter H. Lindert, "Unequal English Wealth since 1670," *Journal of Political Economy* 94, no. 6 (1986): 1127–62.
4. Thomas and Dimsdale, "A Millennium of Macroeconomic Data."

5. Thomas and Dimsdale, "A Millennium of Macroeconomic Data."
6. A. E. Feavearyear, *The Pound Sterling: A History of English Money* (Oxford: Clarendon Press, 1931), 304–5, as cited in A. Arnon, *Monetary Theory and Policy from Hume and Smith to Wicksell: Money, Credit, and the Economy* (New York: Cambridge University Press, 2010), Table 10.4.
7. Imlah, "British Balance of Payments."
8. Imlah, "British Balance of Payments."
9. Anderson, *English Questions*, 144.
10. Hobsbawm, *Industry and Empire*, 170, 233–35.
11. Stephen Broadberry, Bruce M. S. Campbell, Alexander Klein, Mark Overton, and Bas van Leeuwen, "Measuring Economic Growth," pt. 1 of *British Economic Growth, 1270–1870* (Cambridge: Cambridge University Press, 2015); Thomas and Dimsdale, "A Millennium of Macroeconomic Data."
12. Hobsbawm, *Industry and Empire*, 233–35.
13. Edward Porritt, "Political Parties on the Eve of Home Rule", *The North American Review,* 195 (1912), 333-342.
14. Cain and Hopkins, *British Imperialism,* 204.
15. Hobsbawm, *Industry and Empire*, 57–58.
16. Witt Bowden, *Industrial Society in England towards the End of the Eighteenth Century* (New York: Macmillan, 1925), 63.
17. Robins, *Corporation that Changed the World*, 88, 110–11.
18. Wilson in Altorfer, *History of Financial Disasters Vol. 1*, 75–83.
19. A. M. Andreadēs, C. M. Meredith, and H. S. Foxwell, *History of the Bank of England* (London: King & Son, 1909), 157.
20. William D. Rubinstein, "The End of 'Old Corruption' in Britain 1780–1860," *Past & Present*, 101 (1983), 55–86.
21. Philip Harling, *The Modern British State: An Historical Introduction* (Cambridge: Polity, 2001), 44–45.
22. Witt Bowden, "The Influence of the Manufacturers on Some of the Early Policies of William Pitt," *American Historical Review*, 29 (1924), 655–74.
23. Bowden, *Industrial Society*, 181.
24. Hobsbawm, *Industry and Empire*, 50; Satia, *Empire of Guns*, ch. 3.
25. Bishop Carleton Hunt, *The Development of the Business Corporation in England, 1800–1867* (Cambridge, MA: Harvard University Press, 1936), 14.
26. Larry Neal, *A Concise History of International Finance: From Babylon to Bernanke* (New York: Cambridge University Press, 2015), ch. 7.
27. E. J. Hobsbawm and George F. E. Rude, *Captain Swing* (New York: Norton, 1975), 49–51.
28. A. Aspinall, *Lord Brougham and the Whig Party* (Hamden: Archon Books, 1972), 43.
29. Harling, *The Modern British State*, 52.
30. Aspinall, *Lord Brougham and the Whig Party*, 43.
31. Aspinall, *Lord Brougham and the Whig Party*, 43.
32. Philip Harling, *The Waning of "Old Corruption": The Politics of Economical Reform in Britain, 1779–1846* (Oxford: Clarendon Press, 1996), 93.
33. Bank of England, Public Sector Net Lending(+)/Borrowing(-) in the United Kingdom [PSNLBIUKA], FRED, Federal Reserve Bank of St.

Louis; ; accessed January 31, 2021, https://fred.stlouisfed.org/series/PSNLBIUKA.

34. Thomas and Dimsdale, "A Millennium of Macroeconomic Data."
35. Bank of England, Wholesale (Producer) Price Index in the United Kingdom [WPPIUKA], retrieved from FRED, Federal Reserve Bank of St. Louis; https://fred.stlouisfed.org/series/WPPIUKA.
36. Bank of England, Bank of England Policy Rate in the United Kingdom [BOERUKM], retrieved from FRED, Federal Reserve Bank of St. Louis; https://fred.stlouisfed.org/series/BOERUKM.
37. Thomas and Dimsdale, "A Millennium of Macroeconomic Data."
38. Bank of England, Unemployment Rate in the United Kingdom [UNRTUKA], retrieved from FRED, Federal Reserve Bank of St. Louis; https://fred.stlouisfed.org/series/UNRTUKA.
39. Hunt, *Development of the Business Corporation*, 14.
40. Neal, *A Concise History*, ch. 7.
41. Neal, *A Concise History*, ch. 7.
42. W. O. Henderson, *The State and the Industrial Revolution in Prussia: 1740–1870* (Liverpool: Liverpool University Press, 1958), 125.
43. T. Tooke, *A History of Prices and of the State of the Circulation from 1793 to 1837; Preceded by a Brief Sketch of the State of the Corn Trade in the Last Two Centuries* (London: Longman, Orme, Brown, Green and Longmans, 1838), 162.
44. Hunt, *The Development of the Business Corporation*, 39.
45. Hunt, *The Development of the Business Corporation*, 49.
46. Hunt, *The Development of the Business Corporation*, 40.
47. Kindleberger, "Germany's Overtaking."
48. Sydney Checkland, *British Public Policy 1776–1939: An Economic, Social and Political Perspective* (Cambridge: Cambridge University Press, 1983), 71.
49. Hobsbawm, *Captain Swing*, 51.
50. Witt Bowden, *An Economic History of Europe since 1750* (New York: American Book Co., 1937), 342–43.
51. Bowden, *An Economic History*, 345.
52. Bowden, *An Economic History*, 346–48.
53. Bowden, *An Economic History*, 351.
54. Hunt, *The Development of the Business Corporation*, 83.
55. R. Harris, *Industrializing English Law: Entrepreneurship and Business Organization, 1720–1844* (Cambridge: Cambridge University Press, 2000), 284.
56. Hunt, *The Development of the Business Corporation*, 102.
57. Cain and Hopkins, *British Imperialism*, 165–66.
58. Cain and Hopkins, *British Imperialism*, 57.
59. Cain and Hopkins, *British Imperialism*, 99.
60. Bowden, *An Economic History*, 358.
61. Hunt, *The Development of the Business Corporation*, 136.
62. Bowden, *An Economic History*, 361.
63. Thomas and Dimsdale, "A Millennium of Macroeconomic Data."
64. Cain and Hopkins, *British Imperialism*, 174.
65. Andreades, *History of the Bank of England*, 345.

66. Hunt, *The Development of the Business Corporation*, 152–53; W. T. C. King, *History of the London Discount Market* (London: Routledge, 1936), 231–35.
67. Hunt, *The Development of the Business Corporation*, 147.
68. Hunt, *The Development of the Business Corporation*, 147.
69. King, *History of the London Discount Market*, 217.
70. *The Economist* 24, no. 1174, February 24, 1866, 221.
71. *The Economist* 24, no. 1174, February 24, 1866, 273.
72. Hunt, *The Development of the Business Corporation*, 148.
73. Andreades, *History of the Bank of England*, 359–60.
74. Imlah, "British Balance of Payments."
75. Hobsbawm, *Industry and Empire*, 198.
76. Cain and Hopkins, *British Imperialism*, 122.
77. Freda Harcourt, "Disraeli's Imperialism, 1866–1868: A Question of Timing," *Historical Journal* 23, no. 1 (1980): 87–109.
78. Pamuk and van Zanden in S. Broadberry and K. H. O'Rourke, *The Cambridge Economic History of Modern Europe* (Cambridge: Cambridge University Press, 2010), 226–27.
79. Harcourt, "Disraeli's Imperialism"
80. Cain and Hopkins, *British Imperialism*, 202.
81. Cain and Hopkins, *British Imperialism*, 202.
82. Cain and Hopkins, *British Imperialism*, 203.
83. Bowden, *An Economic History*, 472.
84. Bowden, *An Economic History*, 473.
85. Cain and Hopkins, *British Imperialism*, 138.
86. Cain and Hopkins, *British Imperialism*, 206–7.
87. Cain and Hopkins, *British Imperialism*, 156.
88. Chamberlain quoted in Cain and Hopkins, *British Imperialism*, 206–7.
89. Cain and Hopkins, *British Imperialism*, 207.
90. Cain and Hopkins, *British Imperialism*, 341.
91. D. C. M. Platt, *Finance, Trade, and Politics in British Foreign Policy: 1815–1914* (London: Oxford University Press, 1968), 154–80, as cited in Cain and Hopkins, *British Imperialism*, 340.
92. Cain and Hopkins, *British Imperialism*, 345.
93. Cain and Hopkins, *British Imperialism*, 347.
94. Checkland, *British Public Policy*, 178.
95. Checkland, *British Public Policy*, 217.
96. Wilkins in A. D. Chandler and B. Mazlish, *Leviathans: Multinational Corporations and the New Global History* (New York: Cambridge University Press, 2005), ch. 2.
97. Checkland, *British Public Policy*, 224.
98. Cain and Hopkins, *British Imperialism*, 138.
99. Smith, *The Wealth of Nations*, bk. III, ch. 4, 389.
100. Smith, *The Wealth of Nations*, bk. III, ch. 4, 389.

## 9. A New Birth of Freedom

1. Hopkins, *American Empire*, 158.
2. Hopkins, *American Empire*, 158.
3. Brian Reinbold and Yi Wen, "How Industrialization Shaped America's Trade Balance," Federal Reserve Bank of St. Louis, February 6, 2020, https://www.stlouisfed.org/publications/regional-economist/fourth-quarter-2019/industrialization-trade-balance.
4. Hopkins, *American Empire*, 145–46.
5. Sven Beckert, *The Monied Metropolis: New York City and the Consolidation of the Bourgeoisie, 1850–1900* (New York: Cambridge University Press, 2001), 25.
6. Cain and Hopkins, *British Imperialism*, 101.
7. Richard B. Sheridan, "The British Credit Crisis of 1772 and the American Colonies," *Journal of Economic History* 20, no. 2 (1960): 161–86.
8. Charles W. Calomiris, "Institutional Failure, Monetary Scarcity, and the Depreciation of the Continental Dollar," *Journal of Economic History* (1988), 47–68, as cited in Jeremy Atack, Peter Passell, and Susan Lee, *A New Economic View of American History from Colonial Times to 1940* (New York: Norton, 1994), 72.
9. Bray Hammond, *Banks and Politics in America: From the Revolution to the Civil War* (Princeton, NJ: Princeton University Press, 1957), 41.
10. Hammond, *Banks and Politics in America*, 48.
11. Hammond, *Banks and Politics in America*, 49; Wilkins, 33.
12. Wilkins, *The History of Foreign Investment in the United States*, 28.
13. US Department of the Treasury, "The Beginning of US Debt," https://www.treasurydirect.gov/kids/history/history.htm; Wilkins, *History of Foreign Investment in the United States*, 29.
14. Wilkins, *The History of Foreign Investment in the United States*, 47.
15. Hammond, *Banks and Politics in America*, 47.
16. Lewis, *America's Stake*, 11.
17. P. H. Burch, *Elites in American History*, vol. 1, *The Federalist Years to the Civil War* (New York: Holmes & Meier, 1980), 53.
18. Burch, *Elites in American History*, 1:55; Wilkins, *The History of Foreign Investment in the United States*, 37.
19. Lewis, *America's Stake*, 18.
20. Sven Beckert, *Empire of Cotton: A Global History* (New York: Knopf, 2014), ch. 5.
21. Burch, *Elites in American History*, 1:59.
22. Wilkins, *The History of Foreign Investment in the United States*, 39.
23. Wilkins, *The History of Foreign Investment in the United States*, 36–39.
24. Lewis, *America's Stake*, 11; Wilkins, *The History of Foreign Investment in the United States*, 40.
25. Burch, *Elites in American History*, 1:88.
26. Beckert, *Empire of Cotton*, ch. 5.
27. Hammond, *Banks and Politics in America*, 146.
28. Hopkins, *American Empire*, 149.
29. Burch, *Elites in American History*, 1:93.

30. Burch, *Elites in American History*, 1:93.
31. Taussig, *The Tariff History of the United States*, 48.
32. Hammond, *Banks and Politics in America*, 148–49.
33. Wilkins, *The History of Foreign Investment in the United States*, 55, 64.
34. Lewis, *America's Stake*, 18.
35. Lewis, *America's Stake*, 18.
36. Lewis, *America's Stake*, 14.
37. Jeffrey G. Williamson, *American Growth and the Balance of Payments, 1820–1913* (Chapel Hill, NC: University of North Carolina Press, 1964), 269.
38. Beckert, *The Monied Metropolis*, 22; Lewis, *America's Stake*, 12.
39. Burch, *Elites in American History*, 1:130.
40. Hopkins, *American Empire*, 154.
41. Peter Temin, *The Jacksonian Economy* (New York: W. W. Norton, 1969), 71, 159, as cited in Atack, *A New Economic View of American History*, 99–100.
42. William B. English, "Understanding the Costs of Sovereign Default: American State Debts in the 1840s," *American Economic Review* 86, no. 1 (1996): 259–75.
43. Phillips Christopher, *The Rivers Ran Backward: The Civil War and the Remaking of the American Middle Border* (New York: Oxford University Press, 2016), 52, 53.
44. Kathleen Smith Kutolowski, "Antimasonry Reexamined: Social Bases of the Grass-Roots Party," *Journal of American History* 71, no. 2 (1984): 269–93.
45. Ariel Ron, "Developing the Country: 'Scientific Agriculture' and the Roots of the Republican Party" (PhD diss., UC-Berkeley, 2012).
46. Ron, "Developing the Country."
47. Phillips, *The Rivers Ran Backward*, 55.
48. Phillips, *The Rivers Ran Backward*, 58.
49. Michael Haines, "The Population of the United States, 1790–1920," in *The Cambridge Economic History of the United States*, vol. 2, *The Long Nineteenth Century*, ed. Stanley L. Engerman and Robert E. Gallman (New York: Cambridge University Press, 2000), 189.
50. Hopkins, *American Empire*, 220.
51. Beckert, *The Monied Metropolis*, 89; Ferguson, *Golden Rule*, 64.
52. Ferguson, *Golden Rule*, 64.
53. Beckert, *The Monied Metropolis*, 91.
54. Sibing He in Kendall Johnson, *Narratives of Free Trade: The Commercial Cultures of Early US-China Relations* (Hong Kong: Hong Kong University Press, 2012).
55. Ferguson, *Golden Rule*, 65.
56. Ferguson, *Golden Rule*, 65–66.
57. Beckert, *The Monied Metropolis*, 23.
58. Hopkins, *American Empire*, 221.
59. Beckert, *The Monied Metropolis*, 90; Ferguson, *Golden Rule*, 66.
60. Beckert, *The Monied Metropolis*, 88; Ron, "Developing the Country."
61. Hopkins, *American Empire*, 170.
62. Terry Reynolds, "'Destined to Produce [a] ... Revolution': Michigan's Iron Ore Industry in the Civil War," *Michigan Historical Review* 39, no. 2 (Fall

2013), 21–49; Frank William Taussig, "The Iron Industry in the United States," *Quarterly Journal of Economics* 14, no. 4 (1900): 475–508.

63. Beckert, *The Monied Metropolis*, 135–36.

64. National Bureau of Economic Research, Miles of Railroad Built for United States [A02F2AUSA374NNBR], retrieved from FRED, Federal Reserve Bank of St. Louis; https://fred.stlouisfed.org/series/A02F2AUSA374NNBR.

65. Atack, *A New Economic View of American History*, 374.

66. Kindleberger, "Germany's Overtaking."

67. Atack, *A New Economic View of American History*, 367.

68. Atack, *A New Economic View of American History*, 374.

69. Hopkins, *American Empire*, 225.

70. Taussig, *The Tariff History of the United States*, 173–74.

71. Hopkins, *American Empire*, 293.

72. Hopkins, *American Empire*, 257–58.

73. Philip H. Burch, *Elites in American History*, vol. 2, *The Civil War to the New Deal* (New York: Holmes & Meier, 1981), 16, as cited in Ferguson, *Golden Rule*, 65.

74. H. George, W. Saunders, and F. G. Shaw, *Social Problems* (New York: Doubleday & McClure Company, 1900), 248.

75. George, *Social Problems*, 248.

76. Daniel B. Schirmer, *Republic or Empire; American Resistance to the Philippine War* (Cambridge, Mass.: Schenkman Pub. Co, 1972); Ferguson, *Golden Rule*, 70, 78.

77. Hopkins, *American Empire*, 294.

78. Schirmer, *Republic or Empire*, 23.

79. Ulysses S. Grant, "Message regarding Dominican Republic Annexation," 1870, https://millercenter.org/the-presidency/presidential-speeches/may-31-1870-message-regarding-dominican-republic-annexation.

80. Schirmer, *Republic or Empire*, 24–28.

81. Hopkins, *American Empire*, 354.

82. Hopkins, *American Empire*, 294.

83. Hopkins, *American Empire*, 295.

84. Hugh Rockoff, "Banking and Finance, 1789–1914," in *The Cambridge Economic History of the United States*, vol. 2, *The Long Nineteenth Century*, ed. Stanley L. Engerman and Robert E. Gallman (New York: Cambridge University Press, 2000), 670.

85. Wilkins, *The History of Foreign Investment in the United States*, 186.

86. Alan Essex-Crosby, "Joint Stock Companies in Great Britain, 1890–1930" (PhD diss., London School of Economics and Political Science, University of London, 1937).

87. Essex-Crosby, "Joint Stock Companies in Great Britain."

88. Wilkins in Chandler, *Leviathans*, 74.

89. Beckert, *The Monied Metropolis*, 241; Alfred D. Chandler, *The Visible Hand: The Managerial Revolution in American Business* (Cambridge, MA: Belknap, 1977), 277–78.

90. Wilkins in Chandler, *Leviathans*, 74.

91. Thomas Childs Cochran and William Miller, *The Age of Enterprise: A Social History of Industrial America* (New York: Macmillan, 1942), 136.
92. Reinbold and Wen, "How Industrialization Shaped America's Trade Balance."
93. National Bureau of Economic Research, Total Exports for United States [M07023USM144NNBR], retrieved from FRED, Federal Reserve Bank of St. Louis; https://fred.stlouisfed.org/series/M07023USM144NNBR; National Bureau of Economic Research, Total Imports for United States [M07028USM144NNBR], retrieved from FRED, Federal Reserve Bank of St. Louis; https://fred.stlouisfed.org/series/M07028USM144NNBR; Louis D. Johnston and Samuel Williamson, "Sources and Techniques Used in the Construction of Annual GDP, 1790–Present," Measuring Worth, 2008, https://www.measuringworth.com/datasets/usgdp/sourcegdp.php.
94. National Bureau of Economic Research, Monetary Gold Stock for United States [M1476AUSM027NNBR], retrieved from FRED, Federal Reserve Bank of St. Louis; https://fred.stlouisfed.org/series/M1476AUS-M027NNBR
95. Ferguson, *Golden Rule*, 76.
96. Ferguson, *Golden Rule*, 78.
97. Hopkins, *American Empire*, 381.
98. Beckert, *The Monied Metropolis*, 330.
99. Lance Davis and Robert Cull, "International Capital Movements, Domestic Capital Markets, and American Economic Growth, 1820–1914," in *The Cambridge Economic History of the United States*, vol. 2, *The Long Nineteenth Century*, ed. Stanley L. Engerman and Robert E. Gallman (New York: Cambridge University Press, 2000), 787.
100. Ferguson, *Golden Rule*, 17, 135.
101. Richard Sylla, "Experimental Federalism: The Economics of American Government, 1789–1914," in *The Cambridge Economic History of the United States*, vol. 2, *The Long Nineteenth Century*, ed. Stanley L. Engerman and Robert E. Gallman (New York: Cambridge University Press, 2000), 540.
102. Gyung-Ho Jeong, Gary J. Miller, and Andrew C. Sobel, "Political Compromise and Bureaucratic Structure: The Political Origins of the Federal Reserve System," *Journal of Law, Economics, & Organization* 25, no. 2 (2009): 472–98.
103. Hopkins, *American Empire*, 312.
104. Rockoff, "Banking and Finance," 674.
105. Bank of England, "Public Sector Net Lending(+)/Borrowing(-) in the United Kingdom [PSNLBIUKA]," FRED, Federal Reserve Bank of St. Louis; accessed January 31, 2021, https://fred.stlouisfed.org/series/PSNLBIUKA
106. National Bureau of Economic Research, Total Exports for United States [M07023USM144NNBR], retrieved from FRED, Federal Reserve Bank of St. Louis; https://fred.stlouisfed.org/series/M07023USM144NNBR; National Bureau of Economic Research, Total Imports for United States [M07028USM144NNBR], retrieved from FRED, Federal Reserve Bank of St. Louis; https://fred.stlouisfed.org/series/M07028USM144NNBR; Louis D. Johnston and Samuel Williamson, "Sources and Techniques Used in

the Construction of Annual GDP, 1790–Present," Measuring Worth, 2008, https://www.measuringworth.com/datasets/usgdp/sourcegdp.php.

107. Stephen Broadberry and Mark Harrison, *The Economics of World War I* (Cambridge: Cambridge University Press, 2005), 3–40.

# 10. American Hegemony and Its Decline

1. James Madison, "Federalist No. 20," 1787, in *Federalist Papers: Primary Documents in American History*, ed. Library of Congress, https://guides.loc.gov/federalist-papers/text-11-20#s-lg-box-wrapper-25493291.

2. J. Israel, *The Expanding Blaze: How the American Revolution Ignited the World, 1775–1848* (Princeton, NJ: Princeton University Press, 2019), 240.

3. United States Census; UK Office for National Statistics.

4. Ferguson, "From Normalcy."

5. Lewis, *America's Stake*, 309.

6. Ferguson, "From Normalcy."

7. Thomas Ferguson and Joel Rogers, *Right Turn: The Decline of the Democrats and the Future of American Politics* (New York: Hill and Wang, 1986).

8. Lewis, *America's Stake*, 218.

9. Lewis, *America's Stake*, 228.

10. Lewis, *America's Stake*, 221–23.

11. Lewis, *America's Stake*, 224.

12. Ferguson and Rogers, *Right Turn*, 48.

13. Ferguson, "From Normalcy."

14. Lewis, *America's Stake*, 197.

15. A. J. Gregor, *Marxism, China, and Development: Reflections on Theory and Reality* (London: Taylor & Francis, 2017), 55.

16. Bank of England, Current Account in the United Kingdom [CURUKA], FRED, Federal Reserve Bank of St. Louis; accessed January 31, 2021, https://fred.stlouisfed.org/series/CURUKA; Bank of England, Public Sector Net Lending(+)/Borrowing(-) in the United Kingdom [PSNLBIUKA], FRED, Federal Reserve Bank of St. Louis; ; accessed January 31, 2021, https://fred.stlouisfed.org/series/PSNLBIUKA; International Monetary Fund, "World Economic Outlook: Coping with High Debt and Sluggish Growth," October 2012, https://www.imf.org/en/Publications/WEO/Issues/2016/12/31/Coping-with-High-Debt-and-Sluggish-Growth.

17. Hobsbawm, *Industry and Empire*, 212, as cited in Charles P. Kindleberger, *The World in Depression, 1929–1939* (Berkeley: University of California Press, 1973), 23.

18. Ferguson, "From Normalcy."

19. Ferguson, "From Normalcy."

20. US Office of the Historian, "Milestones: 1921–1936," in *Milestones in the History of US Foreign Relations*, US Department of State, https://history.state.gov/milestones/1921-36/foreword.

21. Ferguson, "From Normalcy."

22. S. Bahcall, *Loonshots: How to Nurture the Crazy Ideas That Win Wars, Cure Diseases, and Transform Industries* (New York: St. Martin's Publishing Group, 2019), 23–24.
23. F. L. Block and M. R. Keller, *State of Innovation: The US Government's Role in Technology Development* (New York: Routledge, 2015), 7.
24. Block, *State of Innovation*, 8.
25. Bahcall, *Loonshots*, 36; D. A. Mindell, *Between Human and Machine: Feedback, Control, and Computing before Cybernetics* (Baltimore: Johns Hopkins University Press, 2004), 178, 212.
26. Robert Skidelsky, *John Maynard Keynes, Vol. 3: Fighting for Freedom, 1937-1946* (New York: Viking, 1986), 150-160.
27. Quoted in B. Steil, *The Battle of Bretton Woods: John Maynard Keynes, Harry Dexter White, and the Making of a New World Order* (Princeton, NJ: Princeton University Press, 2013), 330.
28. United States Office of Management and Budget.
29. Charles Noble, *Welfare as We Knew It: A Political History of the American Welfare State* (New York: Oxford University Press, 1997), 86.
30. Ferguson and Rogers, *Right Turn*, 52.
31. Ferguson and Rogers, *Right Turn*, 52.
32. World Bank, World GDP Growth (annual %), retrieved from https://data.worldbank.org/indicator/NY.GDP.MKTP.KD.ZG
33. Michal Kalecki, *Collected Works of Michal Kalecki*, vol. 2, *Capitalism: Economic Dynamics*, ed. Jerzy Osiatynski, trans. Chester Adam Kisiel (Oxford: Clarendon Press, 1991), 405.
34. US Bureau of Labor Statistics, All Employees, Government [USGOVT], retrieved from FRED, Federal Reserve Bank of St. Louis; https://fred.stlouisfed.org/series/USGOVT
35. Federal Reserve Bank of St. Louis, Velocity of MZM Money Stock [MZMV], retrieved from FRED, Federal Reserve Bank of St. Louis; https://fred.stlouisfed.org/series/MZMV; Board of Governors of the Federal Reserve System (US), Capacity Utilization: Total Index [TCU], retrieved from FRED, Federal Reserve Bank of St. Louis; https://fred.stlouisfed.org/series/TCU
36. Kalecki, *Collected Works*, 2:405; Mariana Mazzucato, *The Entrepreneurial State: Debunking the Public vs. Private Myth in Risk and Innovation* (London: Anthem Press, 2015), 44–45.
37. Brenner, *The Economics of Global Turbulence*, 58, 119.
38. Brenner, *The Economics of Global Turbulence*,
39. Brenner, *The Economics of Global Turbulence*,
40. John Kenneth Galbraith, *The New Industrial State* (Boston: Houghton Mifflin, 1967), 339.
41. Ferguson and Rogers, *Right Turn*, 65.
42. "Nixon Reportedly Says He Is Now a Keynesian," *New York Times*, January 7, 1971, https://www.nytimes.com/1971/01/07/archives/nixon-reportedly-says-he-is-now-a-keynesian.html.
43. Kalecki, *Collected Works*, 2:407.
44. Brenner, *The Economics of Global Turbulence*, 5.

45. Jeremy J. Siegel and Jeremy D. Schwartz, "Long-Term Returns on the Original S&P 500 Companies," *Financial Analysts Journal* 62, no. 1 (2006): 18–31.
46. Brenner, *The Economics of Global Turbulence*, 59.
47. Ferguson and Rogers, *Right Turn*, 59.
48. Michael D. Bordo, Eric Monnet, and Alain Naef, "The Gold Pool (1961-1968) and the Fall of the Bretton Woods System. Lessons for Central Bank Cooperation," *National Bureau of Economic Research Working Paper Series* No. 24016 (2017), http://www.nber.org/papers/w24016.
49. B. J. Eichengreen, *Globalizing Capital: A History of the International Monetary System* (University Press, 1996), 120–21.
50. Jamie Powell, "The Not-So-Nifty Fifty," FT Alphaville, *Financial Times*, May 29, 2018.
51. George Jerome Waldo Goodman, *Supermoney* (New York: Random House, 1972), 298.
52. Bank for International Settlements, Total Credit to Private Non-Financial Sector, Adjusted for Breaks, for United States [QUSPAM770A], retrieved from FRED, Federal Reserve Bank of St. Louis; https://fred.stlouis-fed.org/series/QUSPAM770A
53. Israel Shenker, "Galbraith: '29 Repeats Itself Today," *New York Times*, May 3, 1970, https://www.nytimes.com/1970/05/03/archives/galbraith-29-repeats-itself-today-galbraith-sees-1929-repeating.html.
54. Brenner, *The Economics of Global Turbulence*, 108.
55. Brenner, *The Economics of Global Turbulence*, 157.
56. Moffitt, *The World's Money* (New York: Simon and Schuster, 1983), 76–84.
57. Sebastian Mallaby, *More Money than God: Hedge Funds and the Making of a New Elite* (New York, NY: Penguin Books, 2011), 74–76.
58. Moffitt, *The World's Money*, 83.
59. Moffitt, *The World's Money*, 143.
60. Barsky and Kilian, "Do We Really Know That Oil Caused the Great Stagflation?"
61. Barsky and Kilian, "Do We Really Know That Oil Caused the Great Stagflation?"
62. Hanson, *The Rise and Fall of the Soviet Economy*, 123–24.
63. Hanson, *The Rise and Fall of the Soviet Economy*, 123–24.
64. Hanson, *The Rise and Fall of the Soviet Economy*, 156.
65. Ferguson and Rogers, *Right Turn*, 106.
66. Ferguson and Rogers, *Right Turn*, 112.
67. Ferguson and Rogers, *Right Turn*, 112.
68. John Brooks, *The Go-Go Years* (New York: Weybright and Talley, 1973), 288.
69. George Soros, *The Alchemy of Finance* (Hoboken: Wiley, 2003), 12.
70. Ferguson and Rogers, *Right Turn*, 90.
71. Ferguson and Rogers, *Right Turn*, 122.
72. Ferguson and Rogers, *Right Turn*, 123.
73. Ferguson and Rogers, *Right Turn*, 124.
74. Ferguson and Rogers, *Right Turn*, 129.
75. Ferguson and Rogers, *Right Turn*, 137.
76. Ferguson and Rogers, *Right Turn*, 130.

77. Ferguson and Rogers, *Right Turn*, 135.
78. Ferguson and Rogers, *Right Turn*, 136.
79. World Bank, United States Domestic Credit to Private Sector, retrieved from https://data.worldbank.org/indicator/FS.AST.PRVT.GD.ZS?locations=US
80. Ferguson and Rogers, *Right Turn*, 146–49.
81. Ferguson and Rogers, *Right Turn*, 154, 185.
82. Ferguson and Rogers, *Right Turn*, 147, 154.
83. Ferguson, *Golden Rule*, 307.
84. Simon Johnson and James Kwak, *13 Bankers: The Wall Street Takeover and the Next Financial Meltdown* (New York: Pantheon Books, 2010), 100.
85. Johnson, *13 Bankers*, 90.
86. Johnson, *13 Bankers*, 90.
87. Johnson, *13 Bankers*, 89.
88. Johnson, *13 Bankers*, 134.
89. Johnson, *13 Bankers*, 136.
90. Simon Johnson, "The Quiet Coup," *Atlantic*, May 2009, https://www.theatlantic.com/magazine/archive/2009/05/the-quiet-coup/307364/.
91. Johnson, *13 Bankers*, 139–40.
92. Michel Fouquin and Jules Hugot, "Trade Globalisation in the Last Two Centuries," *VoxEU*, September 17, 2016, https://voxeu.org/article/trade-globalisation-last-two-centuries.
93. Robert Edward Rubin and Jacob Weisberg, *In an Uncertain World: Tough Choices from Wall Street to Washington* (New York: Random House, 2003), 182–83.
94. Csilla Lakatos and Franziska Ohnsorge, *Arm's-Length Trade: A Source of Post-Crisis Trade Weakness* (World Bank, 2017).
95. Nicholas R. Lardy, "Trade Liberalization and Its Role in Chinese Economic Growth" in *India's and China's Recent Experience with Reform and Growth* (New York: Palgrave, 2005), pp. 158–69.
96. Brenner, *The Economics of Global Turbulence*, 325.
97. World Bank.
98. Ben Inker, "Bigger's Been Better," *GMO Quarterly Letter*, 2019; Thomas I. Palley, "The Fallacy of the Natural Rate of Interest and Zero Lower Bound Economics: Why Negative Interest Rates May Not Remedy Keynesian Unemployment ," *Review of Keynesian Economics* 7, no. 2 (April 2019): 151–70.
99. Thomas Ferguson, "Financial Regulation? Don't Get Your Hopes Up." TPM Café Book Club April 17, 2008; reprinted in Naked Capitalism, May 25, 2012, https://www.nakedcapitalism.com/2012/05/tom-ferguson-financial-regulation-dont-get-your-hopes-up.html; Johnson, *13 Bankers*, 185.
100. Alan Greenspan, "The Federal Reserve's Semiannual Monetary Policy Report," Testimony before the US House Committee on Banking, Housing, and Urban Affairs, February 26, 1997, https://www.federalreserve.gov/boarddocs/hh/1997/february/testimony.htm.
101. Kevin Phillips, *Bad Money: Reckless Finance, Failed Politics, and the Global Crisis of American Capitalism* (New York: Viking, 2008), 100.

102. Heather Long, "Every American Family Basically Pays an $8,000 'Poll Tax' under the US Health System, Top Economists Say," *Washington Post*, January 7, 2020, https://www.washingtonpost.com/business/2020/01/07/every-american-family-basically-pays-an-poll-tax-under-us-health-system-top-economists-say/.

103. Simeon Alder, David Lagakos, and Lee Ohanian, "The Decline of the US Rust Belt: A Macroeconomic Analysis," FRB Atlanta CQER Working Paper No. 14-5, August 1, 2014; Adam Dean and Simeon Kimmel, "Beyond the Sacklers: Free-Trade Policies Contributed to the Opioid Epidemic," *STAT*, October 8, 2019, https://www.statnews.com/2019/10/08/free-trade-policies-opioid-epidemic/.

104. Anne Case and Angus Deaton, "Rising Morbidity and Mortality in Midlife among White Non-Hispanic Americans in the 21st Century," *Proceedings of the National Academy of Sciences of the United States of America* 112, no. 49 (2015): 15078–83.

105. Thomas Ferguson, Paul Jorgensen, and Jie Chen, "Industrial Structure and Party Competition in an Age of Hunger Games: Donald Trump and the 2016 Presidential Election," *Institute for New Economic Thinking Working Paper Series*, 2018.

106. David Streitfeld, "Peter Thiel to Donate $1.25 Million in Support of Donald Trump," *New York Times*, October 15, 2016, https://www.nytimes.com/2016/10/16/technology/peter-thiel-donald-j-trump.html.

107. Anonymous Employees of Microsoft, "An Open Letter to Microsoft: Don't Bid on the US Military's Project Jedi," Medium, https://medium.com/s/story/an-open-letter-to-microsoft-dont-bid-on-the-us-military-s-project-jedi-7279338b7132, as cited in J. S. Tan, "Big Tech Embraces New Cold War Nationalism," *Foreign Policy*, August 27, 2020, https://foreignpolicy.com/2020/08/27/china-tech-facebook-google/.

108. Tan, "Big Tech Embraces New Cold War Nationalism."

109. Eric Schmidt, "Eric Schmidt: I Used to Run Google. Silicon Valley Could Lose to China," *New York Times*, February 27, 2020, https://www.nytimes.com/2020/02/27/opinion/eric-schmidt-ai-china.html.

110. Ross Andersen, "The Panopticon Is Already Here," *Atlantic*, September 2020, https://www.theatlantic.com/magazine/archive/2020/09/china-ai-surveillance/614197/.

111. World Bank.

112. Nicholas R. Lardy, *The State Strikes Back: The End of Economic Reform in China?* (Washington, DC: Peterson Institute for International Economics, 2019), ch. 1.

113. Jamil Anderlini, "China Has 'Wasted' $6.8tn in Investment, Warn Beijing Researchers," *Financial Times*, November 27, 2014.

114. See in general Lardy, *The State Strikes Back* about the end of market reform and the recentralization of economic authority.

115. Sidney Leng, "Can Xi Jinping Revive China's Dream of Turning Its Poor West into an Economic Powerhouse?" *South China Morning Post*, June 24, 2020, https://www.scmp.com/economy/china-economy/article/3090273/can-xi-jinping-revive-chinas-dream-turning-its-poor-west;

Matt Schiavenza, "Mapping China's Income Inequality," *Atlantic*, September 13, 2013, https://www.theatlantic.com/china/archive/2013/09/mapping-chinas-income-inequality/279637.

# 11. Conclusion

1. *Reuters*, "TSMC Says Latest Chip Plant Will Cost around $20 Bln," December 7, 2017, https://fr.reuters.com/article/tsmc-investment-idUS-L3N1O737Z; Raymond Zhong, "In US-China Tech Feud, Taiwan Feels Heat from Both Sides," *New York Times*, October 1, 2020, https://www.nytimes.com/2020/10/01/technology/taiwan-china-tsmc-huawei.html.
2. Harry Stevens and Aman Sethi. How Some of India's Biggest Companies Route Money to Political Parties. Hindustan Times. April 14, 2017. https://www.hindustantimes.com/interactives/electoral-trusts-explained/
3. Stephanie Findlay and Hudson Lockett, "Modi's 'Rockefeller': Gautam Adani and the Concentration of Power in India," *Financial Times*, November 12, 2020.
4. Tim Buckley and Simon Nicholas, "The Economic Case for Adani to Lead India's Domestic Energy Strategy: A Coal Power Phaseout to Align the Group's ESG Commitments with India's Renewables Future," Institute for Energy Economics and Financial Analysis, 2020, https://ieefa.org/wp-content/uploads/2020/11/The-Economic-Case-for-Adani-To-Lead-Indias-Domestic-Energy-Strategy_November-2020.pdf
5. Stephanie Findlay and Hudson Lockett, "Modi's 'Rockefeller.'"
6. Una Galani, "Breakingviews – India Insight: Ambani, a Maverick Rockefeller," *Reuters*, August 24, 2020, https://www.reuters.com/article/us-reliance-m-a-breakingviews/breakingviews-india-insight-ambani-a-maverick-rockefeller-idUSKBN25L08M.
7. Smith, *The Wealth of Nations*, bk. 4, ch. 9, 634.
8. J. Dewey, J. A. Boydston, and S. Ratner, *The Later Works of John Dewey, 1925–1953: 1931–1932, Essays, Reviews, and Miscellany* (Carbondale: Southern Illinois University Press, 2008), 163.
9. Smith, *The Wealth of Nations*, bk. 4, ch. 2, 438.
10. Lawrence H. Summers, "Reflections on the New 'Secular Stagnation Hypothesis'", October, 30, 2014, *VoxEU*, https://voxeu.org/article/larry-summers-secular-stagnation.
11. United Nations, "World Population Prospects 2019," https://population.un.org/wpp.
12. Michaela Grimm, Janine Junge, Arne Holzhausen, and Patricia Pelayo Romero, "Allianz Global Wealth Report 2020," Allianz, 2020, https://www.eulerhermes.com/en_global/news-insights/economic-insights/Allianz-Wealth-Report-2020.html.
13. Amartya Sen, *Development as Freedom* (Oxford: Oxford University Press, 2001), 8.
14. Lindblom, "Market and Democracy."
15. John Maynard Keynes, *The Collected Writings of John Maynard Keynes*, vol. 25: *Activities 1940–1944: Shaping the Post-War World: The Clearing Union*, ed.

Elizabeth Johnson and Donald E. Moggridge (Cambridge: Cambridge University Press, 2013), 28.

16. Keynes, *Collected Writings*, 25:30.

17. Palley, "Fallacy of the Natural Rate of Interest."

18. Olivier Blanchard, Giovanni Dell'Ariccia, and Paolo Mauro, "Rethinking Macroeconomic Policy," *Journal of Money, Credit and Banking* 42 (2010): 199–215.

19. Matt Bruenig, "Social Wealth Fund for America," People's Policy Project, 2018, https://www.peoplespolicyproject.org/projects/social-wealth-fund/.

20. Thomas I. Palley, *From Financial Crisis to Stagnation: The Destruction of Shared Prosperity and the Role of Economics* (New York: Cambridge University Press, 2012), 183.

21. Polanyi, *Great Transformation*, 76.

22. Jerry Evensky, "Theory of Moral Sentiments: On Morals and Why They Matter to a Liberal Society of Free People and Free Markets," *Journal of Economic Perspectives*, 19, no. 3 (2005): 109–130; Palley, *From Financial Crisis*, 212.

23. Adam Smith, *The Theory of Moral Sentiments*, ed. Amartya Sen (New York: Penguin Books, 2009), pt. 2, sec. 2, ch. 3, 104.

24. Smith, *Theory of Moral Sentiments*, pt. 4, ch. 2, 218, as cited in Evensky, "Theory of Moral Sentiments"; Palley, *From Financial Crisis*, 213.

25. Smith, *The Wealth of Nations*, bk. 4, ch. 9, 634.

# BIBLIOGRAPHY

Adler, Gustavo, Camila Casas, Luis Cubeddu, Gita Gopinath, Nan Li, Sergii Meleshchuk, Carolina Osorio-Buitron, Damien Puy, and Yannick Timmer. "Dominant Currencies and External Adjustment." *IMF Staff Discussion Note*, 2020.

Alder, Simeon, David Lagakos, and Lee Ohanian. "Competitive Pressure and the Decline of the Rust Belt: A Macroeconomic Analysis." Working paper no. 20538, National Bureau of Economic Research, 2014. https://www.nber.org/papers/w20538

Altorfer, Stefan. *History of Financial Disasters 1763–1995*. Vol. 1. London: Pickering and Chatto, 2006.

Anderlini, Jamil. "China Has 'Wasted' $6.8tn in Investment, Warn Beijing Researchers." *Financial Times*, November 27, 2014.

Andersen, Ross. "The Panopticon Is Already Here." *Atlantic*, September 2020. https://www.theatlantic.com/magazine/archive/2020/09/china-ai-surveillance/614197/.

Anderson, Jonathan. "How to Think about Emerging Markets." Emerging Advisors Group, 2017. https://emadvisorsgroup.com/.

Anderson, Perry. *English Questions*. London: Verso, 1992.

Andreadēs, A. M., C. M. Meredith, and H. S. Foxwell. *History of the Bank of England*. London: King & Son, 1909.

Arestis, Philip, Michelle Baddeley, and John McCombie. *Globalisation, Regionalism and Economic Activity*. Cheltenham: Edward Elgar Pub., 2003.

Arnon, A. *Monetary Theory and Policy from Hume and Smith to Wicksell: Money, Credit, and the Economy*. New York: Cambridge University Press, 2010.

Ashton, Robert. *The Crown and the Money Market, 1602–1640*. Oxford: Clarendon Press, 1960.

Aspinall, A. *Lord Brougham and the Whig Party*. Hamden: Archon Books, 1972.

Aston, T. H. *Crisis in Europe 1560–1660*. New York: Basic Books, 1965.

Atack, Jeremy, and Larry Neal. *The Origins and Development of Financial Markets and Institutions: From the Seventeenth Century to the Present*. Cambridge: Cambridge University Press, 2009.

Atack, Jeremy, Peter Passell, and Susan Lee. *A New Economic View of American History from Colonial Times to 1940*. New York: Norton, 1994.

Avdjiev, Stefan, Robert N. McCauley, and Hyun Song Shin, "Breaking Free of the Triple Coincidence in International Finance," *BIS Working Papers*, 524 (October 2015).

Bahcall, S. *Loonshots: How to Nurture the Crazy Ideas That Win Wars, Cure Diseases, and Transform Industries*. New York: St. Martin's Publishing Group, 2019.

Bank of Japan Currency Museum. "The History of Japanese Currency." https://www.imes.boj.or.jp/cm/english/history/content/#Ancient.

Barbour, Violet. *Capitalism in Amsterdam in the 17th Century*. Ann Arbor: University of Michigan Press, 1963.

Barsky, Robert B., and Lutz Kilian. "Do We Really Know That Oil Caused the Great Stagflation? A Monetary Alternative." *NBER Macroeconomics Annual* 16 (2001): 137–83.

Beckert, Sven. *Empire of Cotton: A Global History*. New York: Knopf, 2014.

Beckert, Sven. *The Monied Metropolis: New York City and the Consolidation of the Bourgeoisie, 1850–1900*. New York: Cambridge University Press, 2001.

Blanchard, Olivier, Giovanni Dell'Ariccia, and Paolo Mauro. "Rethinking Macroeconomic Policy." *Journal of Money, Credit and Banking* 42 (2010): 199–215.

Block, Fred L., and Matthew R. Keller. *State of Innovation: The US Government's Role in Technology Development*. New York: Routledge, 2015.

Blok, P. J., O. A. Bierstadt, and R. Putnam. *History of the People of the Netherlands: Frederick Henry, John De Witt, William III*. New York: Putnam's Sons, 1907.

Bogart, Dan. "The East Indian Monopoly and the Transition from Limited Access in England, 1600-1813." *National Bureau of Economic Research Working Paper Series* No. 21536 (2015). http://www.nber.org/papers/w21536. o

Borio, Claudio, and Piti Disyatat. "Global Imbalances and the Financial Crisis: Link or No Link?" *BIS Working Papers* 346, May 2011.

Bordo, Michael, Eric Monnet, and Alain Naef. "The Gold Pool (1961-1968) and the Fall of the Bretton Woods System. Lessons for

Central Bank Cooperation." *National Bureau of Economic Research Working Paper Series* No. 24016 (2017). http://www.nber.org/papers/w24016.

Bowden, Witt. "The Influence of the Manufacturers on Some of the Early Policies of William Pitt." *American Historical Review* 29, no. 4 (1924): 655–74.

Bowden, Witt. *An Economic History of Europe since 1750*. New York: American Book Co., 1937.

Bowden, Witt. *Industrial Society in England towards the End of the Eighteenth Century*. New York: Macmillan, 1925.

Brandt, Loren, and Thomas G. Rawski. *China's Great Economic Transformation*. Cambridge: Cambridge University Press, 2008.

Brenner, R. *Merchants and Revolution: Commercial Change, Political Conflict, and London's Overseas Traders, 1550–1653*. New York: Verso, 2003.

Brenner, R. *The Economics of Global Turbulence: The Advanced Capitalist Economies from Long Boom to Long Downturn, 1945–2005*. New York: Verso, 2006.

Broadberry, Stephen, and K. H. O'Rourke. *The Cambridge Economic History of Modern Europe*. Cambridge University Press, 2010.

Broadberry, Stephen, and Mark Harrison. *The Economics of World War I*. Cambridge: Cambridge University Press, 2005.

Broadberry, Stephen, B. M. S. Campbell, A. Klein, M. Overton, and B. van Leeuwen. *British Economic Growth, 1270–1870*. Cambridge: Cambridge University Press, 2015.

Brooks, John. *The Go-Go Years*. New York: Weybright and Talley, 1973.

Bruenig, Matt. "Social Wealth Fund for America." People's Policy Project, 2018, www.peoplespolicyproject.org/projects/social-wealth-fund/.

Buckley, Tim, and Simon Nicholas. *The Economic Case for Adani to Lead India's Domestic Energy Strategy: A Coal Power Phaseout to Align the Group's ESG Commitments with India's Renewables Future*. Institute for Energy Economics and Financial Analysis, November 2020. https://ieefa.org/wp-content/uploads/2020/11/The-Economic-Case-for-Adani-To-Lead-Indias-Domestic-Energy-Strategy_November-2020.pdf.

Burch, P. H. *Elites in American History*. Vol. 1, *The Federalist Years to the Civil War*. New York, Holmes & Meier, 1980.

Burch, Philip H. *Elites in American History*. Vol. 2, *The Civil War to the New Deal*. New York: Holmes & Meier, 1981.

Burke, P. *Venice and Amsterdam: A Study of Seventeenth-Century Élites*. London: Temple Smith, 1974.

Burns, Tom. "Organization and Social Order." Unpublished manuscript. Retrieved from http://www.sociology.ed.ac.uk/tomburns/manuscript.html. Accessed February 19, 2021.

Buyst, Erik, and Ivo Maes. "Central Banking in 19th Century Belgium: Was the NBB a Lender of Last Resort?" *Financial History Review* 15, no. 2 (2008): 153–73.

Cain, P. J., and A. G. Hopkins. *British Imperialism: 1688–2015.* New York: Routledge, 2016.

Calomiris, Charles W. "Institutional Failure, Monetary Scarcity, and the Depreciation of the Continental." *Journal of Economic History* (1988): 47–68.

Case, Anne, and Angus Deaton. "Rising Morbidity and Mortality in Midlife among White Non-Hispanic Americans in the 21st Century." *Proceedings of the National Academy of Sciences* 112, no. 49 (2015): 15078–83.

Chandler, A. D., and B. Mazlish. *Leviathans: Multinational Corporations and the New Global History.* New York: Cambridge University Press, 2005.

Chandler, Alfred D., Jr. *The Visible Hand: The Managerial Revolution in American Business by Alfred D. Chandler, Jr.* Cambridge, MA: Belknap, 1977.

Chang, Ha-Joon. *Kicking Away the Ladder: Development Strategy in Historical Perspective.* London: Anthem Press, 2002.

Checkland, S. George. "The Birmingham Economists, 1815–1850." *Economic History Review* 1, no. 1 (1948): 1–19.

Checkland, Sydney. *British Public Policy 1776–1939: An Economic, Social and Political Perspective.* Cambridge: Cambridge University Press, 1983.

Christopher, Phillips. *The Rivers Ran Backward: The Civil War and the Remaking of the American Middle Border.* New York: Oxford University Press, 2016.

Clarkson, Iain. *The Industrial Revolution: A Compendium.* Basingstoke, Hampshire: Macmillan, 1990.

Cochran, Thomas Childs, and William Miller. *The Age of Enterprise: A Social History of Industrial America.* New York: Macmillan, 1942.

Cook, B. A. *Belgium: A History.* New York: Peter Lang, 2002.

Cooper, Randolf G. S. *The Anglo-Maratha Campaigns and the Contest for India: The Struggle for Control of the South Asian Military Economy.* Cambridge: Cambridge University Press, 2003.

Curran, James, and Jean Seaton. *Power without Responsibility: Press, Broadcasting and the Internet in Britain.* London: Routledge, 2010.

Davey, Mike. "The European Tobacco Trade from the 15th to the 17th Centuries." University of Minnesota Libraries. Accessed January 29, 2021, https://www.lib.umn.edu/bell/tradeproducts/tobacco.

Davids, Karel. *The Rise and Decline of Dutch Technological Leadership Technology, Economy and Culture in the Netherlands, 1350–1800.* Leiden: Brill, 2008.

Davis, Lance, and Robert Cull. "International Capital Movements, Domestic Capital Markets, and American Economic Growth, 1820–1914." In *The Cambridge Economic History of the United States.* Vol. 2, *The Long Nineteenth Century.* Edited by Stanley L. Engerman and Robert E. Gallman, 733–812. New York: Cambridge University Press, 2000.

De Vries, Jan, and Ad van der Woude. *The First Modern Economy: Success, Failure, and Perseverance of the Dutch Economy, 1500–1815.* Cambridge: Cambridge University Press, 2010.

Dean, Adam, and Simeon Kimmel. "Beyond the Sacklers: Free-Trade Policies Contributed to the Opioid Epidemic." *STAT,* October 8, 2019. https://www.statnews.com/2019/10/08/free-trade-policies-opioid-epidemic/.

Dornbusch, Rudiger and Jacob A. Frenkel. "The Gold Standard and the Bank of England Crisis in 1847." In *A Retrospective on the Classical Gold Standard, 1821-1931.* Edited by Michael D. Bordo and Anna J. Schwartz, 233-273. Chicago: University of Chicago Press, 1984.

Edelstein, Michael. "Realized Rates of Return on UK Home and Overseas Portfolio Investment in the Age of High Imperialism." *Explorations in Economic History* 13, no. 3 (1976): 283–29.

Edwards, Elizabeth Clare. "Amsterdam and William III: The Role of Influence, Interest and Patronage on Policy-Making in the Dutch Republic, 1672–1684." PhD diss., University of London, 1998.

Eichengreen, B. J. *Globalizing Capital: A History of the International Monetary System.* Princeton, NJ: Princeton University Press, 1996.

Eichholtz, Piet M. A. "A Long Run House Price Index: The Herengracht Index, 1628–1973." *Real Estate Economics* 25, no. 2 (1997): 175–92.

English, William B. "Understanding the Costs of Sovereign Default: American State Debts in the 1840s." *American Economic Review* (1996): 259–75.

Essex-Crosby, Alan. "Joint Stock Companies in Great Britain, 1890–1930." PhD diss., London School of Economics and Political Science, University of London, 1937.

Evensky, Jerry. "Adam Smith's Theory of Moral Sentiments: On Morals and Why They Matter to a Liberal Society of Free People and Free Markets." *Journal of Economic Perspectives* 19, no. 3 (2005): 109–30.

Farmer, Roger. "Post Keynesian Dynamic Stochastic General Equilibrium Theory." *National Bureau of Economic Research Working Paper Series* No. 23109 (2017). https://www.nber.org/papers/w23109.

Fearon, Peter, and Derek Howard Aldcroft. *British Economic Fluctuations, 1790-1939.* London: Macmillan, 1972.

Feavearyear, A. E. *The Pound Sterling: A History of English Money.* Oxford: Clarendon Press, 1931.

Fendel, Ralf, and David Maurer. "Does European History Repeat Itself?: Lessons from the Latin Monetary Union for the European Monetary Union." *Journal of Economic Integration* 30, no. 1 (2015): 93–120.

Ferguson, Thomas, and Joel Rogers. *Right Turn: The Decline of the Democrats and the Future of American Politics.* New York: Hill and Wang, 1986.

Ferguson, Thomas, Paul Jorgensen, and Jie Chen. "Industrial Structure and Party Competition in an Age of Hunger Games: Donald Trump and the 2016 Presidential Election." *Institute for New Economic Thinking Working Paper Series*, no. 66 (2018).

Ferguson, Thomas. "Financial Regulation? Don't Get Your Hopes Up." TPM Café Book Club, April 17, 2008. Reprinted in Naked Capitalism, May 25, 2012, https://www.nakedcapitalism.com/2012/05/tom-ferguson-financial-regulation-dont-get-your-hopes-up.html.

Ferguson, Thomas. "From Normalcy to New Deal: Industrial Structure, Party Competition, and American Public Policy in the Great Depression." *International Organization* 38, no. 1 (Winter 1984): 41–94.

Ferguson, Thomas. *Golden Rule: The Investment Theory of Party Competition and the Logic of Money-Driven Political Systems.* Chicago: University of Chicago Press, 1995.

Findlay, Stephanie, and Hudson Lockett. "'Modi's Rockefeller': Gautam Adani and the Concentration of Power in India." *Financial Times*, November 12, 2020.

Finkelstein, Andrea. *Harmony and the Balance: An Intellectual History of Seventeenth-Century English Economic Thought.* Ann Arbor: University of Michigan Press, 2003.

Fischer, David Hackett. *The Great Wave: Price Revolutions and the Rhythm of History.* New York: Oxford University Press, 1999.

Flandreau, Marc, and Juan H. Flores. "Bonds and Brands: Foundations of Sovereign Debt Markets, 1820–1830." *Journal of Economic History* 69, no. 3 (2009): 646–84.

Fouquet, Roger, and Stephen Broadberry. "Seven Centuries of European Economic Growth and Decline." *Journal of Economic Perspectives* 29, no. 4 (2015): 227–44.

Fouquin, Michel, and Jules Hugot. "Trade Globalisation in the Last Two Centuries." *VoxEU,* September 17, 2016. https://voxeu.org/article/trade-globalisation-last-two-centuries.

Galani, Una. "Breakingviews – India Insight: Ambani, a Maverick Rockefeller." *Reuters*, August 24, 2020.

Galbraith, John Kenneth. *The New Industrial State.* Boston: Houghton Mifflin, 1967.

Gelderblom, O. *The Political Economy of the Dutch Republic.* Farnham: Ashgate, 2009.

Gelderblom, Oscar, and Joost Jonker. "Exploring the Market for Government Bonds in the Dutch Republic (1600–1800)." November 2006. http://pseweb.eu/ydepot/semin/texte0607/GEL2006EXP.pdf

Gelderblom, Oscar, and Joost Jonker. "Public Finance and Economic Growth: The Case of Holland in the Seventeenth Century." *Journal of Economic History* (2011): 1–39.

George, H., W. Saunders, and F. G. Shaw. *Social Problems.* New York: Doubleday & McClure Company, 1900.

Gerrard, Christine. "Poems on Politics." In *The Oxford Handbook of British Poetry, 1660-1800.* Edited by Jack Lynch. Oxford: Oxford University Press, 2016.

Gomes, L. *Foreign Trade and the National Economy: Mercantilist and Classical Perspectives.* London: Palgrave Macmillan UK, 1987.

Goodman, George Jerome Waldo. *Supermoney.* New York: Random House, 1972.

Grant, Ulysses S. "Message regarding Dominican Republic Annexation," 1870. https://millercenter.org/the-presidency/presidential-speeches/may-31-1870-message-regarding-dominican-republic-annexation.

Grantham, Jeremy, and Ben Inker. *GMO Quarterly Letter* (2017).

Greenspan, Alan. "The Federal Reserve's Semiannual Monetary Policy Report." Testimony before the US House Committee on Banking, Housing, and Urban Affairs, February 26, 1997. https://www.federalreserve.gov/boarddocs/hh/1997/february/testimony.htm.

Green, Timothy. *Central Bank Gold Reserves: An Historical Perspective Since 1845.* London: World Gold Council, 1999. https://www.gold.org/goldhub/research/central-bank-gold-reserves-historical-perspective-1845.

Gregor, A. J. *Marxism, China, and Development: Reflections on Theory and Reality.* London: Taylor & Francis, 2017.

Grimm, Michaela, Janine Junge, Arne Holzhausen, and Patricia Pelayo Romero. *Allianz Global Wealth Report 2020.* Allianz, 2020. https://www.eulerhermes.com/en_global/news-insights/economic-insights/Allianz-Wealth-Report-2020.html.

Habib, Maurizio. "The Exorbitant Privilege from a Global Perspective." *VoxEU,* March 29, 2010. https://voxeu.org/article/how-exorbitant-dollar-s-exorbitant-privilege.

Haines, Michael. "The Population of the United States, 1790–1920." In *The Cambridge Economic History of the United States.* Vol. 2, *The Long Nineteenth Century.* Edited by Stanley L. Engerman and Robert E. Gallman, 143–206. New York: Cambridge University Press, 2000.

Hammond, Bray. *Banks and Politics in America: From the Revolution to the Civil War.* Princeton, NJ: Princeton University Press, 1957.

Hanson, P. *The Rise and Fall of the Soviet Economy: An Economic History of the USSR 1945–1991.* New York: Routledge, 2014.

Harcourt, Freda. "Disraeli's Imperialism, 1866–1868: A Question of Timing." *Historical Journal* 23, no. 1 (1980): 87–109.

Harline, C. *Pamphlets, Printing, and Political Culture in the Early Dutch Republic.* Dodrecht: Nijhoff, 1987.

Harling, Philip. *The Waning of "Old Corruption": The Politics of Economical Reform in Britain, 1779–1846.* Oxford: Clarendon Press, 1996.

Harris, R. *Industrializing English Law: Entrepreneurship and Business Organization, 1720–1844.* Cambridge: Cambridge University Press, 2000.

Heller, H. *Labour, Science and Technology in France, 1500–1620.* Cambridge: Cambridge University Press, 2002.

Henderson, W. O. *The State and the Industrial Revolution in Prussia: 1740–1870.* Liverpool: Liverpool University Press, 1958.

Hill, Christopher. *God's Englishman: Oliver Cromwell and the English Revolution.* New York: Harper, 1972.

Hill, Christopher. *Reformation to Industrial Revolution: The Making of Modern English Society.* New York: Pantheon Books, 1967.

Hill, Christopher. *The Century of Revolution, 1603–1714.* New York: Norton, 1982.

Hobsbawm, E. J. *Industry and Empire: From 1750 to the Present Day.* London: Penguin, 1990.

Hobsbawm, E. J., and George F. E. Rude. *Captain Swing.* New York: Norton, 1975.

Homer, Sidney, and Richard Eugene Sylla. *A History of Interest Rates.* Hoboken: Wiley, 2005.

Hopkins, A. G. "American Empire: A Global History." Princeton, NJ: Princeton University Press, 2019.

Hunt, Bishop Carleton. *The Development of the Business Corporation in England 1800–1867.* Cambridge, MA: Harvard University Press, 1936.

Imlah, Albert H. "British Balance of Payments and Export of Capital, 1816–1913." *Economic History Review* 5, no. 2 (1952): 208–39.

Inker, Ben. "Bigger's Been Better." *GMO Quarterly Letter* (2019).

International Monetary Fund. "Namibia: Financial System Stability Assessment." Washington, DC: IMF Publication Services, 2018. https://www.imf.org/en/Publications/CR/Issues/2018/03/15/Namibia-Financial-System-Stability-Assessment-45723

International Monetary Fund. "World Economic Outlook: Coping with High Debt and Sluggish Growth." October 2012. https://www.imf.org/en/Publications/WEO/Issues/2016/12/31/Coping-with-High-Debt-and-Sluggish-Growth

Israel, Jonathan. *Dutch Primacy in World Trade, 1585–1740.* Oxford: Clarendon Press, 1989.

Israel, Jonathan. *Empires and Entrepots: The Dutch, the Spanish Monarchy and the Jews, 1585–1713.* London: Bloomsbury, 1990.

Israel, Jonathan. *The Dutch Republic: Its Rise, Greatness, and Fall, 1477–1806.* New York: Oxford University Press, 1995.

Israel, Jonathan. *The Expanding Blaze: How the American Revolution Ignited the World, 1775–1848.* Princeton University Press, 2019.

Jeong, Gyung-Ho, Gary J. Miller, and Andrew C. Sobel. "Political Compromise and Bureaucratic Structure: The Political Origins of the Federal Reserve System." *Journal of Law, Economics, & Organization* 25, no. 2 (2009): 472–98.

Johnson, Kendall. *Narratives of Free Trade: The Commercial Cultures of Early US-China Relations.* Hong Kong University Press, HKU, 2012.

Johnson, Simon, and James Kwak. *13 Bankers: The Wall Street Takeover and the Next Financial Meltdown.* New York: Pantheon Books, 2010.

Johnson, Simon. "The Quiet Coup." *Atlantic,* May 2009. https://www.theatlantic.com/magazine/archive/2009/05/the-quiet-coup/307364/.

Johnston, Louis D., and Samuel Williamson. "Sources and Techniques Used in the Construction of Annual GDP, 1790–Present." MeasuringWorth, 2008. https://www.measuringworth.com/datasets/usgdp/sourcegdp.php.

Kalecki, Michal. *Collected Works of Michal Kalecki.* 7 vols. Edited by Jerzy Osiatynski. Translated by Chester Adam Kisiel. Oxford: Clarendon Press, 1991.

Keynes, John Maynard. "The General Theory of Employment." *Quarterly Journal of Economics* 51, no. 2 (1937): 209–23.

Keynes, John Maynard. *The Collected Writings of John Maynard Keynes.* Vol. 25, *Activities 1940–1944: Shaping the Post-War World: The*

*Clearing Union.* Edited by Elizabeth Johnson and Donald E. Moggridge. Cambridge: Cambridge University Press, 2013.

Keynes, John Maynard. *The General Theory of Employment, Interest, and Money.* Cham: Palgrave Macmillan, 2018.

Kindleberger, Charles P. "Germany's Overtaking of England, 1806–1914." *Review of World Economics* III, no. 2 (1975): 253–81.

Kindleberger, Charles P. "The Economic Crisis of 1619 to 1623." *Journal of Economic History* (1991): 149–75.

Kindleberger, Charles P. *The World in Depression, 1929–1939.* Berkeley: University of California Press, 1973.

Kindleberger, Charles P. *World Economic Primacy, 1500 to 1900.* New York: Oxford University Press, 1996.

King, W. T. C. *History of the London Discount Market.* London: Routledge, 1936.

Koehler, Benedikt. *History of Financial Disasters.* Vol. 2. London: Pickering & Chatto, 2006.

Kohler, Karsten. "Gross Capital Flows and the Balance-of-Payments: A Balance Sheet Perspective." Post Keynesian Economics Society Working Paper Series, October 2020. http://www.postkeynesian.net/downloads/working-papers/PKWP2019.pdf.

Krugman, Paul. "The Myth of Asia's Miracle." *Foreign Affairs* (1994): 62–78.

Kutolowski, Kathleen Smith. "Antimasonry Reexamined: Social Bases of the Grass-Roots Party." *Journal of American History* 71, no. 2 (1984): 269–93.

Lakatos, Csilla, and Franziska Ohnsorge. *Arm's-Length Trade: A Source of Post-Crisis Trade Weakness.* World Bank, 2017.

Lardy, Nicholas R. *The State Strikes Back: The End of Economic Reform in China?* Washington, DC: Peterson Institute for International Economics, 2019.

Leng, Sidney. "Can Xi Jinping Revive China's Dream of Turning Its Poor West into an Economic Powerhouse?" *South China Morning Post,* June 24, 2020. https://www.scmp.com/economy/china-economy/article/3090273/can-xi-jinping-revive-chinas-dream-turning-its-poor-west.

Lewis, Cleona, with Karl T. Schlotterbeck. *America's Stake in International Investments.* Washington, DC: Brookings Institution, 1938.

Lindblom, C. E. "Market and Democracy—Obliquely." *PS: Political Science & Politics* 28, no. 4 (1995): 684–89.

Lindblom, C. E. *Politics and Markets: The World's Political Economic Systems.* New York: Basic Books, 1977.

Lindert, Peter H. "Unequal English Wealth since 1670." *Journal of Political Economy* 94, no. 6 (1986): 1127–62.

Lindert, Peter, and Jeffrey Williamson. "Unequal Gains: American Growth and Inequality since 1700." *VoxEU*, June 16, 2016. https://voxeu.org/article/american-growth-and-inequality-1700.

Lipson, Ephraim. *The Economic History of England.* Vol. 3. London: Black, 1943.

List, Friederich. *The National System of Political Economy.* Translated by Sampson S. Lloyd. London: Longmans, Green, 1909.

Long, Heather. "Every American Family Basically Pays an $8,000 'Poll Tax' under the US Health System, Top Economists Say," *Washington Post*, January 7, 2020, https://www.washingtonpost.com/business/2020/01/07/every-american-family-basically-pays-an-poll-tax-under-us-health-system-top-economists-say/.

Mackay, Charles. *Extraordinary Popular Delusions and the Madness of Crowds.* New York: Barnes & Noble Books, 2004.

Madison, James. "Federalist No. 20," 1787. In *Federalist Papers: Primary Documents in American History*. Edited by Library of Congress. https://guides.loc.gov/federalist-papers/text-11-20#s-lg-box-wrapper-25493291.

Mallaby, Sebastian. *More Money than God: Hedge Funds and the Making of a New Elite.* New York: Penguin Books, 2011.

Matsui, Yoko. "Japanese-Dutch Relations in the Tokugawa Period." *Transactions of the Japan Academy* 72, special issue (2018): 139–54.

Mazzucato, Mariana. *The Entrepreneurial State: Debunking the Public vs. Private Myth in Risk and Innovation.* London: Anthem Press, 2015.

McCauley, Robert N., and Michela Scatigna. "Foreign Exchange Trading in Emerging Currencies: More Financial, More Offshore." *BIS Quarterly Review, March* (2011).

McCusker, John. *Essays in the Economic History of the Atlantic World.* London: Routledge, 2005.

McLeay, Michael, Amar Radia, and Ryland Thomas. "Money Creation in the Modern Economy." *Bank of England Quarterly Bulletin* (2014): Q1, https://www.bankofengland.co.uk/quarterly-bulletin/2014/q1/money-creation-in-the-modern-economy

Mehrling, Perry. "Financialization and Its Discontents." *Finance and Society* 3, no. 1 (2017): 1–10.

Mill, J. S. *Principles of Political Economy: With Some of Their Applications to Social Philosophy.* New York: Appleton, 1895.

Millard, Anne Mary. "The Import Trade of London 1600–1640." PhD diss., London School of Economics and Political Science, University of London, 1956.

Mindell, D. A. *Between Human and Machine: Feedback, Control, and Computing before Cybernetics.* Baltimore: Johns Hopkins University Press, 2004.

Minsky, H. *John Maynard Keynes.* New York; London: McGraw-Hill, 2008.

Minsky, H. "Prices in a Capital-Using Capitalist Economy I" (1976). Hyman P. Minsky Archive. Paper 37. http://digitalcommons.bard.edu/hm_archive/37.

Minsky, H. "Prices in a Capital-Using Capitalist Economy II" (1992). Hyman P. Minsky Archive, 36. https://digitalcommons.bard.edu/hm_archive/36.

Minsky, H. *Stabilizing an Unstable Economy* New York: McGraw-Hill, 2008.

Moffitt, Michael. *The World's Money.* New York: Simon and Schuster, 1983.

Morgan, Edward Victor. *The Theory and Practice of Central Banking, 1797–1913.* New York: Kelley, 1966.

Murau, Steffen, Joe Rini, and Armin Haas. "The Evolution of the Offshore US-Dollar System: Past, Present and Four Possible Futures." *Journal of Institutional Economics* 16, no. 6 (2020): 767–83.

Nash, Gary B. *The American People: Creating a Nation and a Society.* New York: Longman, 1998.

Neal, Larry. "The Financial Crisis of 1825 and the Restructuring of the British Financial System." *Review-Federal Reserve Bank of Saint Louis* 80 (1998): 53–76.

Neal, Larry. *A Concise History of International Finance: From Babylon to Bernanke.* New York: Cambridge University Press, 2015.

*New York Times.* "Nixon Reportedly Says He Is Now a Keynesian." January 7, 1971.

Noble, Charles. *Welfare as We Knew It: A Political History of the American Welfare State.* New York: Oxford University Press, 1997.

Obstfeld, Maurice. "Does the Current Account Still Matter?" *American Economic Review* 102, no. 3 (2012): 1–23.

Ormrod, D., O. David, C. Feinstein, P. O'Brien, B. Supple, P. Temin, and G. Toniolo. *The Rise of Commercial Empires: England and the Netherlands in the Age of Mercantilism, 1650–1770.* Cambridge: Cambridge University Press, 2003.

Paas, Martha White, and John Roger Paas. *The Kipper und Wipper Inflation, 1619–23: An Economic History with Contemporary German Broadsheets.* New Haven: Yale University Press, 2012.

Palley, Thomas I. "Export-Led Growth: Evidence of Developing Country Crowding-Out." In *Globalization, Regionalism, and Economic Activity.* Edited by Philip Arestis, Michelle

Baddeley, and J. S. L. McCombie, 175–97. Cheltenham, UK: Edward Elgar, 2003.

Palley, Thomas I. "The Fallacy of the Natural Rate of Interest and Zero Lower Bound Economics: Why Negative Interest Rates May Not Remedy Keynesian Unemployment." *Review of Keynesian Economics* 7, no. 2 (April 2019): 151–70.

Palley, Thomas I. *From Financial Crisis to Stagnation: The Destruction of Shared Prosperity and the Role of Economics.* New York: Cambridge University Press, 2012.

Palmer, Robert Roswell, and Joel Colton. *A History of the Modern World to 1815.* New York: Knopf, 1971.

Petram, Lodewijk Otto. "The World's First Stock Exchange: How the Amsterdam Market for Dutch East India Company Shares Became a Modern Securities Market, 1602–1700." PhD diss., Universiteit van Amsterdam, 2011.

Phillips, D. L. *Well-Being in Amsterdam's Golden Age.* Amsterdam: Amsterdam University Press, 2008.

Phillips, Kevin. *Bad Money: Reckless Finance, Failed Politics, and the Global Crisis of American Capitalism.* New York: Viking, 2008.

Pierenkemper, T., and R. H. Tilly. *The German Economy during the Nineteenth Century.* New York: Berghahn Books, 2004.

Piketty, T. *Capital in the Twenty-First Century.* Translated by Arthur Goldhammer. Cambridge, MA: Harvard University Press, 2014.

Pistor, Katharina. *The Code of Capital: How the Law Creates Wealth and Inequality.* Princeton: Princeton University Press, 2019.

Platt, D. C. M. *Finance, Trade, and Politics in British Foreign Policy: 1815–1914.* London: Oxford University Press, 1968.

Polanyi, Karl. *The Great Transformation: The Political and Economic Origins of Our Time.* 2nd ed. Foreword by Joseph Eugene Stiglitz, new introduction by Fred L. Block. 1944. Reprint, Boston: Beacon Press, 2001.

Porritt, Edward. "Political Parties on the Eve of Home Rule." The North American Review 195, no. 676 (1912): 333-42.

Posthumus, N. W. *Inquiry into the History of Prices in Holland.* 2 vols. Leiden: Brill, 1946.

Powell, Jamie. "The Not-So-Nifty Fifty." *Financial Times,* May 29, 2018.

Qian, Y. *How Reform Worked in China: The Transition from Plan to Market.* Cambridge, MA: MIT Press, 2017.

Rabb, T. K. *Enterprise and Empire: Merchant and Gentry Investment in the Expansion of England, 1575–1630.* Cambridge, MA: Harvard University Press, 1967.

Reinbold, Brian, and Yi Wen. "How Industrialization Shaped America's Trade Balance." Federal Reserve Bank of St. Louis, February 6, 2020.

https://www.stlouisfed.org/publications/regional-economist/fourth-quarter-2019/industrialization-trade-balance.

Reinbold, Brian. "Trade and Gold Reserves after the Demise of the Classical Gold Standard." Federal Reserve Bank of St. Louis, September 1, 2020. https://www.stlouisfed.org/on-the-economy/2020/september/trade-gold-reserves-decline-gold-standard.

Reinert, Erik S. "Diminishing Returns and Economic Sustainability; the Dilemma of Resource-Based Economies under a Free Trade Regime." The Other Canon, 1996. http://othercanon.org/wp-content/uploads/2020/02/Diminishing-Returns-and-Economic-Sustainability-The-Dilemma-of-Resource-based-Economies-under-a-Free-Trade-Regime.pdf.

*Reuters.* "TSMC Says Latest Chip Plant Will Cost around $20 Bln." December 7, 2017. https://www.reuters.com/article/tsmc-investment/tsmc-says-latest-chip-plant-will-cost-around-20-bln-idINL3N1O737Z.

Reynolds, Terry. ""Destined to Produce [a]... Revolution": Michigan's Iron Ore Industry in the Civil War." *Michigan Historical Review* 39, no. 2 (Fall 2013): 21–49.

Robins, Nick. *The Corporation That Changed the World: How the East India Company Shaped the Modern Multinational.* London: Pluto Press, 2006.

Rockoff, Hugh. "Banking and Finance, 1789–1914." In *The Cambridge Economic History of the United States.* Vol. 2, *The Long Nineteenth Century.* Edited by Stanley L. Engerman and Robert E. Gallman, 643–84. New York: Cambridge University Press, 2000.

Ron, Ariel. "Developing the Country: 'Scientific Agriculture' and the Roots of the Republican Party." PhD diss., University of California, Berkeley, 2012.

Rubin, Robert Edward, and Jacob Weisberg. *In an Uncertain World: Tough Choices from Wall Street to Washington.* New York: Random House, 2003.

Rubinstein, William D. "The End of 'Old Corruption' in Britain 1780–1860." *Past & Present* 101, no. 1 (1983): 55–86.

Satia, Priya. *Empire of Guns: The Violent Making of the Industrial Revolution.* Stanford: Stanford University Press, 2018.

Saez, Emmanuel, and Gabriel Zucman. Trends in Us Income and Wealth Inequality: Revising after the Revisionists. Working paper no. 27921. National Bureau of Economic Research, October 2020, https://www.nber.org/papers/w27921.

Sawyer, Malcolm. "Kalecki on Imperfect Competition, Inflation and Money." *Cambridge Journal of Economics* 25, no. 2 (2001): 245–61.

Schama, Simon. *The Embarrassment of Riches: An Interpretation of Dutch Culture in the Golden Age.* Berkeley: University of California Press, 1988.

Scheifley, William H. "The Father of French Agriculture." *Sewanee Review* 29, no. 4 (1921): 467–71.

Schiavenza, Matt. "Mapping China's Income Inequality." *Atlantic*, September 13, 2013. https://www.theatlantic.com/china/archive/2013/09/mapping-chinas-income-inequality/279637.

Schirmer, Daniel B. *Republic or Empire: American Resistance to the Philippine War.* Cambridge, MA: Schenkman Pub. Co., 1972.

Schmidt, Eric. "Eric Schmidt: I Used to Run Google. Silicon Valley Could Lose to China." *New York Times*, February 27, 2020. https://www.nytimes.com/2020/02/27/opinion/eric-schmidt-ai-china.html.

Scott, W. R. *The Constitution and Finance of English, Scottish and Irish Joint-Stock Companies to 1720.* Vol. 1, *The General Development of the Joint-Stock System to 1720.* Cambridge: University Press, 1912.

Sen, A. *Development as Freedom.* Oxford: Oxford University Press, 2001.

Shenker, Israel. "Galbraith: '29 Repeats Itself Today." *New York Times*, May 3, 1970. https://www.nytimes.com/1970/05/03/archives/galbraith-29-repeats-itself-today-galbraith-sees-1929-repeating.html.

Sheridan, Richard B. "The British Credit Crisis of 1772 and the American Colonies." *Journal of Economic History* (1960): 161–86.

Siegel, Jeremy J., and Jeremy D. Schwartz. "Long-Term Returns on the Original S&P 500 Companies." *Financial Analysts Journal* 62, no. 1 (2006): 18–31.

Skidelsky, Robert. *John Maynard Keynes, Vol. 3: Fighting for Freedom, 1937-1946.* New York: Viking, 1986.

Smith, Adam. *An Inquiry into the Nature and Cause of the Wealth of Nations.* Edited by Edwin Cannan, with an introduction by Max Lerner. New York: Modern Library, 1937.

Smith, Adam. *The Theory of Moral Sentiments.* Edited by Ryan Patrick Hanley. Notes by Ryan Patrick Hanley. New York: Penguin Books, 2009.

Soltow, L., and J. L. van Zanden. *Income and Wealth Inequality in the Netherlands, 16th–20th Century.* Amsterdam: Het Spinhuis, 1998

Soros, George. *The Alchemy of Finance.* Hoboken: Wiley, 2003.

Soundtoll Registers Online.
    http://www.soundtoll.nl/index.php/en/over-het-project/str-online.

Spiegel, Henry William. *The Growth of Economic Thought.* Durham:
    Duke Univ. Press, 1991.

Steil, B. *The Battle of Bretton Woods: John Maynard Keynes, Harry Dexter
    White, and the Making of a New World Order.* Princeton, NJ:
    Princeton University Press, 2013.

Stiglitz, J. E., B. C. Greenwald, P. Aghion, and K. J. Arrow. *Creating a
    Learning Society: A New Approach to Growth, Development, and
    Social Progress.* New York: Columbia University Press, 2014.

Streitfeld, David. "Peter Thiel to Donate $1.25 Million in Support of
    Donald Trump." *New York Times*, October 15, 2016.
    https://www.nytimes.com/2016/10/16/technology/peter-thiel-
    donald-j-trump.html.

Summers, Lawrence H."Reflections on the New 'Secular Stagnation
    Hypothesis'." *VoxEU*, October 30, 2014.
    https://voxeu.org/article/larry-summers-secular-stagnation.

Supple, Barry Emanuel. *Commercial Crisis and Change in England,
    1600–1642.* Cambridge: University Press, 1959.

Suzuki, Y. *Japan-Netherlands Trade 1600–1800: The Dutch East India
    Company and Beyond.* Kyoto: Kyoto University Press, 2012.

Sylla, R. E., and G. Toniolo. *Patterns of European Industrialization: The
    Nineteenth Century.* London: Routledge, 1991.

Sylla, Richard. "Experimental Federalism: The Economics of
    American Government, 1789–1914." In *The Cambridge
    Economic History of the United States.* Vol. 2, *The Long
    Nineteenth Century.* Edited by Stanley L. Engerman and
    Robert E. Gallman, 483–542. New York: Cambridge
    University Press, 2000,

'T Hart, Marjolein. *The Dutch Wars of Independence Warfare and
    Commerce in the Netherlands 1570–1680.* New York:
    Routledge, 2014.

Tan, JS. "Big Tech Embraces New Cold War Nationalism." *Foreign
    Policy*, August 27, 2020.
    https://foreignpolicy.com/2020/08/27/china-tech-facebook-
    google/.

Taussig, Frank William. "The Iron Industry in the United States."
    *Quarterly Journal of Economics* 14, no. 4 (1900): 475–508.

Taussig, Frank William. *The Tariff History of the United States.* New
    York: The Knickerbocker Press, 1931.

Teich, M., R. Porter, and B. Gustafsson. *The Industrial Revolution in
    National Context: Europe and the USA.* Cambridge:
    Cambridge University Press, 1996.

Thirsk, Joan. *Economic Policy and Projects: The Development of a Consumer Society in Early Modern England.* Oxford: Clarendon, 1978.

Thomas, Ryland, and Nicholas Dimsdale. "A Millennium of Macroeconomic Data." Bank of England, 2017. https://www.bankofengland.co.uk/statistics/research-datasets.

Thompson, A., and C. R. Hickson. *Ideology and the Evolution of Vital Institutions: Guilds, the Gold Standard, and Modern International Cooperation.* New York: Springer, 2001.

Tooke, T. *A History of Prices and of the State of the Circulation from 1793 to 1837; Preceded by a Brief Sketch of the State of the Corn Trade in the Last Two Centuries.* London: Longman, Orme, Brown, Green and Longmans, 1838.

Tseng, Wanda, and David Cowen. *India's and China's Recent Experience with Reform and Growth.* New York: Palgrave Macmillan, 2005.

United Nations. "World Population Prospects 2019." https://population.un.org/wpp.

US Department of State Office of the Historian. "Milestones: 1921–1936." In *Milestones in the History of US Foreign Relations.* US Department of State. https://history.state.gov/milestones/1921-36/foreword.

US Department of the Treasury. "The Beginning of US Debt." https://www.treasurydirect.gov/kids/history/history.htm

Van Dillen, Johannes Gerard. *History of the Principal Public Banks, Accompanied by Extensive Bibliographies of the History of Banking and Credit in Eleven European Countries.* Collected by J. G. Van Dillen. London: Cass, 1964.

Van Oosten, Roos. "The Dutch Great Stink: The End of the Cesspit Era in the Pre-Industrial Towns of Leiden and Haarlem." *European Journal of Archaeology* 19, no. 4 (2016): 704–27.

Van Zanden, Jan Luiten. "Prices and Wages and the Cost of Living in the Western Part of the Netherlands, 1450–1800." International Institute of Social History. Accessed January 29, 2021. http://www.iisg.nl/hpw/brenv.php.

Van Zanden, Jan Luiten. "Tracing the Beginning of the Kuznets Curve: Western Europe during the Early Modern Period." *Economic History Review* (1995): 643–64.

Victoria and Albert Museum. "Flintlock Pistol." http://collections.vam.ac.uk/item/O97426/flintlock-pistol-monlong-pierre/.

Wallerstein, I. *The Modern World-System I.* Berkeley: University of California Press, 2011.

Wallerstein, I. *The Modern World-System II: Mercantilism and the Consolidation of the European World-Economy, 1600–1750.* Berkeley: University of California Press, 2011.

Wilkins, M. *The History of Foreign Investment in the United States to 1914.* Cambridge, MA: Harvard University Press, 1989.

Williamson, Jeffrey G. *American Growth and the Balance of Payments, 1820–1913.* Chapel Hill, NC: University of North Carolina Press, 1964.

Wilson, Charles. *England's Apprenticeship 1605–1763.* London: Longmans, 1965.

Wilson, Charles. *Profit and Power: A Study of England and the Dutch Wars.* The Hague: Nijhoff, 1978.

Xu, Chenzi. "Reshaping Global Trade: The Immediate and Long-Run Effects of Bank Failures." Proceedings of Paris December 2020 Finance Meeting EUROFIDAI – ESSEC, October 13, 2020. https://ssrn.com/abstract=3710455.

# Index

Spinoza, Baruch, 49
stadtholder, 3, 91–92, 94,
100, 102–103, 106–107,
113–114
stagflation, 32–33, 196, 198
Stalin, Joseph, 86
Standard Oil, 159, 187–188
States Party, 17, 48, 139, 204
Stop of the Exchequer, 130,
132
strong dollar policy, 208
Stuart monarchy, 75, 127
sugar, 84, 95, 106, 113, 128,
173
Sulphur Crisis of 1840, 150
superabundance of bullion in
the Dutch Republic, 3
supply inelasticities, 38, 60
syndicates, 118, 125

**T**
tariffs, 80–81, 83, 87, 93, 113,
149, 151, 156, 159, 166, 171–172,
176, 178–179, 183, 187, 190–193,
213
taxes, 12, 34, 54, 91, 93, 105, 108,
110, 124, 131, 141–143, 166, 190,
193, 201–202, 214
technological progress, 6–7,
14, 17, 43, 51, 77, 80, 89, 162–163
technology, 6–8, 42–44, 75, 82,
88, 101, 106, 192, 200, 209, 212,
214, 216
textiles, 47, 75–76, 82, 85, 94,
98, 100, 106, 110–111, 120, 128,
141–142, 154, 162, 167, 169, 172,
180, 187, 208
textile machinery, 82, 167
*The Theory of Moral
Sentiments*, 225
*The Wealth of Nations*, 6,
159, 218, 225
Thornton, Henry, 45
tobacco, 74, 93, 99, 106,
123–125, 128

tonnage, 122
Tory Party, 18, 40, 49–50, 126,
139, 143, 147–151, 155–156, 168,
182, 205, 213
trade deficit, 199, 209, 220
trade unionism, 140, 159
trade war, Franco-Dutch, 113
transcontinental railroad,
175–176
Treasury Mind, 139
Treaty of Munster, 106
triangular trade, 105
Trip brothers, 102
Trump, Donald J., 213–214
tulip mania, 26

**U**
uncertainty, 11, 13, 25–27, 29, 31,
33–35, 37, 39, 41, 45–46, 97
unemployment, 12, 26–27, 30–
33, 38–40, 48, 110, 121, 144, 148–
149, 159, 197–198, 202–203, 213
Union of Utrecht, 91
upswing, 43–45, 143
USAID, 193

**V**
van den Enden, Franciscus,
49
van Oldenbarnevelt, Johan,
100, 102
Venetian Republic, 73
VOC (Dutch East India
Company), 98–100, 111–112,
126, 135
Volcker, Paul, 145, 200, 203
vroedschap, 92

**W**
Wagner Acts, 191
Walker Tariff, 174
Walpole, Robert, 50
War of the Spanish
Succession, 21, 35, 47,

CPSIA information can be obtained
at www.ICGtesting.com
Printed in the USA
LVHW091300120821
695167LV00009B/63/J

9 781736 603932